... something special about my child . . . I knew it from the moment she was born. . . . A minute morsel, she weighed under two pounds, and measured nine inches from the tip of her tiny head to her infinitesimal toes. . . . I lay back still, bathed in happiness. It was like a brittle shell, this happiness, and I felt that motion or sound might shatter it. . . . I could still feel the surge of unbelievable wonder and joy evoked by the baby's lusty yell.

"What do you think of our child? Is she as pretty as Marie? Did you count her fingers and toes?" . . .

He sat down at the foot of the bed and I waited for him to express his delight.

"You must realize"—John spoke gently—"she's not out of the woods yet."

A gust of cold air entered my sun-drenched room and I shivered. . . .

KAREN

Marie Killilea

LAUREL-LEAF BOOKS bring together under a single imprint outstanding works of fiction and nonfiction particularly suitable for young adult readers, both in and out of the classroom. Charles F. Reasoner, Professor Emeritus of Children's Literature and Reading, New York University, is consultant to this series.

Published by
Dell Publishing
a division of
Bantam Doubleday Dell Publishing Group, Inc.
666 Fifth Avenue
New York, New York 10103

Dedication: TO MY BLESSED MOTHER

ISBN: 0-440-94376-0

RL: 7.0

Reprinted by arrangement with Prentice-Hall, Inc.
Printed in the United States of America
One Previous Laurel-Leaf Edition
New Laurel-Leaf Edition
December 1983

20 19 18 17 16 15 14 13 12

KRI

after thirty years

In the thirty years since our books *Karen, Wren,* and *With Love from Karen* were first published, we have received over 100,000 letters and our "family" has indeed been extended. It reaches into more than sixty countries and communicates in twenty-nine foreign languages. We have come to love people we have never met, nor shall ever meet, but their letters are tender and personal and many send tokens of their affection. Our involvements have developed in most unlikely places and encompass a wide variety of situations. I have a key ring made for me by an inmate of a federal prison; a finely lettered prayer from a Carmelite cloister in Johannesburg, South Africa; beautiful handcrafted porcelain angels for our creche from a farmer in Idaho; hundreds of pictures of babies, cats, dogs, rabbits, horses, goats, entire families for two or even three generations, weddings, christenings, graduations from kindergarten and university, rivers, mountains, ranches, Far Eastern bazaars, Japanese temples, an Indian hospital in Jamshedpur.

When *Karen* was published the response of the reviewers was most gratifying, but it was the ardent enthusiasm of many, many book-loving salespeople who made it a success. I can testify to this, since I traveled throughout the country meeting those who are on the front line of selling. Consequently, there were the usual numbers of interviews. On a warm October day a reporter and I were on the porch and my son, Rory, was sitting on the floor building a horse with Tinkertoys. The reporter had been querying me about my previous writing experience. I gave him my complete tally: grocery lists, legislative reports, and letters to friends. The phone rang and I excused myself to answer it. As I was returning, my visitor said to Rory, sotto voce: "Tell me, sonny, Mummy didn't really write that book alone?" Rory put another stick into another hole. He was thoughtful. "No," he finally answered. The reporter, intent on a hot tip, pursued the lead. "She had help—a ghost writer?" Rory stopped building, squirmed around to face his inquisitor. "Yes, of course," he answered with a wide smile. "Who?" the reporter asked in a conspiratorial whisper. Delighted by his integration into the interview and sure of his knowledge, my son announced, "The Holy Ghost," and turned back to his Tinkertoys.

v

We have answered 15,000 letters. In our hundred-year-old house, I worked in a room converted into an office. There are rows of files and supply cabinets, and Jimmy removed part of the window seat to make room for a desk in the bay window from which I could look out to the sea and down on the dogwoods.

After many months we came to realize that correspondence had taken over our lives. We did not have the funds for a full-time secretary or the necessary household help. A form letter was suggested, but it would have been monstrous to reply in this way to the loving and frequently intimate revelations that came to me; nor could I turn them over to someone else to answer. We were driven to two painful decisions. 1) We could not continue responding, and 2) in due time we would write a sequel, since most writers asked "What happened next?"

There would always be some individuals to whom we felt we must respond—parents who demonstrated a life-threatening depression; a *single* parent who had a handicapped child; an unmarried mother who had kept her child; people in the armed services; people in prison.

Into this last category of prisoners fell Robert (not his real name), the maker and giver of my cherished key ring. He wrote to say he had read *Karen* and *With Love from Karen.* He had been in a federal prison for many years and the books had given him a feeling of family. He thanked me for writing them. I answered this letter promptly. Robert replied even more promptly. His vocabulary was adequate but his sentence structure was strange. I was puzzled, because it seemed that he had read a good deal. His script was generous and attractively formed. His second letter said he was honored by my reply, but that in fairness he should tell me about himself. He was born a deaf-mute and he was in prison for murder and would understand if he did not hear from me again. I wrote again, giving him family news, and sent him some books. It was a long time before I ferreted out the story of his crime, and I did not learn it from him. Over the years, a woman in his hometown had found great sport in taunting this man when she met him in a store or on the street. There came a day when, driven beyond endurance, he struck her. She fell backwards against a building, fractured her skull, and died.

At the time we began corresponding, Robert had served twenty-one years "in the Walls" and had a blameless prison record. Despite many recommendations for his parole, it was repeatedly denied. We did some more ferreting. The husband of the dead woman was a politician with power and influence. He swore that he would see to it that Robert spent the rest of his life behind bars.

After many months we decided on a campaign. We wrote the politician. Our letter went unanswered. We wrote again and yet again, asking him to talk to the warden. He did not reply, so we switched to the Probation and Parole Commission. Over the years we have accumulated a file over an inch thick of correspondence with them. As the months wore on, his optimism unclouded by repeated failures, Robert was preparing himself for his "release," being far more sanguine than I. His preparation consisted of teaching himself Braille so that when he was free he could teach the blind deaf-mute. All of this intelligence we passed on to the politician and the Probation and Parole Commission.

I glean excerpts from Robert's correspondence to me that reveal what manner of man he is. "Now, about speech class before parole. Good idea. I welcome your suggestion. Dr. J. of the State University has become my friend and is so kind, like you, writing many letters. I know how to converse with deaf and blind, also not hard to teach the retarded deaf. I have read a lot of books. I want to help unfortunate deaf pupils. I am patient. Many thanks for writing to the Governor." (I sent Robert copies of some of my letters.) ". . . If it wasn't for Dr. J's effort to help me I would be turned into vegetation, maybe like green collards. Bless him. He will see me the second week in September. . . . I have no family but seems like you and Jimmy and Karen adopt me and some day I will dance across the street to you without handcuffs just like other people."

The next letter: "I wrote you about Lottie coming into my life. She is a fighter like in Book of Esther. One day we will marry. She has sold her house and takes apartment in town to be near me. . . . I work with that young boy who came in here. Can you believe how much signing he learns in two weeks! So smart. I talk a lot to him. Does he want to spend years in prison like me? He doesn't think so. I pray for him." (I sent this letter to the Governor, the politician, and the Probation and Parole Commission.) "I can't wait to buy me a puppy when I hit the street."

Dec. 10: "Got your Christmas package today. Thank you a million." (Jimmy had found a set of crèche figures, which looked like ivory but were not.) "It is an unusual gift. At first I thought they were chocolate candies with white coverings, ha! One I tried to bite almost cracked old aged tooth. I am going to see the chaplain to let me put these little biblical toys on table in front of platform so people can see them while praying, to lift up their holiday fervor. Bless you again. I will take them home with me when I am paroled and Lottie will put them on a corner shelf of wall. Nice decoration."

A bulky envelope came from him: "Merry Christmas! Here enclosed LIFE SAVER KEY HOLDER—more protection than St. Christopher medallion (pardon me) *because* any criminal will know key holder with *lacing* like this only made by the inmate in the U.S. Prisons."

After several more hard-fought years, owing mainly to Dr. J's unstinting efforts, Robert got his parole. Dr. J got him a job teaching Braille at the university, and I have several pictures of our friend, nattily dressed, sitting at a table on campus surrounded by students, their faces a study in puzzlement, amazement, and admiration. This was the first time I had seen Robert. He is handsome with deeply etched laugh lines, a generous mouth, a well-trimmed mustache, brown eyes, white hair, and an almost military carriage.

Robert and Lottie were married, and on a lovely day in late July came the letter we had all worked and prayed for for so long. "I AM FREE! Lottie and I are on our way to Atlantic City, then on to Larchmont for the joy of walking through your sacred door. We will be there three weeks from Saturday. How I want to embrace you all. I will hug like the big bear. HA!"

We made signs; we festooned the porch with crepe paper, wrapping it around the columns; we blew up dozens of balloons and they danced in the sea breeze. We made a casserole and a salad and set the table with the Spode and silver and crystal around kerosene lamps. Not having any clear idea of when they might arrive, we were ready by noon. The afternoon moved on. On the beach across the street, families began packing up blankets and pails and shovels and sail boats began drifting in to their moorings. The shadows grew longer and paler. We leaned over the rail-

VIII

ing to scan every car that came up the street. The sunset gun sounded. The birds sang their vespers. We lit the lamps. Moonlight rippled on the water. We paced the porch and the yard, someone always standing by the phone—for word of an accident? We waited—and waited. In the small hours of the morning we blew out the lamps and went to bed. I could not sleep. If only I had had the wit to send Robert a card with my name, address, and telephone number to carry in his wallet, saying IN CASE OF ACCIDENT NOTIFY THE ABOVE. Robert did not come. The days, the weeks, the months passed with no word. That is two years and nine months ago. I'm afraid we'll never get to hug each other.

Many of the letters we receive bring comfort. From Mexico: "I have read your books . . . now I have hope in my heart for my son." From Australia: ". . . I am working to help build the first clinic *and* school in this country." From a high school freshman: "I have just read your wonderful books and realize they came out thirty years ago. If you are still alive, will you write me."

There were many foreign languages, and being no linguist, I enlisted the help of the Assumptionists in Worcester to translate. From Italy came a deluge of mail. Karen had been abroad and both times had spent three weeks in Italy. If there is a totally absorbent ear, it has been given to Karen. In those comparatively brief stays in Italy she had acquired a serviceable knowledge of the language and, I am told, a flawless pronunciation. She was able to give me functional translations.

From Austria: ". . . We want to thank you for sharing your family with the world. We now want to share our lives with someone who needs us. . . ." A twelve-year-old youngster wrote: "My mother would never tell the world about me."

Wishing to maintain our privacy, I had written the first book with false names and camouflaged geography and even locations. The sole purpose in writing the first book was to give to the reader an understanding of cerebral palsy, the potential of the affected person, and how to deal with the problem. We wanted understanding to replace prejudice, and dignity to be accorded each individual.

The manuscript completed, I sent it to Fr. McSorley, who had guided us through days of doubt, discouragement, and near-despair. He believed that unless we stuck to real names, real places, and real people, the book would not be believable and would negate the very purpose for which it was written. This is hard to realize now, but I was writing about events that had taken place over forty years ago. During the ensuing years the mail proved Father's thinking to be absolutely correct.

Many letters were laudatory and many carried burdens of grief, which, in a real way, became ours. We were like sponges absorbing tragedies and tears until we could hold no more.

Jimmy and I decided to take a vacation that would afford us as much isolation as we wished. We went to Canada to a remote spot in the wilds on the Saguenay River. We stayed at an inn called Tadoussac, located where there had once been an Indian village.

Late in the afternoon of the first day a gentleman arrived who was warmly greeted by the staff who expressed their sympathy over the death of his wife. At dinner that evening we noticed this gentleman sitting alone. Jimmy went over to his table, introduced himself, and invited him to join us. Returning, Jimmy presented Mr. Dodd, who proved to be a delightful companion. He and his wife had been coming to this inn for many years. He was familiar with the river and the forested land. He took us deep into the woods to a tiny chapel built by the Indians several hundred years ago. Its walls were crudely painted with religious figures colored, Mr. Dodd explained, with fish blood and berry juices.

A few days into our stay, there arrived a gentleman from Montreal with whom I had worked to establish a Cerebral Palsy Association and a treatment center. The next day Mr. Dodd referred to our book *Karen,* about which my friend from Montreal had told him. At luncheon Mr. Dodd suggested that I rewrite *Karen* for children—he knew it would do well in the juvenile market. He spoke with such authority that I asked him how he could be so positive. He explained that he was Frank Dodd of Dodd, Mead & Company publishers, and urged me to do it. We clearly saw the advantages of educating youngsters before they had acquired any prejudice toward any disability. And so it was that in a remote inn, in the wilds of Canada, *Wren* was born.

On the same day that a letter arrived from Madame Chiang Kaishek, there was a letter from a child named Tommy. On heavy wide-lined paper he printed: DEAR MARIE KILLILEA MY NAME IS TOMMY I AM SEVEN YOURS IS THE BEST BOOK I HAVE EVER READ I HAVE READ 2 LOVE TOMMY.

Letters from children all over the world warmed our hearts. For example, from England: "We in the fourth grade have read WREN. We had a fair for cerebral palsied and raised 3 pounds"; from Oklahoma a fourteen-year-old writes: ". . . I am baby-sitting for the parents of a C.P. kid because they cannot afford a sitter. That's because I read your books and know it is expensive to have a C.P. and they need some relief"; from Brooklyn: "Dear Karen. I read WREN. I hope you are still alive and have rabbits"; from Alabama: ". . . . I would like to invent some things to help kids and adults that are handicapped. That would be a good project. . . ."

Wren was published in 1954. It is still in print. In the summer of 1981 Jimmy and I were at the Bronx Zoo with Jason, our youngest grandchild. We were in the train that goes around the park. Waiting on the platform was a group of youngsters who were physically handicapped. In the seat ahead of us was a woman of about forty, expensively accoutered, and opposite her was a girl of about ten. Looking at the crowd on the platform, the woman spoke disgustedly in a carrying voice: "They shouldn't let such defectives and idiots out." The girl looked straight and hard at the woman and said with great feeling: "They are *not* defectives or idiots. They are physically handicapped." Jimmy and I wondered if she had read *Wren*, for she had expressed exactly what we hoped the book would do.

Readers not only wrote, some came to see us. "We just dropped in. We're from Nebraska and are on our way to Florida." Scores telephoned. Although this measure of interest was gratifying beyond measure, it grew to the point that our personal lives and all social activities were so completely taken over that finally we had to set limits.

To bring a light note into our lives, Walter Slezak, who was going abroad to make a film, gave us his mynah bird. It had been given to Walter by Ezio Pinza. The bird looked like black satin, with golden eyes, and our cats were fascinated. We removed temptation and settled him on top of the refrigerator well out of reach. We named him Gazebo in honor of Walter's most recent Broadway hit. Owing to the linguistic expertise of his former owners,

Gazebo had things to say in Italian, French, Dutch, and German, and now, at a somewhat advanced age, he was plunged into the company of peasants who spoke only English. But he was, like his owner, a quick study and on the first day he learned to coo "I love you!" His imitative skills grew apace; he whistled for the cats and meowed; he whistled for the dogs; he perfectly copied the laugh of each family member; he picked phrases out of our conversations and threw them back; Marie had a heavy bronchial cough—so did Gazebo and for a while we were concerned that he had caught her infection. She stopped coughing and so did he.

We were plagued for some weeks by a gentleman caller who wanted to speak to me to plan a visit. Everyone came to recognize his voice and defended me against these repeated onslaughts. We came home from Mass one Sunday morning to be followed into the kitchen by a man and his two kids. He greeted me: "I've called so often and you were never home so I thought I'd catch you in on a Sunday morning." As we stood in stunned silence the telephone rang and before the receiver could be lifted, came the sweet regretful voice of Gazebo: "I'm sorry, Mother isn't home."

Often we are praised as co-founders of the United Cerebral Palsy Association. As to that, if we hadn't been involved, very soon there would have been others to work for the cerebral palsied. It was like a spontaneous combustion. Parents all over the country were in the throes of the agitation that brings the seed to flower.

We are often asked, "Don't you question why God gave your family this burden?" Frequently that question is coupled with the thought that we must be proud of what the books have accomplished. I find this juxtaposition amusing, for it is as though a patient were coming through a most complicated and dangerous operation and saying of the successful outcome: "I had a wonderful scalpel!" The scalpel itself is but a tool, the surgeon is the master, and so we see ourselves—we are the scalpel and God is the surgeon.

Scalpels have been wielded close by and in remote places. One day there was a letter from a young woman named Barbara (not her real name) who lived in a remote part of New England. She had read *Karen* and wrote to say that she had a two-year-old son

XII

who could not sit up, who could only drink from a bottle, whose head lolled, and who did not speak. At the end of a long letter she said she would like to hear from me. She did not think I would want to write to her, since the baby was illegitimate. She believed that her son's affliction was a punishment for her sin. My immediate reaction was to send a telegram saying "NONSENSE." Instead, I called a friend of mine, a priest who lived about eighty miles from her, and read him the letter. He didn't wait to be asked but said he would go and see her the following day. On his return he called me. Barbara was twenty. They lived in a trailer on the side of a mountain. The baby was as she described him. She had no running water—water was delivered in a five-gallon milk can. She had no telephone. The baby and the trailer were immaculate. He visited with her for several hours and found her highly intelligent, although she had had only a brush with high school education. He left her with some understanding of God as He is—infinitely loving, infinitely forgiving. Father said Barbara would need some bolstering of these ideas and he would return. She told him that she was a pariah in her village and that even her mother and grandmother were ridiculed when they went shopping for her. Her family had little money and she was on welfare.

Barbara and I were now writing several times a week since there was no way to reach her by phone. I enclosed stamped envelopes for her replies.

It was only two weeks to Christmas. Kathy Cassidy and Dorothy Haigney, two close friends who had been involved since the first book, joined me in purchasing and wrapping enough gifts to crowd the back of the station wagon; soft and cuddly animals of various sizes, mobiles, wind chimes, clothes, blouses, sweaters, skirts, jackets, and a beautiful robe for Barbara and things for her home that the observant priest reported lacking. On a brisk winter day we drove to the mountains.

When I met Barbara I was impressed by her quiet dignity and composure, her tender gentleness with her son, Billy. There was an air of indefinable resoluteness about her. Billy looked like the model for the original Hummel angel. After I had spent some time with the youngster, I knew it was imperative that we get a dependable evaluation. From our own experience, and others', I knew how undependable many evaluations are. To get to the right evaluation center would necessitate a trip of five hundred miles with six changes of buses and trains. With the burden of carrying the boy and all the necessary paraphernalia, the journey would be impossible without help, and even then, so exhausting for both that no testing would be valid.

I appealed to a friend of ours, who appealed to a friend of his and it was arranged that Barbara and Billy would take a taxi to the airport and be flown in a private DC 3 to the airport near the diagnostic center. Jimmy and I drove and arrived in time to meet the plane. Sharp is my picture of the smartly uniformed crew of three as they came down the steps carrying a sterilizer, a brown grocery bag of baby food, a container of bottles, a very large bag of fresh diapers, a bag of clothes for Billy, an old straw suitcase of clothes for Barbara, a large blanket; and of the navigator carrying Billy most tenderly. Barbara followed, looking dazed. As they came up to us, the captain saluted smartly and said Mr. Skakel had instructed him to stand by for as long as we needed him.

It was necessary for them to stay three weeks. They stayed with friends we had come to know through the book *Karen* but whom we had never met. When the diagnosis was completed, Jimmy and I released the plane and crew and drove home.

It developed that Barbara was a fantastically quick study. Eight hours a day she attended lectures, observed, studied, and was tutored in the various therapies Billy would need. In one conversation she said that learning was so exciting—she had never known this in school.

When it was time, we drove her home. At the end of a month she had her routine established and now needed a team of volunteers to help her with the therapy. Where to find them? She called a minister, thinking that he might know someone who was suicidal and who would be helped by joining in the therapy for a disabled child. Did he know such a person? He did, and several other people who were miserable because no one needed them. She got to make a presentation on a local radio station. The word spread and Billy had his corps of two dozen volunteers. In time, this therapy became a cause célèbre and this once-ostracized girl was invited to speak at the church, then at the high school assembly, and later she was to lecture at colleges and a state university. Spreading the gospel — another "scalpel."

Her living in such an isolated spot with no telephone worried us. We petitioned our veterinarian, who found her a splended watch dog (the victim of a broken home) with a voice like thunder, and also found a veterinarian near Barbara who would generously give any medical care needed. Welfare could not cover dog food, and a kind merchant was glad to be the supplier. The large beast stood guard over Billy, came to know the volunteers, and so watchful was he that Barbara had to introduce replacements very carefully.

Billy made slow but steady progress. In the winter of his fourth year Billy developed pneumonia. I received a call from Barbara: "Billy is an angel now." She came to stay with us for a bit and two years later married a lovely man and had a daughter who also looked like a Hummel figure.

We were surprised at the amount of reader interest in our menagerie. One of our Newfoundlands, Ch. Little Bear's Bona-vista, had died during one of my lengthy hospitalizations. She could not be coaxed from her spot beside my bed. She refused all food. She was not comforted by her companion New-foundland or her beloved Persian cat. She waited and waited and before I could get back to her she died. No autopsy can show death from a broken heart.

People still write and ask: "Are you still showing prize-winning dogs?" After Bonnie's death we looked for a breed ideally suited to our present circumstances. Roger Caras suggested a Keeshond — a decision based on breeding, intelligence, temperament, beauty, and size. Of this breed the "dog bible" says "no negative characteristics." The Keeshond is a spectacularly beautiful creature with a profuse stand-up black and silver coat, a mask that gives great expression to the face, and eyes as dark as forest pools. We found our dog, Tryon's Wrocky Road, in Portland, Oregon, and had him flown in to Kennedy Airport. The whole family went to fetch him. He greeted us cordially, then flung himself into Karen's lap where he stayed during the ride home — all forty-five pounds of him. He proved to be a real showman — one might even say "ham." He made two appearances on *Good Morning America* that he enjoyed as much as he did strutting around the show ring. We gave him the call name of "Drummer." Kristin, our youngest, handled him to an International Championship.

At this time Kristin had adopted a racing whippet whose owner was going to "put him down" because he was going blind and was losing. In the same week we fell heir to a miniature French poodle. Its family could not keep the dog, had read *Karen,* and could only bear the parting if the dog came to us. What a fortuitous circumstance this proved to be, for Karen, from her wheelchair, undertook to train the dog in what is officially recognized as "Obedience."

To train the dog on a six-foot lead *and* propel the chair without entanglement was a task I believed to be beyond her. She was unalterably determined, so we scanned the field of teachers and got her George Cowton, the best. Unlike us, George had absolute confidence in her ability to do what we thought to be impossible. The usual time for training is twenty minutes in the morning and twenty minutes in the afternoon. It would sometimes take Karen twenty minutes just to untangle the lead from the spokes or to clip the catch to the collar. She was, after all, dealing with a *miniature* poodle. The dog, Tam Tam, solved this last problem by pushing her muzzle *between* the spokes, which put her neck right under Karen's hand. I watched a few of Karen's solitary sessions, then retreated. The superhuman patience, the physical struggle with what seemed to me to be insurmountable difficulties, were more than I could watch. The session at an end, I would find Karen, her color high, drenched with perspiration. Her comment: "I don't perspire—I sweat—most unladylike!"

The only assistance we gave was to set up a series of jumps. Imagine, if you can, what is required to handle the six-foot leash, guide the dog over jumps without getting caught on them, and propel the wheelchair at the same time. There was an exercise in retrieving. Karen would be given a dumbbell to handle, then someone would place it among a cluster of dumbbells some twenty feet away. At command, Tam Tam would be "sent" to select the only dumbbell touched by Karen and return it to her with "straight sit," and hold it in her mouth until the command "out"; then, without command, return to her position beside the chair. The training in all its complications was completed when Karen was able to cease voice commands and the dog responded to hand signals alone.

After two years, at the invitation of Mr. Cowton, Karen was giving demonstrations at Obedience classes where able bodied people were ready to give up because it was all too difficult. Her last demonstration before Tam Tam died was at an American Kennel Club show in Boston. I say "demonstration" for the AKC Judges refused to judge her in competition because she was handicapped. Privately she scored 198! We battled that one for years without success. Today there is the pleasurable excitement of seeing handicapped people competing. There is a plethora of wheelchairs at shows and in the rings. One young lady who is blind is scoring very well.

In the last three decades there has been a great psychosociological alteration in the attitude toward disability, greater than in all the preceding thousands of years. Witness the Special Olympics — restrooms to accommodate wheelchairs, inclines instead of curbs, designated parking for the disabled, and lower telephone booths and water fountains. Buildings using federal funds have many mandates: handrails along the walls, elevator buttons in Braille, etc. Now there are special vans to taxi the disabled and, most important, the handicapped are being integrated into the school system.

Mea culpa! I am told that throughout the books I frequently mentioned the solace I found in smoking. Would that I could undo such a bad example.

The phrase "prayers for you all" runs through hundreds of letters. In no small measure I credit these prayers as the greatest assist to my doctor in the treatment of my lung cancer. So also does my doctor, for I had a secondary solid tumor of the trachea that proved inoperable. In June of 1971 I was told there was little hope of my surviving past Labor Day. Treatment was started on June 28, 1971, my fifty-seventh birthday. There was chemotherapy, radiology, and immunology. I was in the care of a crew of talented, loving professionals, and I was cured. I spent most of five years in the hospital (including three Christmases), and one of my brief R and R's allowed me to be at home, it was Barbara who came to take care of me. Robert wrote: ". . . Lord not ready for you—wait for me."

It has been reported to me that McGill University was the first medical school to make our books required reading. Over the years we have had letters attesting to the fact that the letter writer first had his attention drawn to cerebral palsy, or, in fact, other disabilities by our story. We have a professional dossier — several neurologists, a half-dozen orthopedists, a pediatrician, psychologists, teachers of Special Education, and a very large number of therapists — physical, occupational, and speech. Each day, I pray for all who have read our books, whether or not we have been in touch with one another.

Readers continue to ask for recommendations as to treatment centers, schools, clinics, residences, and hospitals. I stick by my policy of never recommending a facility that I have not visited within six months.

"... I feel I am part of your family" is perhaps the most pleasing phrase, and from those who write thus, the salutation is the intimate "Dear Marie." One of the most moving experiences is to be told "I *heard* your books." A college junior wrote: "I am totally blind. In high school I went through quite a self-pity routine. My teacher gave me talking books of *Karen* and *With Love from Karen*. The story gave me Faith, hope, and courage. I knew that, like all of you, with God, I could do anything."

I speak with gratitude of many letters from third-generation readers: "... little did I think when my grandmother gave me *Wren*, that I would one day have a cerebral-palsied child."

Our circle of friends and acquaintances was ever widening. We received a call one day from an English priest. He apologized profusely for the intrusion, we had a short and pleasant chat, and I invited him to visit. There are rare meetings when both parties sense that they were never strangers.

He told me that last year, on vacation, he was taking a walking tour of Ireland. He had started out on a country road in a drizzle that had become a pelting rain. A car came along, stopped beside him, and the two ladies in it offered to take him to his destination. He most gratefully accepted. They said they were from the United States and had always dreamed of visiting Ireland. Father told them he had dreamed of visiting the United States since he had read a booked called *Karen*. He longed to visit the Killilea family, but as he had taken a vow of poverty, such a visit could never be. His benefactors looked startled—they lived only a few miles from the Killileas. In parting they said they hoped that one day his dream would come true. When they arrived home they wasted no time, and it was arranged that their pastor would gladly have Father take the place of his vacationing curate. So, from a country lane in Ireland to our kitchen. Mirabile dictu!

The country to most recently publish our books is Poland and there is considerable letter response. "Dear Lady, I have greatly impresse by your books because they give hope in which lately was lacking quite often. I have a two year old little son with spastic palsy. . . I want advice how to manage him. I want spiritual support. This, alas, the doctors who treat him don't do it. I am told only unpleasant things with not any view on the future. . ." I have Mark's picture before me. He has his mother's auburn hair, he is handsome and is laughing up into the face of his daddy, who is holding him. ". . . His development is extremely slow . . . many visits to physicians. He is unable to sit up until now. . . . All prognosis for future have been unpropitious. . . . I would like to correspond with you. Your wisdom and experience of the past years are very precious for me."

We answered this letter, asking the questions that would be asked in this country by a knowledgeable doctor. When the answers came we were inspired to turn them over to Karen's pediatrician of many years ago, Dr. John Gundy. Out of the generosity of his heart, he has directed and offered the spiritual support one seeks from one's physician. Following pages of medical advice, he wrote: "Answers lie in prayer, expectations, patience and *communication of love*." The italics are his.

There came other letters in Polish. Here was an opportunity to put parents in touch with each other and we knew how salvific this could be. I sent them to Danuta, our first correspondent, for translation. She sent them back; I sent her the answer in English, which she translated into Polish and passed on to the writer. The first translation from Polish informed us that the mother was a professional woman whose husband had left her and the disabled child "at the urging of his parents." Ignorance breeds attendant tragedies that are incalculable. From subsequent letters: ". . . . We think about you often and in the same way as we think about our nearest, and we enjoy every contact with you very much. We pray for your good health and many smiling days. Now we don't feel so lonely and lost in our worries. Kisses to the whole family and warm wishes for Dr. Gundy." There is none of us who is not in need of prayer and support and I, in turn, am immeasurably comforted by my "family" in Poland. I just mailed them copies of *May's Boy*. That will do more for them than it is in my power to do.

The mail can be a surprise. On the outside of an envelope from New Waterford, Canada, is written *"Karen* and *With Love from Karen* are the 'Pillars of Hercules' to the Handicapped." Which boosted my ego. From the letter within: "I had an English assignment to write to an author so I am writing to you, though I did not want to."

Through Karen, more beauty was brought to the world. Alastair Cassels-Brown composed a concerto, inspired by and dedicated to Karen. W. C. Handy, the father of the Blues, had lost his sight and the books were read to him. He asked to come and "see" us. He brought with him his manuscript of the Twenty-third Psalm, which he dedicated to Karen. He said he found much laughter in the books, a comment which always pleases me. We spoke of laughter as one of God's greatest gifts. Asked to define Karen's courage, I see it as a welding of faith and humor. To the many who want to know ". . . and what is Karen doing now?" I reply—and with profound gratitude to those whose prayers have supported all of us over the years. Karen lives alone in a lovely apartment, which she keeps herself. She's a top-notch secretary donating her time to one of the busiest priests in the world, as he is a psychologist, runs a Retreat house, teaches, writes, and gives retreats all over the country, indeed around the world. She is on the Board of the Cardinal Hayes Home for Children. To this establishment she brings an understanding of the emotional, spiritual, physicial, and social needs of the disabled.

It is only a brief four decades since several hundred thousand, in this country alone, found these needs unmet. One is impelled to think again of the Surgeon and His "Scalpels."

As we begin the thirty-first year of the first publication of our story, we thank all those who gave to us and we continue to pray for all who care.

Chapter I

THE FIRST STAG LINE in my daughter's life was composed of eleven men, varying in age from twenty-four to sixty.

Few debutantes have been the recipients of such mass masculine interest upon their presentation. Few have received such careful scrutiny, evoked such exclamations of admiration, such expressions of welcome.

All eleven were unaware of the myriad charms of the other young ladies present. Karen had a quality of attractiveness, which, since the time of Adam and Eve, has not been surpassed.

What new baby hasn't?

This somewhat unusually large attendance at a rather usual miracle was due to the fact that, like any prima donna, she heralded her arrival and then kept her public waiting almost two weeks. The stage was set, the stagehands ready, the actors knew their lines and places. Then, with true Gaelic dramatic timing, she arrived just when the audience had hit its peak of anticipatory excitement. Contrary to custom the drama was enacted almost three months before the announced date.

Ten of the assembled men were medical doctors. The eleventh could also rightly be called "doctor," since his degree was Doctor of Divinity. He was a priest and was present by special invitation. If Karen's appearance on stage was to be brief and fleeting, as predicted, Jimmy and I wanted to make sure she made her exit straight back to where she came from. We wanted her baptized.

Karen was born a few minutes before noon. A minute morsel, she weighed under two pounds, and measured nine inches from the tip of her tiny head to her infinitesimal toes. She squalled immediately and energetically, in what may have been an indictment of the many dire prophesies concerning her survival.

I was wheeled back to my room. The early sun bounded off the cretonne curtains and put a frosty veneer on the maple chairs and bureau. The nurse helped me brush my hair and tie a ribbon around it.

"We put on my bed jacket" and "We put on some powder and lipstick." And then she left. I now understood what a friend of mine meant when he said that nurses lead plural lives.

I lay back still, bathed in happiness. It was like a brittle shell, this happiness, and I felt that motion or sound might shatter it. A very big part of it was the vast relief that Jimmy would not have to experience again the agony of bereavement of last year when our second daughter died. Today was a miracle and I could still feel the surge of unbelievable wonder and joy evoked by the baby's lusty yell.

My mind flitted from one thought to another and finally fastened on little Marie's striking resemblance to me and the wish that this little mite would look like her daddy.

"Girls should look like their fathers," I muttered sleepily.

If she did she'd be lovely. Jimmy has a long face that is both strong and sweet, a "Barrymore" nose, firm chin with a deep cleft, and eyes that are blue as a summer sky, very deep-set and slanting just a little to follow the fine line of high cheekbones. His ears are set well back, beautifully shaped and close to the head.

She could adopt any coiffure and if her hair were rich and wavy like his— What more could a girl ask?

We had been married six years and my heart still picked up tempo when I thought of Jimmy. I certainly knew what I was doing when I proposed to him.

I heard a step and a gentle knock and I opened my

8

eyes to see him hesitating at the door. He was carrying a huge box and I knew from my previous confinements that Jimmy's pleasure could only find expression in four-foot gladioli of the more vivid hues.

He came over to me quickly, put the flowers on the foot of the bed and wrapped his arms around me.

"You're prettier than ever," he said and pulled a chair beside the bed. He took my hand and held it in both of his.

There was a knock and I called, "Come in."

It was Dr. John Gundy, our pediatrician.

"What do you think of our child? Is she as pretty as Marie? Did you count her fingers and toes?"

"Yes, yes, and blue eyes—what else?" he answered, smiling.

He sat down on the foot of the bed and I waited for him to express his delight.

"Good heavens, is that all you have to say?" I asked him, laughing a little since his enthusiasms are more tempered than ours.

Jimmy got up, picked up the flowers and handed them to me. I took off the lid and there they were, all eighteen of them, a dozen blooms to the stalk, salmon, yellow and crimson.

"They're exquisite. You may kiss me again."

John took the box and put it on the bureau.

"You're quiet—even for you," I chided him.

Jimmy sat down again and picked up my hand.

John came back and stood leaning on the foot of the bed.

"Did you ever see anything so tiny?" I asked him.

"Never," he answered and looked at me with curious intentness.

"While you were making yourself beautiful," he smiled, "Jimmy and I were talking."

Jimmy gave my hand a little squeeze.

"You must realize, Marie"—John spoke gently—"she's

9

not out of the woods yet. As I told Jimmy, we've been friends for a long time, I know the best policy for all of us is an honest evaluation of Karen's chances."

I had been right—it was a brittle shell, and sound had smashed it.

The room had grown very warm. It was going to be a scorcher. John shifted his weight and it occurred to me that everything he did seemed slow until I realized he never made a superfluous motion.

I looked at Jimmy. He was watching John and he was pale. I suddenly remembered that he'd been pale when he came in.

John's voice was calm and soft. "I've already told Jimmy that no premature baby is considered a well baby and the chances for survival are pretty much determined by weight. Any infant under a five-pound birth weight is considered premature, even if it's a full-term baby."

Jimmy lit a cigarette and put it between my lips.

"It will be a day or so," continued John, "before we know whether her lungs will fully expand, or whether she can take nourishment."

"What else may go wrong?" I asked.

"Honey, we can't be sure of her vision for some months," Jimmy replied. "As John has explained it to me we have a real struggle on our hands. Every ounce gained is a battle; a pound a victorious campaign. At best, she has a twenty to forty chance for survival."

We talked for about an hour and John got up to leave. In spite of everything his honesty and air of natural confidence were reassuring.

"I've ordered three nurses for round-the-clock duty with Karen," he said at the door. "I'll be back a little later."

Long after, and quite by accident, I found out about the many hours, especially at night, that Dr. John sat with Karen.

After he left I turned to Jimmy. "Thank God for John. If anyone can pull her through he can. He'll work hard, we'll pray hard, and one fine day she'll leave here fat and round."

"Of course," said Jimmy, and meant it.

My hospital stay was difficult. Each time I heard wheels roll in the corridor I knew (rightly or wrongly) it was a fresh tank of oxygen for Karen. Any conference in the hall, I thought must be an emergency discussion. Any footsteps hurrying down the corridor tapped out "danger."

The rising bell on the maternity floor comes earlier than on the other hospital floors, about 5:15 a.m. to be exact. On maternity, however, it is not the dismal knell it is elsewhere, but a joyous ring of a new day and a new life.

The babies are brought to the mothers between 5:00 and 6:00. I would lie there in the dim morning and listen to the vibrating, noisy trains of youngsters as they were wheeled down the corridor and halted for transfer from cart to mother. When they went unhesitatingly by my door, I would try to think only of how lucky we were that she was holding her own and even gaining a little. But there are six feedings in twenty-four hours and I found it rough going.

I was impatient to "meet" my daughter, even if the meeting would be through a window. On the 22nd of August, when she was four days old, the meeting took place.

I had made up very carefully, brushed my hair and tied it back with a Kelly green ribbon to match my robe. Gingerly I slid off the bed and, leaning heavily on the nurse, eased myself into a wheel chair. This was several years before science had advanced to the present procedure of sending mama on a hike the day after the baby is born.

The nurse was sweet and just a little anxious. She propelled me out of the room and down the hall to the nursery. The door was in the middle, and the walls on either side, facing the corridor, were plate glass. It was

11

a cheerful room of many windows, and the morning sun shone brightly on the soft yellow walls. Sinks and tables with the accouterments for the first handling were at the extreme right. The babies' baskets were in neat four-tiered rows, each row four baskets long. To the left and just under the window where I stood, were three oblong metal and glass boxes with a confusing profusion of dials and tubes. These were the incubators.

My daughter and I were introduced by the baby's nurse, Jackie Bayha, who smiled at me with her eyes (the lower part of her face was totally concealed by a mask). She pointed to my daughter's couch in the nearest incubator. I rose carefully from the wheel chair, and joyful and fearful bent for my first look at our wee bairn.

She was covered from chin to toe with cotton. The first glance was a rude shock; she was so tiny. How could anything so minute be alive, I wondered as I watched the still little form. Why, she's smaller than any of Marie's dolls. I gripped the ledge under the window and waited to catch the tiniest movement of breathing. After a little I was sure I saw one; then I considered her from an esthetic point of view. I believe she was the most exquisite morsel of humanity ever fashioned. I feasted my eyes. How I yearned to touch her, to hold her.

I must have stood a long time, when I suddenly began to feel faint. Reluctantly I slid my eyes away from her and sank back into the chair. The nurse wheeled me back to my room, helped me into bed, left me for a moment, and returned with something that tasted awful but revived me somewhat. After she left I lay with my eyes closed, trying to recall every detail of the little head.

Three days later I was discharged. Before I left I spent a long time at the window, memorizing the baby features to take home with me. I remarked to one of the nurses that Karen's head was no bigger than the orange I'd had for breakfast.

"It's not," she replied, "and she weighs less than the broiler I bought for dinner last night. But you wait and see. Before long she'll be the size of a turkey gobbler."

A hospital, for most people, is a robber's den, holding them hostage and appropriating something before releasing them—an appendix, tonsils, or pounds of flesh after an illness. But the hospital, like Robin Hood, seeks to redeem itself through what it gives to others. For example, a woman forgets everything when she is wheeled to the door and the nurse walks beside her holding a small, soft bundle.

Off the record, any similarity to Robin Hood ends here, for he gave gladly, whereas nurses seem most reluctant to part with their bundle—which seems to indicate unmistakably lack of faith in a new mother's ability to do anything but lie abed and modestly receive congratulations.

Grandma, who bore her children in the large front bedroom at home, surrounded by steaming pans of hot water (I have never been able to find out what it's for, nor have I ever seen any in a hospital) did miss something. She missed the thrill of bringing the baby home.

Jimmy and I had relished this homecoming with our first baby Marie. He had carried her into the house not as easily as he carries a football, but a little stiffly and not a little proudly.

That first time I came home, two and one-half years before, I felt as though I'd been away from it for a long time. The house looked strange and at the same time warmly familiar. He had pushed the thermostat up to eighty degrees so we should not "chill." The elaborate bassinet was in place beside our bed. Mountains of diapers were on the bureau. In the bathroom, tins and bottles of talc and baby oil had replaced Jimmy's shaving things and my boxes and bottles and jars. The baby scales were on the table. The folding bath usurped the tub. There was confusion in the house, there was a baby in the house, and it was wonderful.

13

This time Marie was waiting for us. As we came around the bend we could see her and Mother on the lawn. Neither had ever looked so good to me. Mother is a woman of rare beauty. She is small, delicately proportioned, her exquisite features perfectly molded. She has brimming dark eyes, and a mouth of infinite sweetness. Her hair has been snow-white since she was twenty-four and that day it gleamed with the blue tinge of fresh snow. I could see that she had Marie scrubbed, starched and shining. We could also see that Mother had been having a time of it keeping her that way till we arrived, because Marie was young, healthy and excited. As we drew up before the house I remember thinking that our street smelled better than any other, for the hot sun drew out the full fragrance of pine, fresh-cut grass, and salt marshes.

As the car stopped, Marie broke loose from her Nana's restraining grasp and raced to meet us. Abruptly she halted in mid-flight and stared at me. Not at my face but at my hanging hands and arms. We had explained to her months ago that when the baby came it would be her baby to care for and that we would do only those things beyond her size and strength. I knew that Jimmy, in an attempt to ward off disappointment, had carefully explained that I couldn't bring the baby home with me.

As I watched her stare at my bundleless arms I could feel my stock go down for that cardinal sin—a broken promise.

"Where's my baby?" she demanded.

"Daddy explained to you," Jimmy said as he moved ahead of me, "that the baby was not strong enough to come home right away."

"Mummy promised."

Jimmy put his hand on her shoulder but she pulled away, a pathetic, tiny figure of disappointment and disillusionment.

I started to speak but she demanded:

"Why can't she get strong here?"

14

I explained that Karen needed doctors and nurses to help her get strong—that we couldn't do it at home.

"I could make her strong. I take care of Susan and she's strong." Susan was her favorite "magic-skin," astigmatic-eyed doll.

Just then Mother came out of the house, whence she had retreated in the face of Marie's hurt.

"I think Mummy should sit down," she said. "Let's help her into the house." Marie turned and walked with us but without any gesture of helpfulness. Mother and I went into the nursery, and Jimmy and little Marie stayed in the living room. Beside Marie's bed was the refurbished bassinet. As I looked at the bed and the bassinet, side by side, I had a frightening feeling of failure.

From the living room came the soothing flow of Jimmy's voice, kind, compassionate and patient.

Susan, the doll, was lying on Marie's bed in that position of abandon peculiar to well-used dolls. I picked her up and brought her with me to the living room.

"Honey, I think Susan's lonesome and a little hungry. Isn't it time for you to feed her?"

"You feed her, Mummy," said Marie dispiritedly.

I went over to the couch and inched in between Jimmy and Marie. Jimmy put his arm around me and Marie squeezed against my side. We three were together in a new closeness. A closeness brought about by hurt and longing, for a member of our family that none of us had even touched.

15

Chapter 2

THE PREVIOUS DAILY ROUTINE was revised.

I would hurry with the housework so that I could be at the hospital for the afternoon visiting hours from two to three o'clock. Marie was too young to take along so I used to farm her out, or a kindly neighbor would come and stay with her until my return. We established a staff of rotating "sitters" for the evening so Jimmy and I could go together and "visit" Karen from seven to eight o'clock. I'd have Marie bathed and pajamaed when he came home. They'd visit a little; then we'd have family prayers which always ended with Marie's "Please, God, make my sister strong quick, and send her home." It was such a hard prayer that she would squeeze her crossed feet, squeeze her folded hands and squeeze her eyes tight shut.

We'd hurry dinner, always afraid we'd miss a few of our minutes with Karen. It was difficult to walk decorously through the corridors; we always felt like running. The first stop was the nurse's station where we studied her chart; how much time under oxygen, how many ounces lost or gained, report on the formula and feedings. No architect designing a skyscraper was more scrupulously concerned with centimeters and ounces.

As we came up to the nursery window we always held hands and Jimmy would usually say, "She looks much bigger and brighter tonight," or "Look at her smile."

"She's talking to the angels," I'd answer, since this was the way Mother interpreted the smiles of all infants and it was certainly logical.

We'd look and look and look. At the slightest motions of arms or legs Jimmy would exclaim, "She's strong!"

"That she is!"

The gallery about any nursery window is probably the proudest assemblage to be found anywhere. Poppas, grandpoppas, grandmammas, sisters, brothers, pizons and gumbods. We used to delight in our anonymity and enjoy their comments on our daughter.

"Al, did you see that wee little thing over there in the incubator? How could anything so tiny live?"

To which Al would reply, "Sure is small. It scares me to look at him."

"Hey, Sis, look at that little one. I wouldn't believe it if I didn't see it."

In the months before Karen graduated from the Nursery to the Pediatric Ward we saw many people and babies come and go. One thing that touched us deeply was the kindly interest these strangers took in our youngster, so that she had in this gallery a series of cheering sections.

Karen's first trip was from the Nursery to Pediatrics in another wing. It was a great moment and conducted with suitable fanfare. The cortege was lengthy and the reception warm. The Nursery staff were loath to lose her to Pediatrics, and behaved much in the manner of a reluctant dowager lending a diamond tiara to a careless cousin.

When the transfer was completed Dr. John turned to Jimmy and me and smiled and left us beside our baby. We both worked hard that we should not weep and then, O wondrous act! we touched her.

"So very, very soft," said Jimmy, as he ran the tip of his index finger lightly across her hand, and then with great excitement, "Hey, honey, she has fingernails."

We looked at each other and knew that we were thinking the same thing. With the surreptitiousness of two thieves escaping with an original Rembrandt we

17

gently loosened the blankets on the side and with quick glances toward the door peered beneath.

"Jimmy," I hissed, "she has toenails, too."

"See how she's grown—her feet must be an inch and a half long."

Jimmy never did get back to the office that afternoon. We stayed all day, reaching hesitant fingers to touch the infinitesimal lobe of an infinitesimal ear, the exquisitely curved chin, even her knee through the blanket.

Marie was kept up very late that night so that we could tell her everything that had happened. At the completion of prayers she instituted a final phrase which has remained the standard closing ever since—

"Thank you, God, for everything."

Our visits were doubly rich now since we had the communion of touch. Karen wouldn't understand stories, and my singing voice is something to be confined to my boudoir, so on my afternoon visits I whistled nursery rhymes. I'd sit my allotted time beside her crib and whistle the hour away. After a while I became really expert.

Christmas came and with it my sister's wedding. 'Twas a delightful matter enhanced by Kay's selection of the groom, Tom Monroe. He was a lovely boy, full of fun and with considerable musical talent. But, as happy as we were for Kay, we didn't have much heart for the prenuptial preparations and festivities.

They were married at a Nuptial Mass at ten in the morning, December 26. Kay, who is dark and beautiful, was gorgeous in white satin.

January sloshed up on the heels of December. February bit at the heels of January; and Karen held her own and gained, fraction by fraction, ounce by ounce. March roughly pushed February aside and her weight was now seven pounds. She was seven months old.

The second Saturday in March, John was with Karen when Jimmy and I arrived for our afternoon call.

"I think it is safe now for us to anticipate Karen's discharge," he said.

I sat down quickly and Jimmy leaned against the wall, looking a little gray.

"If she holds her rate of gain," John continued, "she may be ready to go home in about a month."

"And her eyes?" I asked, and prayed as I spoke.

"So far as we can tell, her vision is perfect. As I told you, at birth I gave her a twenty to forty chance for survival. Well, I think it is safe now to say she's made it." Dr. John has that quality of imperturbability, so highly rated by Sir William Osler. It forsook him then and he grinned.

We three sat quietly around her bed. Gradually we became aware of a high, light, delicately sustained sound. Simultaneously we gasped. It was Karen. She was whistling. Jimmy and I gawked and John started to laugh. "I'll have to go and apologize to quite a few nurses," he said. "About a week ago they told me about this—this—unusual activity at seven months." He started to laugh again. "The story spread all over the hospital and frankly, I took it with a tablespoon of salt. Oh, dear. It's amazing. Simply amazing."

March was a long month in that Year of Our Lord, one thousand nine hundred and forty-one. The first weeks of April moved sluggishly too, and then, suddenly, in riotous celebration, our tulips, jonquils and violets rushed through the earth in phalanxes of color and shot skyward as never before.

One brittle Sunday morning, Jimmy and Marie and I were standing in awe before the violet bed. (Violets always make me think of babies and I was regretting the lost, sweet months of Karen's infancy.) Dr. John drove up in his car. Marie ran to him and hand in hand they walked over to us. One look at him and there was no need for him to say: "This is a happy errand. Karen is eight months—weighs eight pounds, and you can bring her home."

19

Jimmy and I exchanged a look and he grabbed Marie and hugged her. She broke away and darted into the house. I started after her and stopped. I went back to Jimmy and John who were sitting on the wall.

"Do we have to bring her home, right away?" I said in panic, and then felt a shock at my question.

Poor Jimmy looked horribly startled. John just nodded and said, "That's a typical reaction under the circumstances. Don't let it disturb you."

My embarrassment at having asked the question receded but the feeling of fright persisted. All of a sudden I had a hundred questions. I acted like a female who had never before handled a baby. After a while John's answers instilled some feeling of competence. I went back into the house and found Marie, standing on her doll's trunk trying to reach the trays, bottles and general miscellany, stored away these weary months. Together we made a list of what we needed and dispatched poppa to the Village.

Marie vanished for a few minutes—I didn't think about where, but I soon found out. She had passed the word to the Vale Place gang, that delightful infantile horde living in our neighborhood. Ten minutes later they started arriving, dancing and yipping their enthusiasm. The dogs stick pretty close to their masters so when we had welcomed twelve young'uns we had acquired five dogs (not counting our own).

As I rushed from kitchen to nursery to bath, I tripped over little ones and trod on their pets. Children and hounds are quick to participate in drama and consider noise a rich contribution. I hurried back to the bath and held my spinning head when I found I had placed the sterilizer and bottles carefully in the middle of the tub. (Several days later I found my hat in the hydrator and a bunch of carrots in the hat box.) I backed out and retreated to the living room. Marie was playing her role for all it was worth. I decided the only way to be sane and productive and not spoil her act was to postpone activities until she had retired.

I sneaked into the bedroom and ever so quietly turned the key. Dizzy, I dropped on the bed and thought of the many folks who would be so very, very happy. Reaching for the phone, I started the gratifying task of relaying word of the miracle. For it was that. A miracle of love, science and prayer.

Jimmy and I didn't sleep much that night. Minds and hearts were much too full of tomorrow's errand.

I don't think we'd dozed more than an hour when there was a tap on the door. I opened my eyes—it was still dark.

"Come in," I called questioningly, thinking I had fancied the knock. Marie bounded into the room and up on the bed.

"It's time to go for Karen. She won't like to wait. I don't. Her crib looks pretty. Did you buy milk? Can I feed her? Can I dress her? I've learned to pin you know." She stopped to breathe and clambered astride Jimmy's chest.

He was grinning sillily.

"You look foolishly happy," I told him.

"Look in your mirror, Ma," he replied and got up.

By eight it was raining sweetly, shiny drops like the blessings that were falling on us. As the morning crawled on, the phone rang a lot and box after box of flowers was delivered. A tiny one arrived and when Marie opened it she clapped her hands.

"Look, Daddy, Karen has a beau." There, nestled in shreds of fine white paper was a corsage of sweetheart buds, a scant three inches in length. It was from my cousin Martin, Karen's godfather.

The day grew warmer but we took with us a good supply of blankets. We arrived at the hospital only ten minutes ahead of the appointed hour. Mother and Marie waited on the lawn and we went into the office to "check out." Jimmy was being nonchalant but I noticed he took the stairs two at a time. The farewell committee on Pediatrics was larger than the reception had been. Dr. John was there and a number of the staff doctors and nurses from the Nursery as well as Pediatrics. When Karen was dressed the nurse held her out to Jimmy to carry but he refused. I think he was both noble and a whit scared. In spite of the number of blankets, she was still a tiny bundle. She was all in white and was truly beautiful. She pursed her lips and made a few little sounds and her eyes sparkled as she glanced brightly from one to another.

The triumphant procession wended its way through the corridors, halted frequently by well-wishers, many of whom did not know us but knew Karen. Dr. John walked to the door with us and his parting words are as bright and clear today as then:

"You know, kids, considering all the rules of science, Karen should not have survived. I believe God has saved her for a very special purpose."

Marie and I took care of Karen in delightful partnership. Karen looked and acted like a brand new infant (except for an occasional whistle). Her diet was the same as it had been in the hospital, but she began to grow very fat. We decided it was the extra love that went into the formula. She was beautiful—a towhead, gray-green eyes, heavy long black lashes, fair complexioned. She had a devastating smile.

When she was about nine months old, we accepted her rotundity and began to watch for development as we had seen it in Marie. I noticed first that Karen failed to perform that most bewitching of all baby activity—little round hand holding an even rounder foot and easily putting the toe in the mouth. Then I noticed that she never kicked off her blankets; and then, that no matter what position I left her in, she was in the same position when I returned to her. She was making no attempt to play with the bright-colored objects I hung on the bars of the crib. She did not get up on her knees and wiggle her bottom like other babies.

I spoke to John, who said it would take Karen a while to catch up because of her prematurity, that there was no timetable for a baby's development, they all did things at a different time and Marie's development had been rapid and could not be a yardstick for Karen. "She's slow," John said. "Just give her time."

It was hard not to make comparisons, so we put Marie's baby book away. But no parent can erase from his mind the budding of his child's mind and body. As the days passed there didn't seem to be any budding with Karen. Most parents (including us) brag about the way their offspring holds its head up in the first week of life—"Look at that—what a strong baby."—unmindful that the other babies on the street do exactly the same thing. That is, all but Karen. Other babies turned over long before this; Karen didn't. As the days passed when others reached out for those bright shiny things that rattle when you bump or grab them, Karen didn't.

I don't know when fear crept in and became a permanent lodger.

Perhaps it was during that most sacred ritual—the queen's bath. Marie and I waited in vain for dripping walls, puddles on the floor, a soaked dress, or that precious trick of all young ones, hauling everything within reach into the tub. She laughed heartily in her tub but her feet and legs didn't churn the water into delightful tides. They moved, but slightly and seemed somewhat stiff. Her hands seemed stiff too and she never grabbed for the cloth or the soap or any of the gay aquatic creatures that floated on the quiet water.

Perhaps it was during her meals when I watched and waited for her hands to close over the bottle, or grab the spoon, shoving them away when they were full and pulling them back when they were empty. With Marie it seemed to us that, as she had been born with large brown eyes, so had she been born with a large sense of

23

contrariness. Not so this second. People referred to her as well-behaved. On these occasions fear spread like a swift stream to every part of my body, for a baby Karen's age does not "behave," it just "is."

Perhaps it was during the luxury hours when we rocked her and she didn't squirm. Perhaps when she didn't grab her daddy's tie and twist it—an annoying, but engaging habit of all babies. Perhaps it was when we bent over her and she didn't pull our hair. I think we missed that most of all.

One evening I was sewing in the living room when I realized that Jimmy had been hunched over a book on the library table for some while.

"What are you reading?" I called as I picked up another sock.

"I'll be with you in a minute," he called back. In a few minutes he rose and went to the bookcase so quietly and guiltily I was suspicious. On the pretext of wanting a cigarette I went into the library. As I suspected, he was pushing Marie's baby book into the back of the case. Not long after, he came home unexpectedly one afternoon. I did not hear him come in and when he walked into the bedroom he caught me lying on the bed, Marie's pink moiré baby book in hand.

Now, on occasion, when the phone rings, I am instantly propelled back to that time. At least once during the day Jimmy would call and say, "Hello, sweetheart, how's Karen?"

"Fine," I'd say, in what I hoped was a bright voice.

"How's Marie?" and I'd recite Marie's activities at great length, postponing as long as possible the next question.

"What did Karen do today?"

"Well," I'd reply, "she ate a good breakfast, had a nice bath and is enjoying her leisure," and then I'd get set, for I knew what came next.

"That's nice, honey, but what did she *do*?"

There was only one answer.

"She didn't *do* anything, but just wait until tomorrow. Give her time." But the tomorrows didn't change my answer.

I began to dread that erstwhile wonderful time of the day when I heard Jimmy's whistling as he came up the street. I did the routine things, checked the gas under the dinner, powdered my nose, smoothed my hair, but I no longer hurried happily to the front door. Daily it grew more difficult to greet him. Marie would leap on him, screaming, and they'd wrestle a moment; then he'd place his paper on the table and come over to me.

"Got a kiss for your best beau?"

I had, several of them.

And then, so casually—

"Did Karen do anything since I called?"

"No, Jimmy, she didn't."

"Well, we'll just have to give her time."

We were not the only ones distressed. After a while, Fear went to live also with others: my mother, Jimmy's mother and father, sisters, brothers, aunts, uncles, cousins, friends and neighbors. Since a contingency as minor as a toothache or a dented fender precipitates a deluge of advice, a situation like ours caused us to be engulfed. We finally developed a fine technique of giving each individual the impression that we considered his efforts at guidance the epitome of wisdom, and then instantly forgetting it.

We continued our fortnightly visits to John, each time asking about all the things we felt she should be doing and wasn't, and each time receiving the same unsatisfactory answers with the admonition: "Don't worry —she's just slow—give her time."

Our fear grew with the hours and became coupled with a constant wondering. The certainty that something was wrong, and the uncertainty as to what it could be, gradually took possession of the hours of the night as well as of the day. This wondering and uncertainty became so agonizing that we believed we would welcome

25

any answer just so long as we knew what we had to face. We had no weapon with which to fight our phantom of ignorance.

On August 26, 1941, a dark, hot morning, when the foghorn seemed to be trying to wake the reluctant day, I rose to feed Karen. Jimmy went to heat her bottle while I provided her with fresh lingerie. As he handed me the bottle, he stated deliberately, "I'm not going to the office this morning." I looked up in surprise.

"I'm going to call John and make an appointment. We're going to get an answer on Karen—today."

"All right," I said, "we can't go on like this." I held Karen rather more tightly than before. She was just a year old and I had had her home just four months.

We asked Hope Lowery to stay with the two youngsters and drove up to John's office about ten-thirty. He was waiting for us, and before he had reached his chair, Jimmy started. "John, I feel we have been remiss in not telling you of the deep, disturbing effect on our whole family which has been produced by our fear and uncertainty. Marie and I have discussed the situation thoroughly and we agree that we can face anything but— not knowing." He sat down and lit a cigarette, never taking his eyes from John's face.

"John," I said, "you *must* believe that we can adjust to any fact, but we cannot adjust to an unknown quantity. We cannot go on living with a shadow. We cannot fight a shadow."

He looked at us both intently and seemed to be taking our measure both as individuals and as a team. I couldn't read his expression, though I did notice a tightening of his lips. His chair creaked as he leaned forward and flattened his hands on the desk with a motion of finality.

"I've suspected for some time that Karen has Spastic Paralysis or, more properly speaking, Cerebral Palsy."

Jimmy and I turned to each other with a blank look. The words held no meaning for either of us.

"What does it mean?" Jimmy asked in a thin voice.

26

John was studying the design on his letter opener. He put it down carefully, aligning it meticulously with the edge of the blotter. He pushed back his chair and turned to the window.

"I had no training in spasticity or cerebral palsy in medical school, nor during my internship," he said slowly. "In fact, in all that time I saw only two cases."

"What were you told about it?" Jimmy broke in.

John seemed entranced by a mosquito that was skating over the windowpane. When he spoke, it was even more slowly than before. "I was told there was nothing we could do about it."

"What does it mean?" I almost shouted the question.

He turned and faced us squarely. "I was told," he spoke as though it required a physical effort to shape his words, "that a cerebral palsied child would never sit up, use his hands, or walk."

"Oh, God!"

Jimmy's face was gray. I saw the sweat break out on his forehead, and his eyes were blank as he stared fixedly at the doctor.

"Of course, this was some years ago," John was saying. "There may have been some progress in the field since then."

"What shall we do?" Jimmy was having difficulty with his articulation and his voice was dry.

"I would suggest you see a specialist."

"Who?"

"I don't know," he said gently, "but I'll find out."

I had a very important question. "What's the life expectancy for the cerebral palsied, John?"

"The same as yours and mine."

Jimmy stood up and came over and put his arm around my shoulders.

"Thank you, John," he said, "I realize this has been most difficult for you."

We walked to the door. I turned and nodded, groped for an amenity, found none.

27

In silence we walked to the car and drove home. One of the license plates was loose and rattled maddeningly. We went directly to the nursery. Hope was just changing Karen's diapers. I picked her up and she smiled and cooed. Hope, very wisely, didn't ask any questions. I carried Karen into our room and put her on the bed. Jimmy and I sat on either side of her. We sat and just looked—at her sparkling eyes, her legs, her arms, her hands and feet.

"We prayed so hard for her to live," I said. "Well, she lived all right. She has existence—but no life."

"Oh, sweetheart, don't—" Jimmy picked her up.

"You know something, honey?"

"What?" He was curling her fingers around his thumb.

"All the happiness we feel when we have a baby is made up of two things. First, the joy that a child is born into the world and we are a part of that miracle, and secondly—" I was sorry I'd started to speak.

"Secondly . . ." he prompted me.

"The second part is the joy of anticipation. I have been looking forward to Karen being as beautiful as Mother, as intellectual as you; I was sure she would be sweet, and popular with girls and boys alike. I knew she'd dance well, be a fine tennis player."

He moved over beside me, with Karen in his arms but I didn't look at either of them.

"Besides," I confessed bitterly, "when I pinned her first diaper in place, I was thinking of her first 'long' dress. It would, of course, be white and diaphanous."

"I know," Jimmy said. "I'd even thought ahead to the day when she'd be a lovely wife and mother." A thin sweet sound interrupted him. We turned and looked at Karen and she was whistling.

The next day Dr. John called and gave us the name of a doctor in New York. He had made an appointment for us for the end of the week. Jimmy took Friday off and we drove into the city. At eleven in the morning the temperature was climbing high in the eighties and the

28

heat stood around us in steaming blocks of concrete. Jimmy let us out in front of the doctor's office and went to park the car. I stood for a moment, staring at the door ahead, supporting Karen's head against my shoulder, and trying to escape the hollow clutch of fear.

The office was on the ground floor and the room I entered was long and pale blue and cool. On the walls were framed camera studies of the New York skyline as seen from the Bay, the Cathedral of St. John the Divine, and a snowbound barn in Vermont. A pleasant young lady, looking chill as a Good Humor in her uniform, asked me a few questions and then offered to hold the baby while I went to bathe my face.

When I returned, Jimmy was holding Karen and standing before the snowbound barn. "I do believe it's made me feel cooler. You ought to try it for a few minutes."

"The doctor is ready to see you." We turned to see a huge man standing in the doorway. He looked more like a wrestler than an M.D. A normally florid complexion was accentuated by the heat and I almost invited him to remove his coat. He held the door for us and as we passed him he smiled and I noticed deep laugh wrinkles at the corners of his eyes.

He started by taking a complete history of previous pregnancies and then dug deep into every phase of my pregnancy with Karen, her birth in its minutest detail, and subsequent difficulties and development. Jimmy fidgeted, mopped and squirmed as the questions went on. Karen alternately fretted and wailed in my arms so I placed her on the cooler leather seat of a chair and perched on its arm. Finally the doctor capped his pen, rose and led the way into the examining room. He walked to the basin to wash his hands. "Get her clothes off, Mother, please."

It didn't take me long to remove a dress and diaper. He came over and stood looking down at her as he dried his hands. She wiggled a little in blissful nudity and

29

smiled up at him. He tossed his towel on a stool, picked up a rubber hammer and started his examination. It was as long and painstaking as his interrogation. Karen began to whimper as he continued to prod, tap, move arms, legs, turn her over and back, over and back. Jimmy was motionless, tense, bent slightly over the table and the perspiration was running freely down the side of his face.

The doctor straightened, walked over to the basin. "You can dress her now." I held her on the edge of the table and Jimmy slipped her dress over her head. I saw his hands were trembling as he pinned her diaper. He picked her up and we followed the doctor back to his office. Jimmy remained standing. I went to take Karen. "I'll hold her," he said and turned to the doctor. "Well?" It was almost a whisper.

The doctor didn't look at either of us, but sat tapping the rubber hammer against the heel of his hand. "I concur with Dr. Gundy's findings. However"—a breath of hope, subtle as a summer breeze, stirred in my heart— "however, I must add something." He was now speaking hastily. "I don't believe that cerebral palsy children have any mentality."

Any decision is subject to appeal. Looking back on the days following the doctor's verdict, I know that Jimmy and I strove for an honest evaluation of our situation. We took our first faltering steps toward objectivity. The difficulties of these steps were increased because we had to take them without the help of Dr. John, who had left to join the 10th Mountain Division. We had found another pediatrician of excellent reputation, but it wasn't the same.

The decision of Karen's mentality was, of course, first in our thoughts. We believed that a mentally retarded child should have a place in society and should be educated to the limit of its ability to absorb education.

But there was evidence that Karen was not retarded.

30

Dr. John, who had exceptionally fine training, vast experience and ability, had said that her intelligence was above normal; as a matter of fact he had kidded us about our Phi Beta Kappa. Karen's eyes were bright, alert, eloquent, as intelligent as Marie's.

We felt the decision must be reversed. We were convinced that somewhere, there must be someone to whom we could appeal.

The opinion on Karen's physical limitations was indisputable—today. But we had been told that there was a possibility of progress in the field and we believed that we had valid grounds for seeking a reversal of the sentence.

"Surely, somewhere, the mind of Research has been directed to this condition," said Jimmy. "We'll keep looking till we find it. Besides, what's the sense of being Irish if you can't be thick?" he added with poor bravado.

"How do we know where to start?" I asked.

"Well," said Jimmy, "she's a baby—so we'll go to the best pediatrician we can find. If the answer isn't in pediatrics, maybe it's in orthopedics, or even neurology if the whole thing is supposed to start in the brain. If not, there are many specialities and *someone* must have the answer."

Our pediatrician recommended that we start with a neurologist and referred us to a doctor who was chief of staff at a hospital about a hundred miles from Rye. Mother came to stay with Marie and we left home with some hope. We felt that if he didn't have all, or some of the answer, he would know someone who did.

Karen was a good traveler and after a three-hour drive we drew up before a veritable monolith. We were both pretty nervous and exchanged smiles, intended to be reassuring.

The hospital smell to which we had grown so accustomed met us at the door. We inquired at the desk and were instructed to proceed to the third floor. Getting off the elevator we followed directions to the fourth room on the right. We were greeted by a harassed looking young lady in a gray and red print dress that looked like tomatoes chasing geraniums interminably through a thick fog.

"Whom do you wish to see?" she inquired in a voice as animated as a postage stamp. Inasmuch as Dr. A's name was the only one on the door, it seemed a little unnecessary.

"Dr. A," I replied.

"By whom were you referred?" she asked.

Jimmy gave her the name of Karen's doctor.

She wrote it down. She sat. We sat. She picked up the phone, nibbled at the receiver and then with a hitch to the print dress, and without a word to us, she rose and left the room. We waited. About a half hour later, a dazzlingly large, white-clad figure entered. She paused at the door, looked from one to the other of us, settled on Jimmy and asked doubtfully, "Will you follow me?"

Jimmy looked as though he'd rather not, but we both said, "Yes," and rose.

It was quite a safari. About ten feet from the door we picked up the first young lady, she of the print. She fell in line behind the one in white, I behind her with Karen, and Jimmy following me. We traversed some fifty yards of corridor, turned through a door to the right, went up three steps and through another door into a delightfully appointed office.

A sweet-looking, red-haired young woman sat behind a desk. She nodded to the two in front of us and they stepped aside. She smiled at us, beckoned us to two chairs in front of the desk. "Good morning," she said, as if it was and she was glad. Jimmy and I sat down. Karen squirmed and cried a little. The young woman came around the desk and stood over the baby. "She's lovely," she said warmly. "I'm going to take what is called a case history." She went back to her desk. I thought: If I could choose someone to take it, it would be such a one.

"I am Dr. X, one of Dr. A's assistants, and you are Mr. and Mrs. Killilea. Help yourselves to a cigarette. There are some in that box." She shuffled some papers.

Jimmy lit one for me and, propping Karen up on my arm, I relaxed against the back of my chair. The doctor asked many questions and she was both considerate and kind. We were with her about an hour. At the end of that time she said, "I know you are anxious to see Dr. A. If you will just go down the hall to Dr. Z's office he will want to ask you a few questions first and then he will take you to Dr. A."

It was all very confusing, Dr. A's secret service. Dr. X pressed an invisible button and a few seconds later the door was opened by a spruce young thing who also inquired, "Will you follow me?" I then realized that the two women who had conducted us in an hour ago had vanished. I knew not the manner of their going.

"Thank you, Doctor," I said as we rose.

"You've been wonderful," Jimmy said.

"Good-by and good luck," she answered and walked around the desk and put her hand lightly and briefly on Karen's head.

We only did about fifteen yards of corridor this time, and were ushered into an office that looked as if it had been whelped in Sloane's. The rug tickled my instep as I waded over to a yellow-leather chair. I could smell the latest application of saddle soap. The young lady nodded, and left. Immediately a large blond man in a doctor's coat entered.

"Good morning," he said as if he didn't know whether it was or not and didn't care.

Three down and one to go before we saw the object of our visit.

"Good morning," we replied in unison. (Soon it will be afternoon, I thought, and we'll get a little variety.)

"I know you're anxious to see Dr. A," he said (he didn't know how anxious). "I will ask you just a few questions first." He pressed one of a row of buttons and

33

a nurse appeared with a Manila folder. He studied its contents for a moment and then— "Just a few questions."

There were more than a few, and most of them we had just finished answering for Dr. X. By this time Jimmy was lighting one cigarette from another and I was shifting Karen back and forth as first one arm and then the other went to sleep. It was getting harder to hold her with every passing hour. She couldn't sit up and held her little body stiffly. Jimmy tried to take her but she protested.

At long last the doctor said, "I think you are ready to see Dr. A now," and laughed heartily. We followed him through a beautifully paneled door and as we left the room the nurse took his place at the desk. We walked into an examining room with two nurses in attendance. I laid the baby on the examining table.

"Undress her, please, Mother," said the one to leeward—I did so. Jimmy stood back, shifting his feet uneasily. There was no chair and of course no ash tray. Poor fellow.

It was cool in the office and when I had stripped Karen I asked for a blanket. I was handed a sheet with which I covered her. We stood close beside her, though there was no danger of her rolling off, since she couldn't wiggle enough. We stood. We stood and stood.

After ten minutes, during which no word was said, the door was opened gently by Dr. Y, who stepped just inside and then turned expectantly toward the door through which he had come. I could swear the two nurses came to attention, and then with measured tread, slowly and majestically, a man entered and walked to the table. Dr. Y closed the door silently and took his place beside the newcomer, then turning to us said, in a hushed voice, "This is Dr. A."

Dr. A. didn't even glance at us. He lifted the sheet from Karen and held it out to his side. One of the nurses glided over quickly and relieved him of it. He stood looking down on Karen. Jimmy moved around

34

beside me and took my hand. Both our hands were cold and wet.

Dr. A looked for about a minute and then, stooping over, ran his index finger across Karen's abdomen—from right side to center—from left side to center. He held out his hand and there materialized a little rubber hammer. He tapped her knees and then her elbows. He extended his hand to his side and the nurse quickly removed the hammer.

He turned to me for the first time and said, "Mother—"

"My name is Mrs. Killilea," I broke in.

"Eh, yes—well, Mother, I shall be honest, there is nothing anyone can do for this child."

I looked at Jimmy. His right fist was grinding into his left. He was staring hard at the doctor's profile.

I felt a strong desire to grab the doctor's arms and beg for one word of hope or encouragement. What I said was, "Surely, Doctor, you have some suggestion for us."

"Yes, I have," he replied. "I suggest you take out a good-size insurance policy so that she will always be provided for. Then take your child to an institution and leave her and forget you ever had her."

Chapter 3

Two AND A HALF YEARS went by. Years in which Marie grew strong and lovely. But they were tortured years of futile searching and alternate hope and despair. We had traveled clear across the country and up into Canada. We'd been to clinics, hospitals, and had seen twenty-three of the top doctors in the country. We'd shackled ourselves to debt for years to come. We'd been away from Marie too much and for what? For an attic full of costly and worthless equipment ordered by a few who lacked the integrity to say, "I don't know."

For a long time now, we had had another lodger— and his name was Doubt. We believed that there was mentality—after all, you just had to look at Karen's eyes. They burned, they sparkled, they were eager. They laughed and they cried. But—could it be that we were wrong, and the doctors were right?

And Doubt presented even more agonizing questions. Privately each considered the other's family—was it hereditary? Or worse—somehow is it my fault? Of what am I guilty?

And the world at large, it regarded our little family with humiliating pity or suspicious scorn.

Karen was now three and a half. She could sit up a little, if packed in well with pillows in a tilted chair. She was beginning to hold up her head and had acquired a kind of locomotion. When we placed her on her stomach, she would cross her arms and hitch herself along with her elbows. She moved about four inches an hour but she was moving. She was learning to reach and grab, slowly and unsurely and as often as not losing the object of her effort. Jimmy developed a gag line which was delivered nightly as he stepped through the front door. "How many pick-ups today?" He would then record in a little black book. Or: "Did she make a first down today?" (A first down was two inches in four tries.)

Karen spoke more often and had increased her vocabulary quite a bit in the last three months. True, she was far behind other three-and-a-half-year-olds, but it was progress.

One Sunday afternoon we sought relief from tension by taking a walk along the beach. It was a bleak, blue day and our hearts were as barren and chill as the frozen earth. The beach was deserted by all save the garrulous gulls. They screamed invectives at us for our intrusion and congregated on the rocks where they held noisy conclave. The currents were strong and the water chased itself like a kitten playing with its tail. It purred against the rocks and stretched felinely across the sand. We climbed the rocks and sat in their rough embrace till long after dark, and the lights from Long Island winked derisively at us across the Sound. Somehow it was soothing.

We walked slowly back across the sand and I turned to Jimmy. "Darling, we can't let our discouragement make us lose sight of the indisputable fact that Karen is intelligent. No matter what anyone says—we have proof. And with our proof it would be less than honest to doubt."

"But, honey, there's nothing left for us to do." His voice was flat and he trudged along with his hands in his pockets, head bent, shoulders a little more stooped than they were a few months ago.

"I've heard of a wonderful doctor in S——."

He interrupted me. "That's quite a trip. It will be expensive. Suppose he charges us $250 like the first guy we saw?"

In addition to our major problems, financial worries were making an old man of my husband who was still in his twenties. We all needed clothes, the house was in dire need of repairs, our Ford had long since become erratic and asthmatic and we had to travel by bus and train except on short hauls.

I decided to drop the doctor in S—— for a little. "At least we now know what cerebral palsy is," I said.

"Yes," he said in mimicking recital, "it is an injury to the brain, affecting muscles. Brain cells, once dead, do not regenerate. They may regenerate in appearance, but never in function," Jimmy chanted in a fair imitation of doctor number twelve. "And how the hell can we be sure he knows what he's talking about?"

"Darling, remember when we thought that cerebral palsy was a rare condition? Think of the hundreds of cerebral-palsied children and adults we've met in our travels and of their parents, all frantically, desperately seeking. And think of the loneliness and frustration of so many cerebral palsied, living behind a wall of silence because their speech is unintelligible or they have none at all. Or those hidden and buried in homes or institutions." This and much more we had learned about the lot of the cerebral palsied.

"I do think about it often," he answered me, "and it makes everything worse. I can't forget that lovely little Mrs. M, whose husband walked out on her because he couldn't take it any more. But what are *we* going to do?"

"Well, I hear that this doctor in S—— is tops and I was told if we had gone to him first we'd have saved ourselves all our searching. They say he knows all there is to know about it."

"We can't quit now, can we, sweetheart? As long as there is a chance left we must grab it."

"That's the way I feel."

We stopped and stood listening to the water.

"Let's go home and write for an appointment," he said and added cautiously, "Maybe this will be the turning point in all our lives. Poor little Marie, her unhappiness is harder to take than our own."

Two weeks later we received a letter making our appointment. My spirits had been rising steadily and Jimmy was more optimistic than he had been for many months.

S—— was an overnight trip. We arrived tired, hopeful, yet fearful. This doctor's office was pretty much like a lot of others, except he didn't keep us waiting. He bounded in and greeted us briefly. He was short and round, dignified but not pompous. He wore a sedate dark-blue suit and a maroon tie. His hair was thick and snow-white, though he was not yet fifty. His eyes were brown and deep-set and he wore old-fashioned steel-rimmed glasses. I realized, with surprise, that they were becoming.

He took us immediately into the examining room and without waiting to be told we began to undress Karen. She started to cry and continued crying all through the examination. While the doctor was using lights, hammer, etc., Jimmy briefed him on our travels.

"We understand, Doctor, that you have the answer," he concluded. The doctor didn't answer, but went right on with his examination. When he was finished, he called his nurse, asked her to dress the baby and said to us, "Come back to my office with me." I was afraid of the hope that was mounting in my heart, as we filed into his room. We sat down and he perched on the edge of his desk.

"Mr. Killilea," he began, "you said you had been told that I had the answer to your problem."

"We heard it from a number of people," I broke in.

He turned and looked directly at me. "In China, they have the answer—"

"Tell us what they do in China and we'll do it." Jimmy jumped up and strode across the room and planted himself in front of the doctor.

39

The doctor uncrossed his legs, removed his glasses and put them carefully on the desk beside him. "In China," he went on, "they take such children up on top of a mountain and leave them."

Chapter 4

At two o'clock in the morning, exactly one week after our return from S——, I was awakened by a sharp cry. Jimmy was lying rigidly on his back. His face was gray and covered with sweat. It was apparent that something was very wrong. I grabbed the phone and called the doctor.

He arrived in something less than ten minutes, and ten minutes after that Jimmy was bundled into an ambulance. He had a ruptured appendix. He was operated on immediately.

While he was in the operating room, I waited in his room. The diamond-shaped pattern of the drapes still comes back to haunt me. Green and rose on bilious yellow. The faucet leaked and with maddening, rhythmic procrastination, dropped the seconds as the hours wore on. At times the noise of the trucks on the Post Road was unbearably loud and flogged me with its stridency.

I sat in an armchair for a while, forcing myself to be quiet, but as the night stretched my vigil, I could not stay still. I began to pace the room. Eleven steps to the door. Eleven steps back.

I doubt if I have ever prayed with such fervor as I did that night. I vividly remember explaining to God that if I had a choice, I'd rather have Jimmy than both the youngsters. They were a most precious part of my life, but Jimmy *was* my life. "Please, please, take care of him, not only for me but for the children. Dear Lord, if anything happens to Jimmy, what will become of Karen?"

Two and a half hours later, I heard the elevator and for the hundredth time rushed into the corridor to see

41

if they were bringing Jimmy back. This time they were. I went quickly to the stretcher and walked beside him. I stood aside while they transferred him to the bed and then I went up to the doctor. He turned to me smiling. "He couldn't be better. If you think he has any secrets, now's the time to find out. Ask him anything you like and he'll tell only the truth. He's had scopolamine." He winked wickedly and left.

I walked over to the bed and leaned my cheek lightly against Jimmy's. "Do you love me?" I whispered.

"Yes." I could barely hear him. "For always."

Jimmy's recovery, though unusually slow, was consistent. Marie, not quite five, was considerably upset and for some reason I couldn't fathom, became more solicitous for Karen.

"When is she going to crawl, Mommy? Barbara is younger and she's been crawling a long time."

"Some doctor will have to tell us, dear, and we haven't found him yet."

"Will she ever sit up—all by herself?"

"If God wants her to, she will," I answered.

"But Mommy, why wouldn't God want her to?"

Surely the answer was beyond her ken, but maybe I could make her feel my implicit confidence in Him. "To understand everything that God does, we would have to have a divine mind. But one thing we know. Because He is infinitely good, anything He does is right. There are many things we cannot understand and will not understand until we get to Heaven."

A week after Jimmy's operation, I was sitting beside his hospital bed reading the evening paper. I had finished the first section and had just finished the sports page in the second.

"Anything else of interest?" he asked rather petulantly. (Jimmy is without doubt the best husband in the world, and without doubt the worst patient. It takes me weeks

42

to recuperate from any of his illnesses.) I turned the pages.

"The Junior League of Morristown gave a tea. A man who gave his name as Brown allegedly went berserk in a bar, forced the bartender to take a drink, in which Brown allegedly placed knockout drops."

I moved faithfully down the page, but halted suddenly at a brief paragraph. I read silently, "Dr. B, cerebral palsy specialist, will be at the clinic at the Medical Center Friday, from one to five o'clock."

Today was Thursday. I looked at my watch—it was five minutes to nine o'clock. Providence intervened in the person of a Gray Lady who stuck her head in the door and said, "Visiting hours are over."

My good-night kiss was rather brief and I left Jimmy looking sulky and injured. I hurried out to the switchboard and asked the girl to call a friend of ours who was a resident physician in the hospital.

He came down shortly and I said, "Bill, I'm not crazy and I haven't had a drink, but I want you to do something for me."

"Sure," he said, and looked a little startled at my urgency.

"Will you get the medical directory out of the library and help me look up the background on someone?"

"Now?" His puzzlement increased.

"Yes, please. Right away."

"O.K." Bill always was a good sport.

He returned with the book and we took it into the waiting room. Dr. B had a wonderful background; Bill was impressed and this impressed me.

"Thanks a million, Bill. Don't mention this to Jimmy."

He looked as though he thought Jimmy had enough trouble and he had no desire to add to it.

"Good night," I said quickly and left him staring at the page.

As soon as I got home I went right to the telephone

and put in a person-to-person call down south to Dr. B. It was now a quarter to ten. I could hear the bell ringing and finally a woman answered the phone. The operator said there was a call for Dr. B.

"Who is calling Dr. B?" the woman asked.

"Mrs. Killilea from Rye." I knew the woman could hear me and I spoke with the deliberate implication that of course Dr. B knew me and would be glad to talk to me no matter what the hour. It worked, and to my joyful surprise I heard a man's voice say, "This is Dr. B."

"You don't know me, Doctor. My name is Mrs. Killilea and I live in Rye. I read in the paper that you were conducting a clinic tomorrow at the Medical Center."

I was so afraid I'd lose him, I raced on, "We have a three-and-a-half-year-old girl with cerebral palsy. We've seen twenty-three doctors in two and a half years. We've been all over the country. They all tell us the case is hopeless—that a person with cerebral palsy has no mentality." I thought I heard a stifled sigh.

"We thought there was no one left for us to see," I hurried on, "and just forty-five minutes ago I read about you. I want to bring her to your clinic tomorrow."

"I'm sorry, Mrs. Killilea," he said kindly, "there wouldn't be time. The schedule is crowded already."

"Oh, Doctor, please," I begged, "couldn't you fit her in somewhere?"

"I know from experience, there won't be a spare minute," he said gently.

"When can you see her?"

"I don't know. Tomorrow evening I leave on an extended trip throughout the West."

I wasn't going to let this chance slip away. I forgot all Mother's teaching and my convent training. I took a grip on the phone and boldly and frantically I said, "Doctor, doesn't your train come into Pennsylvania Station?"

"Yes, it does."

"Doctor, I believe you're our last hope. I feel that if you say our case is hopeless, we must accept the verdict.

44

But, I also feel that if you saw Karen you would not say so."

"But—"

I interrupted him and went on. "If you'll tell me what time your train gets into Penn Station, I'll get a redcap to take Karen into the baggage room. If you'll just look at her for five minutes, that's all I ask."

"But—"

Again I interrupted. "Oh, Doctor, please, please. Just to tell me—shall we keep on looking or is it hopeless. Is it as they say?"

There was a long pause. A life hung suspended in the silence, to be saved or shattered by his reply. "Dear God, make him say yes!"

"Very well, Mrs. Killilea"—his voice was sweet—"bring her to the clinic tomorrow and we'll see if we can't fit her in."

"Oh, thank you, Doctor, thank you—"

"No need for thanks. I'll see you tomorrow then. Good night."

"Good night, and God bless you."

I didn't want anyone to know about this trip since, with the exception of our mothers, there was a pretty general opinion that we had carried this searching business a bit too far. Certainly beyond the realm of good sense. "You must learn to accept and stop fighting this thing," was the usual advice.

My thoughts were in a tumult as I prepared for the trip. I had never taken such a trip without Jimmy. The physical aspects of the journey were not frightening but rather the ordeal of facing a verdict without his moral support.

It was only a week before Christmas and we were involved in the welter of preparation peculiar to families with children. We were hoping that Jimmy would be home before Christmas, but the only thing we could count on him for was expert direction in the concoction

45

of egg-nogs, from a horizontal position on the couch. As long as Marie would be home without my supervision, I had to scurry around that morning before she was up and bury interesting packages and boxes in closets and drawers, like a diligent squirrel before the first frost.

It was always a great pleasure to dress my little ones because they were so beautiful (if I do say so, as shouldn't). Karen was ravishing in her blond loveliness. I selected a pale yellow voile which was very feminine, brushed her hair till it sparkled, and zipped her snugly into a soft yellow snow suit. So attired she always made me think of the first daffodil of the year.

All nature appeared involved in a gigantic conspiracy to make my trip as unpleasant and hazardous as possible. Several days before it had snowed, then melted, and then frozen. Today it was sleeting and the radio had been brightly suggesting that no one should travel unless it was absolutely necessary. Every time I heard the sober announcement, I thought there was no trip more necessary than mine; for didn't I have a chance in a million of bringing my husband a Christmas present beyond compare—a future for his child. I didn't allow myself to dwell on this thought, but each time it would sneak into my consciousness, I would get a tingling feeling all over.

The car I borrowed was lovely, and equipped with everything but a waffle iron. The windshield wipers were as sleek and slim as two fine scalpels, but after the first two blocks I realized that with wipers, like scalpels, appearance isn't everything. They perform only as well as the impulses they receive, and somewhere along the line impulses were being detoured and delayed.

If only Jimmy were here! I thought for the first of many times during the day.

Every community was gay in its Christmas masquerade. The sleet freezing on the pavements was trampled into slush by armies of shoppers; all their usual emotions

46

veneered with that bright look of holiday expectancy and good will, which seems to settle into place on or about December 15 and evaporate about January 3. Indignant drivers didn't swear at stalled cars, but rather shouted mild denouncements, as though they felt that if they allowed the incident to pass without umbrage they would be playing traitor to their code.

As I watched so many hurrying along the streets, I wondered if any ever paused and gave thought to the miracle that took place each time he *put* one foot in front of the other; each time he *picked up* a bundle and *held* it securely; or that greatest miracle of all, when without any conscious effort, he could pronounce "Merry Christmas."

I prayed a lot during that ride. I prayed that, if it would be best for our whole family, the Infant Savior would bring with Him this birthday a gift beyond price —a gift of thought and motion for our daughter.

The nearer I came to the hospital, the more apprehensive I became. I was not at all sure of my resiliency in the face of another knockdown.

This clinic, like so many we had waited in, was crowded with children of all ages. Some stiff like Karen, some with exaggerated constant movements, some with facial grimaces, some who drooled, others staggering around with unbalanced gait, and many in wheel chairs. They all had some type of cerebral palsy.

Finally our turn came. I cared not how it was arranged. I was asked to take Karen into one of many little curtained alcoves in which there was an examining table and one small white enameled stand. Immediately a man entered. He was tall and slender and carried himself superbly. I thought he looked tired. As he came over I extended my hand. "I am Mrs. Killilea and this is Karen." I watched him closely to detect any slight change of expression. There was none that I could see. "I can't thank you enough for seeing her."

47

"I'm happy to meet you," he said as he supported Karen on the edge of the table. "Did you drive down?" He handed her a lollypop and laid her on her back.

"Yes, we did, Doctor."

He glanced over at me and smiled and started unlacing her shoe. I stepped forward and went into Karen's stripping routine.

"Tell me all about her," he invited in a well-modulated voice.

I'd given so many histories that I had grown quite adept at knowing just what was considered important and reciting concisely. He started examining Karen as I was talking and when I finished asked a number of questions. Most of them were questions I had not been asked before. I tried to be intelligent and objective and succinct. I was so nervous I was not very articulate, but he gave the impression of finding my answers satisfactory.

He took a long, long time with his examination and did many things I had never seen done before. He did one very strange thing. When he was through, he helped me dress her. When she was dressed he supported her in a partially sitting position on the edge of the table.

"Well, Doctor, what's your verdict?" I heard myself stress the "your." Karen was smiling at him and he was smiling back at her.

"Mrs. Killilea"—he began quietly and confidently. I was totally rigid and I could feel the perspiration running down my back. This was my first verdict alone. He went on: "Karen is a fine healthy child. She needs help and a great deal of it. My verdict is—that she can be taught to sit up and use her hands. And Karen is going to walk. In addition there is no question that she is mentally very alert. Normal IQ or higher."

In all the years of defeated dreams and vain searching I had not cried—but I cried now, and the tears were warm and sweet, because they were tears of happiness.

Chapter 5

IN THE PAST FEW YEARS, there has been much discussion of a comparatively new field in medicine: the field of psychosomatics. Being one of the few individuals uninformed on the subject, I can hold no opinions nor express any belief. I feel, however, that the exponents of this science might be glad to include in their reports a record of Jimmy's rapid recovery following Dr. B's prognosis.

As soon as Jimmy was well enough, late in January, we three set out for Dr. B's office in the south. A two-day jaunt seems to require the same amount of luggage as a two-week trip. For several years this had puzzled and irritated my efficient spouse, but he had gradually become reconciled. This time he did rather more beefing than usual over the Gladstone and overnight bag. He pointed out that we were totally dependent on porters, since the doctor would still not permit him to lift or carry and it was up to me to handle Karen.

No honeymoon ever paralleled this trip of ours in the happy confidence of a bright future. We were going to find out how to teach Karen to sit up, use her hands, walk. This journey was in sharp contrast to others we had made. We must have looked different somehow, because instead of the usual quick glance or rapidly averted head or the bemused stare of pity, passers-by nodded, grinned, or spoke a friendly and happy "hello." We were entranced by people's responsiveness and discussed it delightedly during the three-hour ride.

It was four o'clock in the afternoon when we arrived. We've made the trip dozens of times since, but I never enter this station without feeling like a character in an

Alfred Hitchcock movie. Vaulted tunnels, spotted with naked bulbs, huge shadows, frozen in weird pattern by clouds of glacial smoke.

The train, like an arthritic giant, groaned its way toward Washington and left us on the wooden platform. We waited optimistically for a redcap. We waited in vain. I beat Jimmy to the punch by saying, "I know 'you told me so,' but it can't be far to the cab stand, so let's go." I clutched Karen tighter and picked up the Gladstone, which felt as if it were full of books or bricks or both. Jimmy sheepishly picked up the small overnight bag, which wasn't heavy because all it had in it was a nightie and my make-up or "face" as Marie called it. We started through the station, Jimmy straight and lithe and I staggering under my load. It was a busy hour and the station was crowded, but here were no friendly nods or smiles but stares and glares. The glances were so obviously hostile I was upset and wondered if we looked like Yankees. We'd never been to this part of the South before and I thought—they're still fighting the Civil War. I looked up at Jimmy and saw that his face was beet red.

"I'm going to sit down," he said. "Put Karen on my lap, leave the bag and for heaven's sake go find a cabby and bring him back. Tell him it's an emergency."

"Jimmy darling, what's wrong, are you ill, does something hurt?" I was terribly frightened.

"You're darn right there's something wrong." He glared at me. "Did you see the way everyone has been looking at us?"

"Yes," I answered, "but I don't know why and I don't care."

"Well, I know why and I do care. There you are, a slight young thing, toting a large child and a heavy bag, while I, obviously masculine and virile, trot along beside you with an overnight bag. It's degrading, absolutely degrading."

The next day was cold and infinitely dreary. We arrived at Dr. B's office fifteen minutes early. Ours was the first appointment and he saw us immediately. The very décor of his office has a soothing effect. Subdued colors against softly shaded walls, a beautiful kneehole mahogany desk, a tall bookcase, several easy chairs and an examining table.

After I had introduced them, Jimmy and Dr. B ribbed me some over my initial telephone call that fateful Thursday night. The doctor took Karen from me and put her on the table. "How's my kitten?"

She smiled sweetly up into his face and said, "'Lo."

Together we undressed her and he re-examined her, talking to us the while, telling us what he was doing and why. He gave us our first real definition of the condition. "First of all," he said, "it's a mistaken idea that all cerebral palsy is from birth. It can happen to anyone at any time. All forms of cerebral palsy are the result of anomaly, injury or disease of the brain, the functions of which are so diverse as to allow for infinite variation of the condition."

"Can you put it a little more simply, Doctor?" Jimmy asked, expressing the bewilderment we both felt.

"Yes, of course," Dr. B answered. "C.P. is any injury to the brain which affects the control of the muscles or joints. It can be the result of a congenital malformation, severe childhood illness, measles, whooping cough, encephalitis, anoxia, a blow on the head, prolonged high fever, or a stroke."

"Gee, I thought if you weren't born with it, you'd never have it," I said in amazement.

"That's a mistake most people make. I don't know how many veterans have C.P."

"Why do some children have excess motion, and Karen not enough?"

"There are five types with different manifestations: spastic, athetoid, ataxia, rigidity and tremor." He then explained the various types and went on to say that for years the condition, regardless of type, had been errone-

51

ously referred to as Little's Disease or Spastic Paralysis. "This is bad," he declared, "because the treatment for each type is different. To have proper treatment, you must have proper diagnosis.

"Here's a simile I've used before," Dr. B told me. "The normal child is born with the physical equivalent of a high-school education. Our cerebral-palsied children are born without it. Just as we have to educate the normal child academically, so we have to educate the cerebral-palsy child physically. If we were to place a normal child on a desert island, at the proper time he would crawl and then walk. He would develop a language from what he heard—the language of the birds and animals. He would know how to reach and grasp and place, and would feed himself; because he was born with the physical education necessary to do these things. The cerebral palsy child is not. He must be taught and he can be taught.

"The earlier treatment is started, the better, for a number of reasons. First, we should be teaching the child at an early age when she has the motivation for speech and movement which nature provides at the time when the child should normally be learning these things.

"Secondly, there is the growth factor. Take a short and a long pencil. It is much easier to stand the shorter one on end. So it is easier for a child to learn to stand before it grows tall.

"Thirdly, if treatment is started at an early age, the minimal C.P., or the child with slight involvement, can be corrected in time so that the layman would never know that there was anything amiss.

"The purpose of treatment is not only corrective but serves to prevent deformities. If we start early stretching a tight hamstring—the muscle up the back of the leg—it will not resist bone growth. If we do not, as the bone grows the muscle gets tighter and tighter and we end up with a permanently bent knee."

"How can we teach Karen?" I asked.

52

"Karen needs physiotherapy to learn to walk; occupational therapy to learn self-help, like feeding and washing and dressing herself and writing. She should have a minimum of each of the treatments at least three times a week. The therapy trains some other part of the brain to do the work of the damaged area, that is, sending out messages."

I quickly computed the fantastic sums we had spent in the past four years and rather hesitantly I said, "But, Doctor, isn't that frightfully expensive?"

"Yes, it is," he answered. "It costs a minimum of five dollars a treatment."

From Jimmy a long-drawn-out "Ohhhhhh."

"Well, you don't have to worry about the cost because as far as I know there are no therapists where you live."

"Well, tell us where there are schools or institutions where we can send Karen to learn," I said.

He answered, "There are a few throughout the country, but the minimum cost is $250 a month and the average waiting list is many years long."

"How are these children going to learn so they can lead useful happy lives?"

He said, "I wish I knew. Today, only one out of a hundred is receiving necessary treatment and education. And every fifty-three minutes another C.P. is born, to say nothing of the tens of thousands who acquire the condition later in life."

He leaned over and picked up a fresh cigarette and lit it from the one he was smoking. Here at long last we had found a solution—and at the moment of finding it, it was snatched away. Jimmy slapped both his hands sharply on the desk and jumped to his feet.

"I don't believe it. This is America—the land of equal opportunity." His voice was raw. "What a laugh!" He marched over to the window and turned. "It's a sin—a shame. By God, we haven't spent all this time finding the answer to forfeit it. There must be something, some way—"

53

His mouth was twisted, his nostrils pinched, his eyes were bleak and hard. I watched an agony beyond anything that had gone before. He came back and threw himself into the chair. His head was bowed between his hands. Suddenly he jerked up—he glanced at me and then faced the doctor.

"Doctor, why can't *we* learn, why can't *we* learn to do therapy ourselves?"

Dr. B stood up and came over to sit on the edge of the desk in front of Jimmy. "You can," he answered.

Jimmy's face was alight with hope. "Doctor, I'll take a leave of absence, we'll come here to live for as long as necessary."

I broke in. "Will you help us, doctor? Will you teach us?"

"I will be happy to." He snuffed out his cigarette. "It is far from the ideal arrangement, but it can be done and I'm sure you two can do it. You come back here and stay and we will show you how to do therapy yourselves, and the equipment you will need and how to use it."

Jimmy and I looked at each other—we turned to look at Karen—our search was over.

He explained many things that had puzzled us these last two and a half years. Doctors and therapists, like lawyers and engineers, know those subjects which are taught or presented to them in school. But—

"Up to the present time," he concluded, "the diagnosis and treatment of cerebral palsy have not been taught in medical schools."

He went over the personal phases of the problem ahead and advised us not only on helping Karen but on helping the rest of the family, and the importance of this phase of our efforts, since Karen's own adjustment would be determined by those around her.

"You make the necessary arrangements and let me know when you can come."

Jimmy took Karen from my lap and his hand pressed

her cheek to his. In a husky voice he said, "Good-by, Doctor, and thank you. Thank you very much."

I was most emotional in expressing our gratitude, but far from being embarrassed, Dr. B accepted our thanks with gracious understanding.

The first week-end after our return, we held a family conclave. We discussed our "situation" (having first decided that we would no longer refer to it as a problem). We analyzed the situation in relation to each of us. It was not something that affected just Karen, but all of us. Each of us had emotional attitudes that needed adjusting but there were some general rules of attitude and conduct that applied to all.

1. Karen was a child with a physical handicap but we must not allow this to make us lose sight of the fact that she was a child, first, with all the needs and desires of all children.

2. Many folk with agile limbs are handicapped in the true sense, by a phony set of values, faulty character, etc.

3. Karen should have compassion—but pity, never.

4. There must never be overprotection. Any fears we have must be conquered or concealed. Fear would undermine and destroy.

5. Our efforts were toward this goal: that Karen would one day be a self-respecting, a self-supporting member of society.

To this end we would in the future refer to Karen, not as being *afflicted* with cerebral palsy, but as being *affected by* cerebral palsy.

Chapter 6

CHRISTMAS 1943 had indeed brought "good tidings of great joy." (I speculated on the phrase—"that shall be to all the people.") Jimmy was like a man reborn and needless to say his recuperation was rapid.

Mother had given the children a canary for Christmas and Karen whistled with its song. We also bought her a turtle, for here was something alive that couldn't move quickly beyond her reach. Just as we were growing accustomed to these two additions to the family, the Balfes presented her with one of their beautiful Angora kittens.

Family and friends appreciated the necessity of bringing action and companionship to her, since she could not yet pursue them.

The kitten grew up and left to seek the company of other cats. The cocker grew old and retired to sleep away her remaining days under the kitchen stove. Replacements were needed, so Jimmy and I bought a beautiful chinchilla rabbit, who was *enceinte* at the time of her purchase.

Marie named her "Babbit," which name was, she explained, a combination of Bunny and Rabbit. Babbit may have appreciated Karen's need, for her contribution was the most generous yet, and she added twelve little "babbits" to the household. To a considerable extent, the pets were Karen's "socialization," and to fill their role had to be in the house during the day. This necessitated housebreaking. It required considerable courage to undertake this chore. I had never before attempted such a task with a rabbit, but surprisingly it was accomplished in a few weeks.

We'd lay Karen on a pad in her playpen and put six or eight of the bunny family in with her, placing a low board on the outside so that they couldn't escape. Marie would wheel the remaining four or six in her doll carriage and everyone was happy. So many things that were done because of Karen's need were so very good for Marie.

When the bunnies were about seven months old, ten of the twelve were suddenly taken very ill. It was late February and very cold. Jimmy called our friend, Walter Miller, who is a "vet." "We have ten very sick little rabbits," he said, and described their symptoms. "We don't know the first thing about nursing rabbits, you'll have to tell us what to do and how to do it."

I think rabbits were a little out of Walter's line, but he has a good memory and obviously was able to think back a number of years to his textbook, for he said, "I don't have any medicine here that would be helpful, but if I remember correctly, they should have dandelion roots."

I could only hear Jimmy's end of the conversation and was somewhat aghast to hear him say, "Did you say dandelion roots?" in a voice of awe. "O.K., if you say so, but I don't relish the job. I'll call you back and let you know how we make out. . . . Anything for the kids," he mumbled as he bundled up. "You'd better bundle up too"—he leered at me—"I'm going to need your help—dandelion roots in February."

We went out to the back yard, which in the summer is an area of dandelion-gold rather than grass-green, but this night they were certainly hard to find. We each had a flashlight and a trowel, and when I finally spotted one I gave a whoop of delight. Jimmy raced over and we attacked the earth. Moving around, it had been cold enough; but kneeling still, the wind tore at our clothes and romped up our sleeves. The ground was frozen hard and we pounded and hammered in an effort to break through. After ten minutes, I broke the handle of my trowel and Jimmy worked on alone, while I held the flashlight. Ten minutes after that, I was stiff and Jimmy had worked up a good sweat but no root.

"I give up," he said disgustedly. "I'm going to call Walter back. There must be another remedy. What happens to sick rabbits in those countries where they don't have dandelions?" He marched into the house.

He glanced at the clock as he went through the kitchen. "Nine-fifteen and poor Walter has probably retired after a hectic day, or he is in the middle of a bridge game. Do I feel silly!" And then—"I'd better see if I can fix your trowel; you'd better call him, honey."

Such nonsense comes easier to women, so I called Walter back and told him of our failure to produce the prescription.

"I've been thinking about it since you called," he said, "and the only other treatment I can recollect is weeping willow limbs, the little tender shoots. I've no idea where you might find them, but good luck and keep me posted. Better dress warmly," he added—with some malice, I thought.

I relayed his message to Jimmy and we stood glumly —where was there a weeping willow tree? Suddenly I remembered. "Jimmy!"—I was exuberant—"I know where there are some, down in the Park by the duck pond. I'll call your mother and tell her we have to go out for a few minutes and I'm sure she will come and stay with the kids."

"Just say we have to go out," said Jimmy. "Don't elaborate until she gets here. I wouldn't want her to think I had suddenly taken to the bottle."

At a quarter to ten, Mother K. was ensconced in front of a blazing fire and we left. Jimmy struggled with the car for a good fifteen minutes, but it just wouldn't start, so we set out to walk the half mile to the Park. We walked briskly, with little conversation as our chattering teeth made words unintelligible. I did understand one sentence enroute: "I wonder if kids ever appreciate the screwy things their parents do for them?" He didn't seem to expect an answer.

The trees were truly beautiful, and irrationally I thought of Lady Godiva. With a gleeful cry I fell to with scissors and Jimmy went to work with his penknife. I don't believe I've ever been so cold. I had goose pimples on my duck bumps. Even my nose was stiff. We had stuffed a paper bag quite full when suddenly from the blackness came a harsh voice.

"You're destroying village property. Come with me." I dropped my scissors, grabbed the flash, directed it toward the voice and there was the *Law*.

"Oh, Officer," I said quickly, "it's for medicine. You see we have sick rabbits."

His expression of stupefaction gave way to one of righteous anger; and more to himself than to us, he said, "Two such nice-looking young people drinking that much, and the night just begun."

I could see our friends calmly opening their papers after dinner tomorrow night—confronted with headlines:

DRUNKEN COUPLE SEIZED

Mr. and Mrs. James Killilea of 40 Hill St. were apprehended last night as they . . .

"Oh, Lord, what do we do now?" I was not long in doubt.

"My car's at the gate. Step lively, I'll have to run you in."

Jimmy signaled that further statements would certainly be held against us. We went quietly. The patrol car was warm and so was the station house. As we entered I experienced a tremendous feeling of relief, for there behind the desk was a sergeant, a young man I had grown up with. We explained the entire situation and finally they were both convinced.

The rabbits recovered, but Jimmy and I never really did.

Some day I shall settle my score with Clare Turlay Newberry who with her adorable illustrations and captivating verse had sold me a bill of goods:

A bunny's a delightful habit
No home's complete without a rabbit.*

Children are born without fear. I've been told that a brand-new infant, if tossed into the water, will swim, but that after the second day of life he cannot. He has acquired fear. And just as a child is born without fear, so is it born without prejudice. Prejudice, like fear, is acquired. This tenet has been graphically demonstrated to us. Over a decade we have learned that kindnesses outnumber occasional cruelties. We have also learned that most cruelties stem from prejudice which has its root in ignorance—an unawareness of the facts.

While engaged in our long search, we found that it was less costly to stay at tourist homes than at hotels. One particular trip took us to a western state. We had an appointment with the doctor early in the morning. So that Karen would not be fatigued before the examination, we came in the night before.

It was raining and Jimmy left me at the door of the house and drove the car around to the back. It had been a long trip and Karen was fussy. The house was lovely—white clapboard, old and with lamplight at the windows, it looked warm and friendly. I rang the bell and the door was opened almost immediately. I stepped in out of the rain and turned to a sweet-looking, middle-aged woman.

"We should like a room for the night," I said, "if you can put a cot in our room for Karen."

"I think I can accommodate you."

She led the way into a tastefully furnished living room and invited me to sit down. I relaxed comfortably, prop-

* From *Marshmallow*, by Claire Turlay Newberry. New York, Harper & Brothers, 1942.

60

ping Karen on my arm. She was, at this time, three and a half years old, small for her age, but still a good-sized youngster.

"Why don't you put the child down, she must be heavy," she inquired.

"That's all right," I said, "I'll hold her."

"Well, sit her in the chair next to you," she suggested. "I don't mind if she gets down and runs around. Traveling is hard on youngsters; she'd probably love to get down."

"Karen can't get down and run around," I explained. "As a matter of fact, she can't sit up alone. Even when I'm holding her you'll notice she has difficulty holding her head erect for any length of time. That's why we're here. We've come to see Dr. C. We hope he may be able to help her."

I suddenly realized that the woman was sitting in an attitude of frozen attention. Her face grew livid and she jumped to her feet. "Get out of my house!" she shouted. "Only bad, dirty people would have a child like that."

I sat stunned.

"Get out, get out!" she shouted again, pointing to the door.

I put Karen over my shoulder and rose and walked to the door, opened it and walked out into the rain. Jimmy was just coming around the side of the house.

"Anything wrong, dear?" he asked.

"They're full," I answered.

"Why didn't you wait for me inside and I'd have brought the car to the door? You're both getting soaked."

"I guess I just wasn't thinking, and I'd get just as wet walking back to the house as to the car."

"Hand over Karen and we'll run for it."

I was shivering as I climbed back into the car. The road was narrow and the old car tracks skiddy. The traffic was heavy and Jimmy was completely occupied with driving. I strained to see through the rain to catch the next *Tourists* sign. We had been driving quite a long time before I stopped shivering and began to recover from the shock of my experience. Two towns later my sense of humor began to revive. A little hysterically, I started to laugh and once started I couldn't stop.

"Oh, Jimmy," I choked, "you really should have been there. It was just like a Grade-B movie. You won't believe it, you really won't." And I told him *All*.

He held the wheel as though he would crush it, and raved and swore with revealing fluency that his wife should be submitted to such indignity—that anyone could think his child was— "I'd like to go back and ram my fist down her throat. That stupid, vicious—"

Far into the night and the next day and night. It took him a good deal longer than me to see what a ridiculous scene it had been. The hurt of someone you love is always much harder to take than your own.

But over the years we found compassion and understanding the rule rather than the exception.

For example: Karen needed a special chair, with a slanting seat, so she would not slide out. Jimmy asked a neighbor of ours, who is a builder, to make it for her. He showed him a picture and Jim Dempsey came over and took Karen's measurements. The chair in the picture was strictly utilitarian, but the chair Jim delivered, less than a week later, was a thing of beauty.

The first of the month came and we received no bill, so one evening Jimmy stopped over at the Dempseys'. Some of our bills had to wait, but Jim had four little ones and we felt he should have priority.

When Jimmy returned he said, "Honey, I want to tell you exactly what Jim said when I asked about his bill. It makes up for that so and so in Ohio."

Almost reverently he repeated Jim's words:

"God has given me four healthy, normal youngsters and two good, strong hands. Don't you think the least I can do is to use my hands for Karen?"

For the most part we found children were careful and

kind. When spring came, and it was safe, we took Karen from the playpen and placed her on the ground.

"Good, Mom Pom," she said, and I knew she was relishing the rough kiss of the earth and its fragrance.

One afternoon I was ironing in the kitchen and watching her and some of the neighborhood children playing in the yard. Our menagerie attracted children, and to add to the attractiveness Jimmy hung a tire from a tree which made a beautiful swing off the side of the hill. He had encouraged sliding on the slope during the winter and as he developed each new lure to entice youngsters to our domain he'd say, "If she can't go after them, we'll bring them to her."

This afternoon I saw a strange child, a lad of about six. He looked like a rugged youngster. I had heard that a new family had moved in on Milton Road and concluded he was their child.

Karen had laboriously worked her way over some three inches of ground to pick up a clothespin I had deliberately placed beyond her reach. As I watched, one of the children, from the house next door, just as deliberately snatched the clothespin from Karen and moved it way beyond her reach. She cried in chagrin and disappointment and then started after it all over again, laboriously inching her way across the ground. The new boy had been standing, watching. He turned, and came up to the kitchen window and knocked. I leaned out and said, "Hello, my name is Marie. What's yours?"

"Dale." He was curt. "What's the matter with her?"— and he pointed to Karen.

"Well, Dale," I answered, "God didn't make her arms and legs as strong as yours and mine. We have to teach her to walk and use her hands. She's learning, but it's very hard work and she needs a lot of help."

As I spoke Dale's eyes grew wider and wider and his bright cheeks lost a bit of their color.

Scratching the calf of his left leg with his right foot,

63

he pondered my remark, looking hard at Karen and the unattainable clothespin.

"Didja see what they done?" he said stiffly.

"Yes," I answered, "but it doesn't happen often and if I butt in, it wouldn't be good for Karen. Besides, it would make the children resent her."

He jerked back to me and spoke savagely, "I'll kill the next brat that teases her," and swung away.

At the offender he yelled, "Yah oughta be ashamed, you stinker. I'll bust you one if ya do that again."

His language wasn't choice but it was effective.

I closed the window and went back to my ironing, while he remained standing over Karen, his fists rolled at his side.

She acquired a champion that day, acceptable to the youngsters because he was one of them. For the six years that Dale lived in our neighborhood she was never teased when he was around.

In the winter when the children were coasting on their sleds—and "slewing" was the popular (and dangerous) variation—Dale stood guard. As soon as Marie or I took Karen out for her sleighing, Dale would bellow in his sweet rough voice, "Karen's out. No more slewin' 'till she goes in." (And there was none who dared to disobey his command; he was tough.) Dale moved away four years ago and I cried when he left.

The financial problem, like Alice, grew and grew, and grew. Our house needed more and more in the way of repairs. We needed a new roof; it leaked badly in the dining room. I can recall one sumptuous Easter dinner (which we had on Holy Thursday, since we do not like to cook on holidays. We always have Thanksgiving dinner the Tuesday before, Christmas dinner the Sunday before, and Sunday dinner, as a rule, on Thursday). Our parents and Marie's godfather and his mother were having dinner with us. A sudden rainstorm started right in

64

the middle of the meal. I excused myself and dashed to the kitchen for the roasting pan and placed it in the strategic spot. Dinner was concluded to the symphony of sound produced by tumbling drops on an aluminum surface.

The gas water-heater also needed replacing. It was the old type that required lighting by hand to meet the demand and turning it off the same way when the supply was adequate. I frequently left it on too long. When I did, the water would boil the rust off the pipes and sometimes the clothes I hung on the line looked as though they had been rinsed in tobacco juice.

With spring came baseball. Always my first love. My obsession with sport was quite normal. Nana's father had been a catcher and had played with the World Champion Cincinnati Red Stockings in 1882. He invented the catcher's mask and his nine daughters never quite forgave him for not patenting it. He also was the first Big Leaguer to use a mitt. I was very young when Grandpa died but I can still remember his hands. Every finger had been broken at least twice.

On Saturday Jimmy and I went to a game with the Groarks and to Jack and Aline McCarthy's for cocktails. Aline was a fine pianist. We stayed for hours, singing the score from *Oklahoma*. Both our mothers were busy and we had Hope's daughter Jeanne, a very capable young lady, "sitting" with the children.

When we left the McCarthys', we were gay as we drove up Hill St. The Giants had shellacked the Dodgers, the singing had been fun and the martinis just dry enough. As we rounded the bend, we were confronted by a terrifying sight.

What appeared to be smoke was pouring from the house and standing in the middle of the street, the center of a rapidly increasing crowd, was a panicked, pathetic group. The sitter stood holding Karen, Maric was pressed against her side; with one hand, Jeanne was steadying the stand of the bird cage; the cat was yowling, the dog was barking and the rabbits thumped and raced and swarmed all over the street.

Jimmy brought the car to a screaming stop and we were both out before it had ceased lurching.

"Are you all right—what's wrong?" we yelled as we charged up to the group.

They had appeared frozen, but at our advent all three started to bawl. The animals joined their voices to the din and the resulting crescendo must have been audible for blocks. Satisfied that they were intact, without wasting time on questions we dashed to the front door. Jimmy flung it open and not smoke, but a wall of steam enveloped us. And then I knew. I had lit the gas heater eight hours before and had forgotten to turn it off.

Marie Groark bundled my family into her car and took them home with her. Tom and Jimmy and I raced around the outside prying open those windows that were closed. In half an hour enough steam escaped to permit us to enter. What havoc! The boiling water had backed up into the cold water pipes and the water tanks in both bathrooms had apparently exploded. Pipes had burst, veneer was peeling off some of the furniture, the curtains hung in limp clods, and all the linoleum was completely ruined.

No one said a word; we just went to work. Sustained partly by desperation and partly by martinis, we kept at it till the wee hours of the morning. I can still see Tom Groark, his clothes limp, his hair plastered to his brow, swinging through the halls with a mop over his shoulder, the remaining steam encompassing his figure like a morning mist, singing at the top of his lungs, "Oh, what a beautiful morning—oh, what a beautiful day."

A few days later, Karen and I were in the kitchen and I was morosely studying the ruined linoleum when there was a knock at the door. It was the United Parcel with a package for Karen.

"This will cheer us up," I remarked, thinking that

nothing less than the Kohinoor diamond or at least a 14' x 14' piece of linoleum could accomplish such a feat.

The box was about nine inches long and five inches deep. It was an exciting size at that and marked FRAG-ILE. With mounting curiosity I unwrapped several layers of heavy paper and opened the box. On top of tightly wadded cotton lay a card. It read, "For Karen—with love from Laurette Taylor." I unfolded the cotton and there was the glass figure of a unicorn from her current Broadway production, *The Glass Menagerie*.

Having seen the play I realized its significance and felt a rush of affection for its wise and kindly donor. Laurette Taylor was not only a great actress but a great woman.

Whenever we had a crisis, and they seemed to occur with satanic regularity, it was inevitably followed by some such nice pick-me-up.

At this time, Karen was gaining speed with her hitching as a means of locomotion. It was now possible, after a few hours' work, for her to travel as far as a neighbor's yard. We concurred that—puddles and barberry bushes, dirt and abrasions, notwithstanding—this was Progress and should not only be allowed but encouraged.

One fine bright noon, I was preparing lunch, meditating happily the while on the fact that my daughter had gone as far as Twomeys' driveway. Helen had called and kept me advised of her progress. The last call had heralded the fact that Karen was approaching her first good-sized mud puddle. I was peeling potatoes when there was a loud quick knock on the back door. I flung it open. There on my doorstep was a man in the familiar uniform of a door-to-door baking service. We didn't use this service and I wondered why he was here. He didn't allow me to wonder long. He was obviously indignant, so indignant he was trembling.

"Mrs. Twomey says that's your child down there in the mud puddle." He was shouting. "She also says that you don't want her picked up—that you don't want her brought home." I opened my mouth, but before I could speak he advanced a step, brandishing an Old-Fashioned Grandma Barrett Home-Cooked Crumbcake under my nose. "I have four children of my own. I cover a lot of neighborhoods, but let me tell you—I have never seen anything like this. You don't deserve to have a child." He had been shouting crescendo and finished fortissimo.

I battled gallantly to recover from the swift and violent attack. It was a shattering transition from a mood of happy pride to an explanation of apparent cruelty. I dropped the vegetable knife, seized the astounded man by the sleeve and propelled him into the kitchen.

"I can explain everything," I cried in a brilliant flash of originality. He backed against the refrigerator door and stood, a stern figure of righteous wrath. "You see my child has cerebral palsy." He looked blank and then suspicious. "You'll understand in a minute," I raced on. "It means—" I launched into my first job of public education and my first study of audience reaction. As the surface of a lake is changed by a fractious wind, so his expression altered as my tale unfolded. "And you can help," I concluded inspirationally. "After all, you come by here every day and you will see her often. Just speak and act as naturally as you would with any child." His apologies were so abject as to be embarrassing. He backed out the door, smiling apologetically, leaving on the table the Old-Fashioned Grandma Barrett Home-Cooked Crumbcake.

The next day it rained, and the day following the puddle in Twomeys' driveway was bigger than before. I dressed Karen in a waterproof suit (guaranteed or your money back) and put her out in the back yard. She started immediately for the driveway and its puddle like a homesick turtle for its pond.

Some two hours later I received a call from Helen. She was laughing so, I could hardly understand what she was saying. It developed that the baker and the milkman had hit her house at the same time. The milkman spotted Karen paddling delightedly in the water, and reacted with proper consternation and disgust. He was quite vocal about it. Whereupon, he was treated to an eloquent lecture on cerebral palsy by our educated baker. The lecture was concluded, she reported, by a stirring description of the proper attitude for the future. Such is the power of public education.

Chapter 7

WHEN THE BUSHES AND TREES were seeking to outdo each other in the color and extravagance of their Easter outfits, Jimmy took a leave of absence and the three of us returned to Dr. B's for our initiation into the mysteries of therapy. As we sped southward there was eloquent evidence of the annual miracle of rebirth and growth. It was in fields, wrenched by the birth of minute green sprouts; in the magnolias, their sensuous cups spilling fragrance; in the azaleas, hurling the violences of their color in successful contradiction of human concepts; in the dogwood—created perhaps that, halfway through the year, man might be reminded of the star over the Stable.

With scheduled daily trips to Doctor B's office, we stayed at a hotel near by. There was to be a session each morning with his therapist, Miss Wenkin. It was her job to teach us how to do therapy.

Miss Wenkin was a pretty, motherly woman in her forties. She had worked with Dr. B for a long time. She greeted us cordially and took us to the therapy room. It was large and well-stocked with equipment. There was a high, padded table, a full-length mirror, long parallel bars, about two feet high, chairs with slanting backs, metronomes, two pieces of wood that looked something like a pair of skis, sandbags, high tables about 2½ feet square with a semicircle cut out on one side. The bars and tables were made so that their height could be adjusted. There were many other things and eventually we came to use them all.

A little overwhelmed, we sat down and put Karen in one of the special chairs. She settled happily and surveyed the room, calling at frequent intervals, "Look, Mom Pom! . . . Look, Daddy!" Miss Wenkin said that before she demonstrated therapy, she wanted to explain to us just what it was.

"Walking is a highly complicated action," she began. "At each step, literally hundreds of muscles in every part of the body are called on to perform in perfect synchronization. Because of damage to certain parts of the brain, many of Karen's muscles do not get the proper messages. The purpose of therapy is to train an undamaged part of the brain to substitute for the damaged area in message sending. There will be exercises for neck, back and stomach muscles so that Karen can hold up her head, sit and stand. Exercises for legs—tight muscles cause Karen's legs to cross in a 'scissors gait.' No one can walk with crossed legs, so muscles must be stretched by pulling the legs apart.

"Reciprocal action of the legs is necessary for crawling, the first step toward walking. Let me amplify a little. If you cover the average child on a hot day, he will kick the covers off, kicking first with one leg and then the other, reciprocally. Not so Karen. If she kicks at all, it is by moving both legs together. So, one of our first assignments, then, will be to teach her reciprocal motion, passively at first, doing it for her and working toward the time when the brain will take over and the exercise then becomes active."

She explained things simply and well, and I thought we should have no difficulty.

"There are exercises for feet, a number of them, and for toes, and so on. I'm not going to confuse you by going into all of them now. Each exercise has its own song and is done in rhythm." We nodded.

She went over and picked up Karen and put her on the table. She undressed her except for pants. "Now I'll show you how to do the exercise for reciprocal motion." Jimmy stood on one side of the table and I on the other.

71

Karen just lay there and smiled and occasionally twisted to look at some new item of interest.

"The first step," said our instructress, "is to teach the child to relax, by your voice, words, by showing her a rag doll." Here she reached behind her, lifted a doll from a shelf and held it in front of Karen. Like all rag dolls it was "relaxed" so that it flopped.

"Pretty doll," exclaimed Karen. "Gimme." Miss Wenkin handed it to her and Karen allowed it to rest on her chest, folding her arms affectionately around it.

"Isn't the dolly *soft?*" asked Miss Wenkin with gentle emphasis on the word. "Soft," she repeated. She gently released the doll from Karen's arms and very slowly she moved its arms and legs, allowing them to fall. "See how soft she is—soft arms, soft legs. Now watch me, honey. See, I'll make my arms and legs soft." And Miss Wenkin did a beautiful take-off on a rag doll. In about half an hour Karen had caught something of the idea.

"Her relaxation before her therapy," Miss Wenkin warned us, "will have to be a conscious effort each time and much of the time she is going to have to work at it during the exercises as well." She returned the doll to the shelf. "Now I'll show you one of the first exercises. This is for reciprocal motion which I talked about before."

She took hold of Karen's feet and slowly moved one so that the knee bent and the heel slid up to within an inch of the buttocks. As she started to bring this one down to its original position, she started the other one up. "This position of the foot is all-important during this exercise, so is the distance between the legs and the rotation of the knees."

Jimmy was watching intently. "I'm beginning to feel a little over my depth," I objected.

She went through the exercise a number of times, explaining just what was happening at each stage of the movement. "You'll want to learn something about muscles so that you will better understand," she advised as

72

she moved aside. "Now, Mrs. Killilea, you move into my place and give it a try."

It had all sounded easy. It had looked easy. It wasn't. There are 110 ways to grasp a foot, 109 of them are wrong.

The first session lasted about two hours. We were given some books and dismissed. We were tired but happy.

Back in our hotel room at night, after Karen had gone to sleep, we put a newspaper over the bed lamp and studied. We devoured all we had been given. It was drink to thirsty people. We had hunted and hunted for material on the subject of C.P. and up to now had found none.

One morning, after weeks of schooling, Dr. B came up to the therapy room. Karen was in the middle of a foot exercise and I was chortling, "Little birdies in their nests, go peep, peep, peep," as I manipulated her toes.

He walked over to the table and picked her up. "How's my kitten this morning?"

She hugged him tightly and laughed up at him, "Fine."

I held my breath for I knew from previous experience what her next move would be. Every time he picked her up she grabbed his glasses, a ritual which upset us considerably and bothered him not a whit.

"Do you think they're pretty?" he asked, as she waved them around making light fairies on the ceiling and walls.

"They are pretty," answered our child, and the four of us grinned smugly at each other.

"I know that one of your greatest concerns has been Karen's slowness in speech."

We nodded. We'd been wondering when he would get around to what we thought the most important aspect of the whole situation.

"Karen's speech problem is environmental rather than organic. Because she has looked and acted like an infant,

73

you have regrettably been treating her like one. Just as soon as you acknowlege her chronological and mental age, there will be rapid progress.

"How would you like to go home and see Marie and Topsy?"

"Yes," she spoke firmly. He turned to us.

"Miss Wenkin and I had a long talk last night," he said, "and we feel that you both are ready to take over the program. We will see you several months from now, at which time we will check Karen's progress. Some of the exercises may be changed, others deleted, and if you are making any mistakes we will correct them. How do you feel about it?" he turned to me.

"I feel confident and at the same time a little nervous. But with Jimmy and me handling it together, I'm sure we'll make out."

"If at any time you come up against a snag, or have any problem whatsoever, I want you to call us," he said. I knew he meant it and it made me feel secure.

"You can plan on leaving this afternoon"—he handed Karen to me; she was still holding his glasses.

"I can't see to walk downstairs without my glasses," he said to her. "I might fall and hurt myself."

"Here." She obligingly handed them over.

"Thank you very much," he acknowledged formally. "You're a good girl; please come back and see me soon."

We rose with him and he shook hands with us. "You two will do a good job," he spoke confidently, and then a little sadly I thought, he added, "I wish all my parents could work together."

"Good-by, Doctor," said Jimmy. "There aren't words with which to thank you."

I added, "What you have done, Doctor, is to help, not only Karen, but our whole family. You undoubtedly know, better than we, how different our future will be as a result of all this."

"It will not always be easy. There will be times when the daily grind will be almost unbearable. Your job will continue, not for months but for years, but the compensations are great. The day Karen takes her first step, you will experience a joy far beyond the joy you knew at Marie's first step." He smiled and left us.

Now a future was being revealed for our daughter, we found ourselves haunted by the tragic figures of the hundreds of helpless and unhelped youngsters we had passed in the night of our search. We now knew that they could be helped too, but by whom, how, and where?

We came home humming the different tunes that we used in therapy. When Jimmy returned to the office, this habit became the source of considerable ribbing. While others whistled or sang the currently popular tunes, Jimmy all unaware, gave forth with:

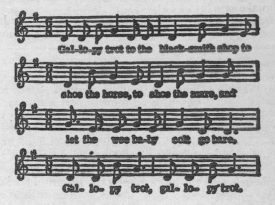

Gal-lo-py trot to the black-smith shop to
shoe the horse, to shoe the mare, and
let the wee ba-by colt go bare.
Gal-lo-py trot, gal-lo-py trot.

It wasn't easy establishing a new household routine to provide for two one-hour periods of therapy each day, six days a week. For Marie, who was almost seven, it meant hours of our time devoted exclusively to Karen. We jumped this hurdle by teaching her the songs (which she loved) and by relying on her help in a number of exercises. She developed a touching sense of responsibility, and as time went on, she acquired a concept of service which, unfortunately, most of us do not have until we are several decades past six.

This was not the only blessing, for if a master mind had contrived a scheme for the perfection of love and unity between husband and wife, this must be it. Heartache, hurt and discouragement there were aplenty, but there was a new, brighter, clearer happiness in our home, and we wouldn't have changed it if we could.

I had never thought that "capable" hands (the tactful way of referring to large hands) would be a source for gratitude. Nor that the years spent on a tennis court and in fencing would produce anything but the problem of covering bulging biceps, summer or winter. That both would one day be a source of facility and strength in teaching my child to walk, would never have occurred to me. God works in mysterious ways. In giving me a passion for sports and an aptitude thereat, He had been equipping me since childhood for a task not entrusted to the average parent.

When I started on the program at home without Miss Wenkin's constant help I realized that, for a while at least, I would need some expert assistance and supervision. I called Dr. Holla, Westchester County commissioner of health, and he arranged to have Lucy Lewandowska, the county orthopedic nurse, visit us once a week. To this wonderful woman we owe a debt we can never repay. Of her experience, kindness and wisdom she taught us well; but more important she instilled an attitude, without which there would have been little value to our efforts.

On her first visit she said to me, "Mrs. Killilea, you should be very proud that God entrusted a cerebral-palsied child to your care. He must have great confidence in you. You must justify that confidence."

Because Karen was barred from most of the average activity of children and therefore could not excel in the usual childhood activities, we sought for a sphere in which she could excel. All young children derive their sense of security (those battered prostituted words) from the home, but as they grow this security must come from their own accomplishments.

We are grateful for our Irish ancestry, for who has known a "Mick" with a sluggish tongue? While other children ran around and played ball and Karen sat and watched, she could be taught to think and speak of them as "youngsters cavorting and hurling an object into space." Stilted today, but tomorrow an excellence—an excellence in language. The family made a pact. To fulfill our pact I must confess we were put to considerable expense for a large dictionary. We would not use a one- or two-syllable word if a four- or five-syllable word would do. As our plan matured, it became a source of endless comic situations which were enhanced by the fact that Karen has always been small, and her stature has been a consistent two years behind the size for her age.

When one of the neighbors offered Karen an orange, she said "Thank you, no. I'm prone to diarrhea." When Marie came in tears and confessed she had had a fistfight with Florence, Karen gave her an icy stare and said, "I am appalled and shocked at your behavior." She told the mailman he was "extremely courteous" and Bob Sherburne, who delivered a pound of butter in an emergency, that he was "most obliging." She was not "hungry" but "famished," not "tired" but "fatigued." One day I chided her about being unusually quiet. She said quite matter-of-factly, "I'm dejected, Mom Pom."

I doubt that there are any that set more store by that precious sixth sense—a sense of humor, than those of Gaelic descent. I grant that not infrequently it is referred to as "that depraved Irish wit"; even so, it is an inheritance that should never be underestimated nor renounced, since by a flick of the tongue it can change tragedy into melodrama and is a reliable immunization against the pervasive illness of self-pity. Jimmy and I watched hopefully for the first indication that Karen had developed this sixth sense. Just before her fourth birthday an incident took place which not only reassured us on this score but demonstrated that, like her father, her sense of humor was somewhat exaggerated.

Our favorite people, George and Aunt Vera, were having dinner with us. With what culinary finesse I could muster, I prepared stuffed veal, several vegetables, mashed potatoes; and as the crowning gesture of my affection, I had baked an apple pie. Karen was wedged into a highchair with a sandbag on her feet to keep her from slipping. I was serving the pie and we were all applauding her because less than half her dinner had been spilled on the floor, when the telephone rang. (I have often noticed that if the phone rings only once a day, it's in the middle of a meal.)

Karen said quickly, "I'll answer it, Daddy."

"Don't run or you might break a leg," Jimmy cautioned, humorously sarcastic.

Karen watched him covertly as he reached for the phone. "And then I couldn't walk," she retorted and burst out laughing. Jimmy's hand stopped in mid-air. The phone kept ringing but no one noticed. We sat for a moment just staring and then we too started to laugh. We laughed till the tears ran down our cheeks but the tears did not entirely spring from amusement.

As soon as dinner was over we sent Nana a night letter reporting the incident, which we ended by saying, "She's on her way." The next morning she wired back, "She's arrived."

Rye is on the Sound and our house is only five minutes from the beach. Marie had learned to swim before she could walk and went fishing before she could talk. We realized that it would be some time before Karen could swim but that summer we took her to the beach as usual. She loved to lie on the water's edge and thoroughly enjoyed the gentle breaking of the tiny waves on her body. We decided that she would be able to go out in a boat to fish long before she could swim, so she should at least know how to hold her breath when submerged.

We bought a bag of brightly colored marbles. These we placed in shallow water and she thought it great sport to pick them up and put them in her pail. By degrees we moved them into deeper water so that to see them and pick them up she had to put her face closer and closer to the surface of the water. Occasionally a wave would slap her and Jimmy taught her how to hold her breath as soon as the water touched her face so it wouldn't go up her nose or make her cough. It was the end of August when he decided she was ready for the final step. He carried her in, laid her on her stomach and placed her favorite bright blue marble deep enough so that in order to seize it she had to put her face into the water. Marie and I watched narrowly. The first four tries she recoiled as she felt the wetness from brow to chin. "You pick it up, Daddy," she told Jimmy.

"If you want it, darling, pick it up yourself. You're big enough now to do things without help. Let's practice holding our breath together and then go after it."

At this point I became aware that a number of people were watching. Their expressions were uniformly disapproving, and a few were quite vocal about it. Ordinarily, I would have explained but I was too engrossed in the outcome to care. "One, two, three," said Jimmy, happily unaware of his audience, and together they held their breath. They did this a number of times and then Jimmy said, "O.K., sweetheart, we'll lose that marble if we leave it, so pick it up and we'll take it home."

"O.K., Daddy," Karen answered and without hesitation she put her head under and went after it. Triumphantly she brought it up and handed it to Jimmy. "Here's the marble, Daddy, and I didn't inhale a drop."

"Good girl," said Jimmy. "Now you're ready to learn to

79

dive. We'll have our first lesson tomorrow." The astounded onlookers dispersed, clucking their way back to their umbrellas.

By the time the summer was over, Karen was completely at home in the water and had no fear whatsoever. This was perhaps the most important step in many things besides swimming. Karen is one of the spastic group of cerebral palsy, and her body, at this time, was very stiff. Fear only made her stiffer. But whether we are teaching our child to swim or walk or use her hands deftly, fear is the monster that can crush and completely destroy: fear of falling, fear of breaking an object, fear of ridicule, fear of being a burden. We learned that with Karen we could never speak without careful thought.

Our house is built on the side of a hill. When you come in the front you are on ground level and when you go downstairs to the back you are on ground level also. It is really very attractive since the house seems to nestle in the land like an angular cocoon. It satisfies our esthetic sense but is physically exhausting because of the ridiculous location of the rooms. First floor: living room, library, bedrooms and bath, and then long steep stairs to the floor on a lower level where we have a dining room, kitchen, bedroom and lavatory. This artistic rather than intelligent layout necessitated many extra trips up and down stairs. Like any other youngster, Karen wished to be with me while I was engaged in household tasks, so I carried her up and down, making extra trips for vacuum, mop and other tools of my profession. As she grew heavier it became necessary to cut down on the times I carried her up and down stairs in a day.

"Bring me up with you, Mummy," she'd ask as I started off to straighten a bedroom.

I couldn't answer without thought because I mustn't plant in her mind the idea that she was heavy for me to carry and therefore a burden. I had no wish to adopt an automatic negative, so many of the requests had to be answered carefully.

"I'm going to air the room and I don't want you to get chilled."

"Watch the potatoes and tell me when they start to boil."

"You can help by drying these dishes." We had bought a plastic set so she'd have no fear of breaking them, and could assume a chore like Marie.

Most of her requests had to be handled with this thoughtful attention. We learned early to avoid the negative approach. One does not say, "Don't be afraid, you won't fall," or "Don't be afraid, the doctor won't hurt you." This only makes the child feel there is something to be afraid of or you would not offer reassurance.

One afternoon in early fall we visited the Healeys in Connecticut. The section in which they live is built around a large and beautiful lake. The homes are spacious, each with several hundred feet of waterfront. Most of the families have a rowboat and canoe since the bass fishing is excellent. It was a cool day, charged with the incipient tang of the first frost. We were sitting on the terrace and Bill asked the children if they would like to go out for a row. I settled Karen and Marie in the stern of the boat facing Bill, Karen right in the middle of the seat with Marie's arm securely around her. The boat was too small to hold seven of us, so Ethel and Jay and Jimmy and I climbed into the canoe and followed behind.

Jay had been discharged from the Army two weeks previously and was wearing a beautiful new Tripler suit. "Don't get cute, this canoe is very tippy," he admonished as he settled himself gingerly in the bow. He paddled along about fifty feet behind the rowboat. I had every confidence in the world in Bill, but still kept my eyes glued on Karen and Marie. We went about half a mile up the lake. The sun beat down in warm embrace, the fish leapt all around us as they always do when you go out without a rod. We waved to a number of people taking their Sunday siestas on their terraces.

"Let's go in to the island," Marie called over to us. "I can watch the fish under the water, and it's fun to hide under the willows."

"All right," I called back and shifted my paddle. I turned to look at the island and at that moment Jimmy stood up and dived over the side. My view of the children was momentarily blocked by Bill, but I knew something had happened to one of them. I didn't wait to stand up but rolled over the side of the canoe and started to swim toward the rowboat.

Bill was poised for a dive and Jimmy yelled to him, "Stay with Marie." So it was Karen we were after. Strange thoughts welled up in my mind as I swam rapidly. "How warm the water is. . . . I'm not excited." Bill was using the oars to keep the rowboat from drifting away from the spot where Karen had fallen over. I saw Jimmy go down, and six feet away, I dived under. The lake was about eleven feet deep at this spot and I had never been able to swim down to such a depth before. That day I did in spite of the fact that I was wearing a tweed suit and heavy oxfords. I swam around, straining my eyes, till I thought my chest would explode. I saw grass and mud but no Karen. I couldn't hold my breath to the surface and came up beside the boat, choking and gasping. I grabbed the side and hung limp.

"I have her," yelled Jimmy, and turning my head I saw him handing Karen in over the stern. She held out her arms to Bill and at first glance I knew she was all right. "She hasn't even coughed," I murmured, as I hung in the water. I was electrified by a sudden thought and scrambled madly over the side. "Please, God, she mustn't be afraid." I fell across the seat and as I got up I called to Karen. "Hey, you. The next time you decide to dive overboard, take your coat off first."

"Couldn't you pick a warmer day?" Jimmy chattered as he climbed in over the stern seat. Marie was huddled on the floor at Karen's feet. I moved to the seat in front of them and Jimmy leaned over and said in an urgent whisper, "We've got to make a joke of the whole thing."

"You look so funny, Karen." I made myself laugh. "You're dripping and you've lost a shoe."

"Your hair looks like a kitchen mop," Jimmy said.

Marie had been staring up at Karen. She turned an ashen, wooden face to me and said, "I couldn't help it, Mommy. Honest, I couldn't." Her words tumbled out. Anxiety creased her eyes. Her arms squeezed tightly around her knees. "She was dragging that long stick and dropped it and pulled right away from me to grab it. I grabbed her leg, but her foot came out of her shoe."

That was quick thinking for a little girl.

"Of course you couldn't help it, darling. I know that." I bent over and kissed her.

Jimmy had been talking to Karen to distract her from what Marie was saying. ". . . and so I have brought half the lake into the boat with me." His saturated trousers clung to his legs.

"Look at Jay and Ethel," I commanded. They were standing about fifteen feet from the island in water up to their thighs. They were a ridiculous sight with their soaking clothes, their hair stringing down over their faces, trying to recapture the over-turned canoe. The mud restrained their every step and they lurched and weaved like a couple of drunks. Both the kids burst out laughing.

"Hey, Daddy," Marie yelled, turning and pointing behind us. "Look at all those people watching us."

"Why shouldn't they?" Jimmy said. "We look very funny indeed." He looked at Bill, who hadn't moved.

"Oh, eh, yes." Bill managed a weak laugh.

Jimmy poked me. "Good Lord, Marie, those people came over to help in time of tragedy and here we are acting gleeful. What must they think?"

We were not long in doubt. It was apparent to the Samaritans that the child was safe and well. They turned their boats where they were, and headed for home. Their final glances at us were ones of revulsion, and made their thoughts all too clear. It was obvious to them that we had over-imbibed (although all we'd had was tea) and risked the lives of our children on an intoxicated sail. Why, we were so far gone, even the near tragedy had not sobered us up! The indictment was on every face.

Jay and Ethel rounded our bow in the captured canoe. They glared in righteous wrath, and all of a sudden I realized that they still didn't know what had happened. That was really funny and this time my laughter was genuine. It may also have been a trifle exaggerated as a result of reaction. I couldn't speak, I could only point them out to Jimmy. In an instant he realized what they were thinking and bellowed like a bull. With a final furious look, they averted their faces and paddled ahead of us, home.

Bill was relieving his tension by rowing like a man possessed. By the way he looked at me when I turned around, I knew what he was thinking. "Don't be an ass," I said sharply. "How could you possibly have foreseen it or stopped it? If you have a dry cigarette, I'd like one."

He shipped his oars and handed me a pack and some matches. "I'm sorry," he said.

"Forget it. You'll have to light the cigarette, I'm too wet."

"Hey, Mom," Jimmy called, "what say, when we get back, you take Marie, and I'll take Karen, and we'll get in a big tub of hot water with all our clothes on."

"But I'm not wet," Marie said. "Would you let me do it anyway?"

"Sure. It'll be crazy and fun."

Karen was snuggled in Jimmy's arms. "Daddy," she said, "you took an awful long time to come and get me." She sighed. "For a while, I thought you weren't coming."

The sun was going down and we were really cold by the time we beached. There was a good bit of spontaneous amusement at Mrs. Healey's expression as five dripping figures marched past her on the way to various baths. I caught up to Jay. I tried to keep a straight face. "Jay, let me explain—"

He ignored me. "Everything's all right, Mother." He articulated each syllable viciously. "Just another example of perverted humor."

"But, Jay—" I tried again. He sloshed off, looking bitterly at his new suit.

The youngsters thought that taking a bath with your clothes on was a wonderful idea. Jimmy reported that Karen suggested that I could, in the future, wash her and her clothes at the same time. We had to borrow clothes for the trip home. Marie and Karen were swallowed up in Ethel's slacks and sweaters. Her clothes were too small for me so I appeared before my startled husband, positively seductive in Jay's Army fatigue duds.

The kids had hot chocolate and we had several cups of coffee and departed. "Don't violate any traffic regulations," I warned Jimmy as we drove off. "We'd have a hard time explaining this setup."

Our technique in handling the accident cost us our reputation in Millbrook, but it was completely successful, for at no time since has Karen shown any fear of the water or a boat. *Te Deum laudamus.*

Marie and Karen talked to everyone about Karen's trick dive "which surprised Mommy and Daddy and made them laugh." About two weeks later, Karen remarked in the middle of breakfast, "You know, when I was lying down there waiting for Daddy to pick me up, it was pretty. There's a lot of grass under the lake."

Chapter 8

As Karen gradually improved, Jimmy and I, in our talks on the matter, spoke more and more of the children and parents who had crossed our path during those dark two and a half years of searching.

"There must be many C.P.'s right here in Westchester," Jimmy concluded. "Why can't something be done?"

"If we could find out how many there were, maybe something could be done."

"Why don't we try."

Jimmy commuted to New York City, so one afternoon I asked a friend to stay with the children and went to see Dr. Holla, the commissioner of health of Westchester County. He is a man with many heavy responsibilities, but he listened courteously while I told him the whole story. "My department is shorthanded now," he said, "but if you wish to work on this, we will give you any help we can. There are no records kept on cerebral palsy," he went on. "You'll have to start from scratch."

"We know," I replied, "that it is sometimes the result of encephalitis. If we could track down the encephalitis records for the past twenty years, we'd be bound to find some."

"I'll give you the names of the patients and the attending physician or hospital and you can go to work. I'll get them to you as soon as possible."

Ten days later the list arrived. There were 270 names on that list. We wrote a sample letter stating the problem and the purpose of our inquiry and sent it to Dr. Holla for approval. He returned it with a brief line: "Good Luck."

We borrowed a typewriter and put it in the library.

We stocked up on paper, carbon, envelopes and stamps. We bought a one-drawer cardboard file. We were very systematic. Jimmy couldn't type, and it took me three weeks to write the individual letters, in my *spare* time.

Meanwhile, we discussed this effort with a friend who suggested we enlist the interest and help of the West-chester County Publishers, who had a chain of papers throughout the county.

Again I lined up a friend as a sitter and went to White Plains to see Bill Fanning and Hugh Robertson. They evinced an immediate interest in the C.P. story and felt we were correct in assuming that there were many parents in the county with the problem and no answers. They said they thought their papers could help. "It is necessary to bring C.P. to the attention of the general public also," Bill said. "We'll run something regularly. We'll advise parents of cerebral-palsied children, and cerebral-palsied adults, to get in touch with you."

I thanked them warmly and started to leave. "One thing more," Bill said. "I think we can have station WFAS help too. If there's anything you want, please call us."

"Don't forget," said Robby.

"Don't worry." I laughed. We shook hands and I left, considerably encouraged.

The following night I rushed for the Port Chester *Daily Item* the minute it was delivered. There it was:

CEREBRAL PALSY NEEDS HELP

Those interested in Cerebral Palsy can call Mrs. J. H. Killilea, Jr., 40 Hill Street, Rye, N. Y., Tel: Rye, 7-0243.

About eight o'clock, I was finishing the dishes when the phone rang. "This is Mrs. Latan," a voice introduced itself when I answered. "I got your name from the paper tonight. Our son has cerebral palsy."

"We have a daughter with cerebral palsy," I said.

"Then I guess you've been through the same mill."

"Did you find a doctor for your son?" I asked.

"Finally," she said. "Did you?"

"Luckily, after a long search. Karen's a spastic. What type is your child?"

"Peter is an athetoid. He's nine and can't speak. We didn't even know what was the matter with him until he was seven. When he was young all the doctors told us he was just slow and then later on, they said, 'Put him away.'"

"Same old story," I muttered. "How is he doing?"

"Physically he's doing quite well, but we can't find anyone to work on his speech. But that's not the worst of it—" Her voice broke and it was several moments before she went on. "He's a sweet child and loves people and wants to play with the other children. But—" she choked up again, "but he drools and the mothers and fathers around here won't let their children be with Peter at all. When he goes up to the youngsters, the mothers yank their children away and then call me and ask me please to keep Peter in his own yard."

I told her about the woman at the tourist rest who had called me "bad" and "dirty."

"Then you know how it feels," she said. "Can you believe it," she then asked, "that this is the first time in nine years that I've been able to talk with someone who really understands? My friends think they do. But how could they? Privately, I think they believe, too, that Peter would be better off away."

"I know about that, too," I said.

"I'd love you to meet Peter. Will you and your husband come down some evening soon?"

"We certainly will. Give me your address." Promising to call within the week I hung up. There was another call later, none the next night, but two the night after.

Every day I waited anxiously for the mail, seizing the letters and quickly running through them for answers to our letters of inquiry. Our mailman was a sweet soul

88

and had known me since childhood. He seemed now to regard me with a new interest, as though wondering why any woman would be so eager and anxious, elated and disappointed over a mail delivery, unless there was *another man*.

It was two weeks before the first answer to our letters had come, and two weeks after that before I received the second. As I had torn open the first, I was thinking, "Jimmy is in the office at this time, I'll call him and read it to him." But I hadn't. The letter had been brief.

> DEAR MADAM:
> We regret that we have no information on this patient.
> > Very truly yours,

The second letter had been substantially the same. Jimmy was pretty crushed when at the end of four weeks we had five answers, and nobody knew nuthin'. In the meantime we contacted orthopedic clinics throughout the county and did uncover a few cases. We wrote follow-up letters on the remaining 265 and wrote also to orthopods, neurologists and pediatricians.

The parents we were in touch with wanted to sit down with us face to face and we had to do something about a sitter for a few hours in the early evening. The school principal recommended a young girl, named Gloria. She said Gloria's mother, who was divorced, was ill and it was necessary for Gloria to earn money. She further said that Gloria had done a lot of baby-sitting and she would give us the names of some people to check with. When we were through checking we decided we would be lucky if we could get this paragon of dependability.

The first night she arrived we were somewhat taken aback. She was small, even for twelve, and her chubbiness made her look younger. "She's going to be a real beauty in a few years," I thought. She had blond hair, green eyes, dimples, high cheekbones that would give her face a look of distinction when she slimmed down. Her complexion was fair and flawless. She had a heart-shaped face, a small straight nose, a sweet mouth with a short upper lip and a fuller lower lip. Her teeth were white, small and even.

We introduced her to the children and hung around for an hour or so before leaving. When we left it was with a feeling that we had stumbled on a gem. She handled the girls as if she had had a dozen of her own and with them it was love at first sight.

We got busier and busier and, as time went on, we came to depend on her more and more. She preferred our house to any other sitting job and handled Karen and Marie with an ideal blend of affection and discipline. "If Marie grows up to be like Gloria, I'll be more than satisfied," Jimmy said more than once.

Every week the papers carried something, and more and more parents called or wrote. Some names came to us from the clinics and to these people we wrote an explanatory letter. A few wrote back: "Please take my name off your list. I am indignant that you should call my child cerebral palsied. He (or she) just can't move much (or just can't walk). I shall take legal action if you make such a statement again."

At the end of eight months we had found 6 C.P.'s as a result of the original 270 letters and had culled an additional 52 from other sources. These cases were distributed throughout the county and gave us a "case." We felt sure there were many more.

Gloria was taking a secretarial course in high school and sometimes after the children were asleep she would type some letters for us, or file.

While we were trying to build toward something for other C.P.'s, our own child was constantly presenting us with new problems.

In raising Karen there were many things to guard

against other than physical deformities. It was a constant job to guard against deformities of character.

The dangers sprang from a number of sources: Karen had to have a great deal of our undivided attention. She had little opportunity to "do" for others and for the same reasons she was constantly being "done for." She was very much limited both in experience and occupation. There was scant opportunity for her to have any responsibility as a member of the family unit.

We did not think of Karen's physical disabilities as a true handicap, but if she were to become a spoiled, self-centered, self-pitying, selfish, dictatorial individual, she would assuredly be handicapped. We knew that an adjusted person, though he travel in a wheel chair or on crutches, can fit well into his niche in society. We also knew that a physically agile person, who is not adjusted, will find that society has no niche for him.

On Washington's Birthday, when Karen was four and a half, we received a solution to some of these problems.

We had a son. James O'Rorke Killilea.

Our great happiness at his birth was immeasurably enhanced by what it would mean to both the girls but especially to Karen. Jimmy was intoxicated with pride and joy.

Rory was born at seven a.m. and at 7:22 Jimmy bounded into my room making the ritualistic presentation of gladioli. I was a bit bruised when he got through hugging and kissing me and, as I massaged my arm, he grabbed the phone and called home. Karen answered and he said, "Hey, sweetheart, the baby's here, it's a boy, Mommy's calling him Rory. Just like you were Marie's baby, he's going to be yours. You're going to have to help Mommy an awful lot."

"Let me speak to her—"

"Hello, darling, isn't it wonderful? Can you believe it?"

"Oh, I love you. It's the bestest present in the whole wide world. Can I feed him?"

91

"Of course. He's yours."

"And change him?"

"Yes—"

"And hold him all by myself?"

"Certainly," I said, laughing happily.

"When will he be home?"

"In a week. You must help get things ready for him."

"I can hardly wait to touch him," and, as an afterthought, "I can hardly wait to see you, too, Mummy."

"Only a week, darling, and we'll both be home. I can hardly wait to see you, too. I miss you both very much. Let me speak to Marie."

But when Marie came on, her words were tumbling around with a lot of tears and I couldn't understand a thing she said. Her reaction was contagious and I started to bawl.

"For the love of Mike!" This from my amazed spouse.

"We'll both be home in a week," I told Marie.

After a few very articulate sniffs, she said, "Do you feel O.K.?"

"Never better, believe me. Kiss Karen and Nana for me, and keep a big one for yourself."

"O.K., Mommy, and hurry home. I love you. Good-by!"

"Good-by, darling, and I love you."

About nine-thirty, Jimmy decided to take a break from telephoning and get some breakfast. "Just one more call," I said, "Florence Healey." Floss is my oldest friend and Karen's doting godmother. She's a precious person with a unique ability to rejoice in others' good fortune.

Jimmy was laughing when he finally said good-by. "She's so happy she's bawling."

"She would. Now go get some sustenance before you faint across my bed." He kissed me and left.

I was making fair progress on the list of announcements when he returned. One glance at his face and I knew something was very wrong.

92

"What is it? What's wrong? Is it—is it the baby?"

He came over and put his arms around me. "Yes. The doctor says that all of a sudden he developed trouble breathing and—he's very bad. I called your mother, but she had already left to come up. I got Mother and Dad and they're on their way now. I want to be sure they see their grandson."

"Did you call the priest?"

"Father Francis was on Wing Two and he baptized the baby about ten minutes ago."

The warm brightness of the morning sun had become flat and steely. It quivered satirically on the gladioli. My mother arrived first. Her white hair was set off effectively by trim blue wool. She was as chic and poised as usual. She came over to the bed and kissed me, bringing with her that calm faith which has supported our family through all its dark hours. I held on to her tightly.

"He's perfectly beautiful," she said proudly, seating herself beside me.

"I know. I saw him two minutes after he was born. Round, plump, a superb head and his eyes—so large and deep violet." My heart ached so it was a physical pain.

Jimmy came in just then, his face a mask of careful control. I knew that he, like me, was thinking of our second, Katherine Anne. He kissed us both and sat on the other side of the bed, holding my hand to his cheek.

"You should be very proud of your son"—Mother's voice was sweet and without a tremor—"and of my daughter." She looked at me, her beautiful eyes shining with pride. "At that, I didn't have to wait so long for a boy to whom I could give Daddy's watch."

"Did you see the doctor—did you speak to him?" It did not seem possible that she could be speaking thus if she understood the situation.

"Yes, I did. He told me to hold no hope, but I think he's mistaken. Oh, medically speaking he's absolutely right, but I think he's overlooked the power of prayer. God knows what this baby boy could mean to Karen. Honey, I have to get back to the children." She rose, drawing on her gloves. "They'll be praying too and remember someone said, 'The prayers of children are always heard.' I believe that." She kissed me again and Jimmy walked out in the corridor with her.

As they left Nancy Florio came in, looking more than ever like an angel in her white uniform. She has abundant black hair, so black it is blue. Her dark eyes with their invincible serenity looked at me levelly as she came across the room. "He's a lovely baby, Marie," she said and her whole attitude seemed to speak: No matter what's ahead you'll not let yourself be found lacking. To all her patients, as to me, Nancy brought a calmness and self-confidence, born of the realization that no matter how slim our own resources of courage, she had a limitless source from which we could replenish ours. "He's very bad," she said quietly, rearranging my pillows as only Nancy can. "The nurse on duty in the nursery didn't wait but baptized him immediately. When the doctor got there, he didn't ask any questions and promptly baptized him. I arrived a few minutes later and, unaware of what had been done before, I baptized him and five minutes after that they brought Father Tully in and he baptized him. Considering your own selection, this four-pound lad of yours is now legally James O'Rorke Thomas Michael Patrick (my choice) Matthew Killilea." She chuckled softly. "If they all cooperate as I expect they should, he may pull through."

My eyes filled with tears of gratitude. "We'll pray with all our might and with the comforting knowledge that God can't make a mistake."

"I'm proud of you—again," she said. "Roll over and I'll rub your back."

Again the carts rolled past my door as they carried the infants to their mothers. Again my hearing became highly educated and I could single out the hushed roll of the two-wheeled cart that brought a fresh tank of oxygen or the hurried, heavier step that brought the doctor to Rory's side.

But Rory held on. Three days, four, a week. Eight days, nine, ten, eleven. And on the eleventh . . . It was seven-thirty and I was just finishing breakfast I didn't want. I looked up to see Nancy at the door. She was smiling beatifically. "They just took Rory off critical," she said and lightly kissed my forehead.

"Thank you, God, thank you," and I began to cry.

Two weeks later Jimmy brought his son home.

There is no question that the parents of C.P. children live with fear, but we condition ourselves to a sense of proportion. We were no exception during the months that we had waited for Rory, nor were we any exception after his birth. "Would he be all right?"

When Rory was three months old, we had a scheduled trip to Dr. B. Mother Killilea had a bad cold and as long as it was a week-end Gloria was able to come and stay at the house with Marie. The Fendlers, Lord love them, knowing that our Ford was unreliable, offered their car and we took Rory with us. The trip had a dual purpose—to check Karen, and more important, to have Dr. B examine Rory. "Would he find anything amiss?" We had pondered this question for many long months.

He evinced no surprise over our request to have him examine Rory. Karen presented her brother with gushing pride. "This is my baby, Doctor, and his name is Rory."

"He's a beautiful baby, kitten, and he looks as though you took good care of him. I'll bet you're a good little mother."

"Oh, I am, Doctor. I feed him. I know how to keep the nipple full of milk, so he won't suck air. I bubble him all by myself. I constantly remind people to support his head"—at this point I thought Dr. B was going to break down, but he covered a chuckle with a cough.

95

"What else do you do?" He managed a serious voice.

"I mind him and Mommy lets me wash a diaper every day. Not the *bad* one." She giggled.

"I'm proud of you. I wish more girls like you had a baby to tend. While you're doing things for him, you're learning other things yourself. I'm proud of you. May I have a look at him?"

"Sure," she said grandly. "I know *you'll* be careful and remember to hold his head. You may give him the baby, Mommy," she said with comical condescension.

Jimmy and I, though apprehensive, were not a little smug as Dr. B. took our son and placed him on the table. There was no denying he was a gorgeous baby. More beautiful than any you see on boxes, tins or jars. The doctor undressed Rory himself, and as I watched his swift, sure and infinitely gentle hands, I thought of the thousands who had been blessed by their touch. Karen was sitting well back in an easy chair watching with absorbed interest. When Dr. B had completed his examination, he lifted Rory, took him over and placed him in Karen's lap.

She looked Dr. B right in the eye and asked, "Does Rory have C.P.?" I almost fainted. Never once had we expressed any doubt in her presence.

"No, he doesn't." Dr. B answered.

"I'm glad," she said, squeezing the baby.

"Where's Mouse?" Dr. B asked, referring to Karen's imaginary playmate of two years' tenure in the household.

"I only play with him when Rory is asleep," she explained. "I'm too busy." She looked down at her burden and started to whistle a lullaby.

An hour and a half later, when Karen had been checked, the nurse took the two children outside and we sat down with the doctor.

"What do you really think, Doctor?" Jimmy asked, coming directly to the point.

"Just what I told Karen," he said. "I can tell you with certainty he is not spastic. I am pretty sure he is not any

96

of the other types, although all infants have involuntary movements at this age. I feel safe in saying that Rory is perfectly normal."

When we returned home with an "all clear" for Rory, a number of parents who had limited their families because they were afraid that a second child might have C.P. took heart and, a few years later, we privately considered ourselves foster parents to several lusty infants.

So much tragedy could have been averted if parents only "knew." I think it was this which provided the final spur to our determination to form an organization and quickly. If nothing else, we would then have a vehicle for the dissemination of facts and the elimination of old wives' tales.

On August 14, 1945—when Karen was just four days short of five years, Rory was six months and Marie was almost eight—the first half of World War II came to an end.

I could not remember the wild celebrations that marked the close of the first world war, but I heard enough and read enough to know that the reaction to the present armistice was altogether different.

The delirious rejoicing of the first armistice was supplanted by reflection, and prayers of thanksgiving and supplication that this peace should be a lasting one.

"Jimmy," I said that night as we walked home from church, "is it amiss to consider that as long as man has been, there has been cerebral palsy; and could it be that after almost two thousand years of nothing being done, there is not a bit of Divine planning in the fact that the cerebral palsy movement is really getting under way at the end of the greatest holocaust that humanity has ever faced?"

"What do you mean?"

"Just this. We cannot do what we are doing and accomplish only the result which started us on our course. Consider the deep spiritual benefits that come to all who

97

work for others. Probably there is a greater need for spirituality today than there has ever been in the history of the world. I wonder if God in His Wisdom has not selected cerebral palsy, at this time, as a tool with which to bring back to many the spirituality that has been lost somewhere along the way."

"That," said Jimmy slowly, "makes a good deal of sense."

On August 28, 1945, John Gundy came home. Our two older children were almost as glad to have him back as were Jimmy and I. Our problems seemed not quite so big when he was around to help.

Every time we visited Dr. B we stayed at the same hotel near his office. We were planning another trip to him in mid-winter, and were looking forward to it, since Karen's progress had been particularly good these last few months. His secretary took care of our hotel reservations for us and when I received a letter from her about two weeks prior to our appointment, I expected it would be the usual confirmation of the hotel arrangements. I began to skim through it and was arrested by the second sentence. She deeply regretted that she had been unable to make the reservations at the same hotel, which was customarily used by most of Dr. B's patients, but the hotel regretted that in the future they would prefer not to handle any of Dr. B's patients, since they embarrassed the other guests.

I could not believe it. If this were true; if this establishment which understood about C.P. did not care, did not accept, what were we working for? To what purpose to train and educate our daughter?

Jimmy wrote to another hotel in the city and gave them the whole story. We received an immediate reply, stating that we would be most welcome and anything they could do to make our stay more pleasant would be a privilege.

When we arrived, with some trepidation, we found this to be the attitude of the entire staff. In the years to come, each time we went, it was like a visit to friends. The bellhops carried Karen lovingly, the waitresses applauded her facility with fork and spoon, the elevator operators asked innumerable questions and the housekeeper added mysterious touches to make our room more homey.

It by no means lessens their kindness or its importance to point out that some others treated us with similar beneficence. The employees of the Baltimore and Ohio Railroad reflected this same attitude of courteous and helpful attention. The steward in the diner on the "Royal Blue" became an ardent admirer of Karen's. He was fascinated by her conversation, sprinkled as it was with words which would be unexpected even from a child twice her size. She had a penchant for crab meat, which she pronounced "delectable."

Chapter 9

No MATTER HOW MUCH we dislike admitting it, we are a nation of conformists. To wit: *"All* women use nail polish." *"Everybody* likes baseball." *"Everybody* has television." As a matter of fact considering styles and habits the only exception I know is the Philadelphia newspaper which advertises: *"Nearly* everybody reads the *Bulletin."*

How many times has it been repeated through the length and breadth of our land: "All children have a right to an education." "All children must go to school—there is a law." All children—except C.P.'s.

The damage is twofold. First, the lack of an education; and secondly, the child who does not go to school is set apart—he is different from the other children. So from the very first year, when the child should be going to school just because he is a child, the C.P. becomes an individual apart. He does not conform to other children's concept of daily pattern.

The loneliness, the lack of stimulation and competition, heartbreaking and harmful as they are, in my opinion do not hurt the child (nor his family) nearly so much as the stamp, "He's different."

Jimmy and I decided that we would do everything within our power to keep Karen from being labeled "different."

Marie attended the parochial school in Rye run by the Sisters of Charity. In late August of 1945, I went to see the principal to talk about Karen, who was five. In spite of the numerous difficulties involved we decided to start her in kindergarten. We had a lengthy discussion with the kindergarten teacher, Sister Rosalie, who was young, very pretty, had lots of personality, was artistic, and patient. Her approach pleased me. "Karen is a child first, and then cerebral palsied."

The day before Karen was to start, I went to the school. It was a "shiny" day as Rory says. The school is located on Milton Road which is a street of wide lawns, patriarchal trees, gracious homes and churches. All the churches in Rye stand in intermittent majesty in a half-mile sweep, their sequence broken by a few houses and acres of sun-flecked lawn.

My errand was in the kindergarten, to speak to the children, only two of whom knew Karen. The quiet orderliness of the building was pleasant as I climbed the stairs to the first floor and classrooms. Slowly I walked down the corridor and knocked at Sister Rosalie's door. She beckoned me in and introduced me to her brood. They had risen as I entered and, acknowledging the introduction, chirped in unison, "Good morning Mrs. Ka-a-l—" Well, they tried and gave it a nice vowel swing.

It was a large sunny room and there were thirty youngsters sitting in groups at little tables, or standing at blackboards, or riding a hobby horse or dabbling in a sandbox. A little redheaded lad with a pug nose and rather prominent ears, dressed in green corduroy shorts and a yellow T shirt, was playing moving man. He had a red express wagon backed up to a doll house and was unloading by the simple expedient of hurling all the furniture through the partly opened roof of the doll house. A sweet little lass, dressed all in blue, was upbraiding him sturdily and snatching at the piles in a vain attempt to create some household order. A chubby fellow stood shyly against the side of the piano, occasionally reaching tentative fingers around the corner to tap the keys. Everything about the room and its occupants was happy and appealing.

I've always enjoyed being in a crowd of children and feel perfectly at home, for some reason (maybe it's obvi-

101

ous). I took a chair, about eighteen inches high, and sat facing them.

"Children, children," Sister Rosalie called, clapping her hands. I was surprised that in less than two minutes the thirty were quiet and were facing me with expressions ranging from curiosity to a hushed expectancy as though they hoped that somehow I'd produce a rabbit and a hat.

"I have a little girl, just your size, named Karen," I began in a conversational tone. "She's nice and laughs a lot and has freckles and pigtails." I turned to a tot at the nearest table. "But her pigtails are not as long as yours." I had done enough public speaking to know when I had established "contact."

"Now God didn't make Karen's legs as strong as yours," I went on, "so we have to help them get strong, so she can walk. Some children wear braces to help their teeth and Karen wears braces to help her legs. There are some things she can't do and some games she can't play. Sister will let some of you help her once in a while. But don't spoil her!" I laughed as I stood up. I went over to the doll house, admired it properly and asked the little lass in blue to show me some of the furnishings. "We have a real bureau with drawers that go in and out that will just fit in the bedroom. Karen will bring it tomorrow. Good-by, Sister, good-by, kids." I waved. "I'll see you tomorrow." Sister walked to the door with me. I was trembling. "How'd I do? Did I sell?" I turned to her anxiously.

"Splendidly. Just wait until tomorrow and then you'll know how well you did."

The next morning we were all in a tizzy. I let Karen select her own dress and ribbons. She chose a gray and yellow plaid with a white piqué collar and cuffs and big yellow taffeta ribbons for her braids. We polished her shoes and the leather on her braces and, as a special surprise, we had bought her a book bag. Everyone had a part in the preparations.

She was far too excited to eat and so were we, if the

truth must be told. I served a double order of vitamin pills by way of compensation. I couldn't leave Rory, who was seven months old, so I took him along and fastened him securely in his car chair.

We drove up in front of the school at exactly eight-forty. The lawn was a teeming vociferous mass of miniature maniacs. The windows winked solemnly at us and I recalled my own first day at school; my mixed-up feelings of frightened excitement, the tenuous fear of so many children in bunches, the titillating delight of the mystery behind the panes. I also remembered how proud I was of my new Mary Jane patent leather pumps, worn only the *first* day of school.

Karen was hard to carry. She squirmed and twisted in delight and in an effort to see everything. We went through the wide doors, up the stairs, and turned right down the corridor with Marie trotting along beside us proudly carrying both book bags, her own and Karen's. It seemed wise for Karen to be in the classroom ahead of most of the others to avoid an "entrance."

Sister showed her to her table and chair, gave her a kiss and said, "Karen, I'm so glad you're in my class."

"So'm I," answered Karen with conviction, looking at her steadily. I tied a new and very pretty scarf around Karen's waist and the back of the chair to keep her from tumbling.

The children were drifting in in snatches and came over and Sister performed the introductions. I handed the bureau to the mistress of the doll house and showed her the real drawers. Some of the children had been staring at Karen's braces curiously but the bureau usurped this interest and they quickly went over to handle it, and discuss with more feeling than tact who would place it in the room. I turned back to Karen who had apparently forgotten me and was talking to a little boy perched on the table beside her. "Mind your manners," I admonished lightly and drifted out without a backward glance.

One of my strongest emotions that morning, as I drove home with Rory beside me, was a deep thankfulness that I still had one in a highchair.

When I got home the phone was ringing, and when I finished with the call I gave the house a "lick and a promise," all the while wondering how things were going in the last room on the right.

At ten forty-five I could stand it no longer. I gathered up my son, parked him across the street with Kavy and tore down to school. I took up a stand outside the door of the classroom where I could see and be unseen. I couldn't hear anything, but the children's gestures were eloquent.

Karen's chair was beside the sandbox and she was leaning forward to dabble with several others of both sexes. As I watched I saw her raise her skirt a little and speak more seriously. She pointed to her knee and kept on talking.

I watched until it was time for dismissal and then retreated a few feet down the corridor so I should not be suspected of hovering. I was on tenterhooks waiting for a report from Sister Rosalie. She was such a diminutive person I stewed over her carrying Karen to and from the bathroom.

She saw me in the hall and came out to me. She looked flushed and happy. "Everything went beautifully," she informed me. We smiled at each other. "The children accepted her completely and she had a wonderful time."

"Was she well-behaved?" Probably the first maternal query to a kindergarten teacher since there have been kindergartens.

"She is a very intelligent and well-behaved child," she told me.

I asked her if she knew what had gone on around the sandbox and she said, "Lucy asked Karen if her braces were broken at her knees."

"A nice healthy interest," I commented. "What was Karen saying?"

"Karen explained that her braces had joints where her legs had joints so she could move right, and then added very matter-of-factly, 'I have cerebral palsy, you know, I'm a spastic. Are you hungry? I am.'"

Thus ended Karen's first day in school.

Chapter 10

ON ONE OF OUR TRAIN TRIPS, there was no unoccupied table in the dining car and we were seated with a solitary gentleman who looked like the popular conception of a big banker. The waiter hurried to place a cushion on Karen's chair. "Hello, sweetheart," he greeted her, "you look real pretty."

"Thank you," smiled Karen, "how do you feel?" The gentleman across the table started. She was five and a half but looked little less than three. As we settled ourselves the waiter moved to take the man's order. "What will you have, sir?" The man studied the menu. Karen leaned across the table. "Have the crabmeat," she advised him. He took a quick gulp of his cocktail and ordered another. "I always order crabmeat," she continued, "the sauce here is so spicy."

"Sounds good," commented the recipient of these suggestions in a dazed tone. To the waiter—"Crabmeat."

The next few minutes were taken up with selecting our luncheon. When all decisions had been made Karen decided to liven up the atmosphere. "Where are you going?" she inquired politely.

"I'm on my way to Washington."

"Do you live there?"

"No, I live in California. Where are you going?"

"I'm going to see Dr. B. I have cerebral palsy and he helps me to learn to walk. Do you know anyone with cerebral palsy?" We had worked hard to make Karen objective about all things medical and she had developed keen, clinical interests, which sometimes required checking.

"Why no-o-o, I don't believe I do."

Jimmy took over at this point and the meal progressed with an animated four-way conversation. By the time we reached the dessert our fellow passenger had fallen hook, line and sinker for our gamine.

"I'm going back to California soon," he spoke to Karen, "and I should like to send you a present. I know where there is the loveliest doll." He described her in detail from the top of her coifed head to kid-clad toes. "If you would rather have something else, just tell me." He sat back satisfied that the shine in Karen's eyes meant that this was a little girl's dream come true.

"Can I truly have anything I want?" Karen was very serious. My mind soared off to scan the wide horizon of her desires.

Mr. Devon (for by this time we had all introduced ourselves) was answering. "Yes, my dear, absolutely anything." He spoke with such simple conviction, I had a moment of panic. Karen was very fond of horses.

"This is what I want, then." She was speaking very distinctly and her voice carried well. Their conversation now had the attention of everyone in the car. "I should like you to send me two enema bags."

Mr. Devon laughed heartily. "Do you know what I thought you said?" he gasped. "I thought you said 'enema bags,'" lowering his voice at the last two words.

"I did," said Karen, "two of them. You said I could have anything I wanted and I want one for Sue and one for Jerry. They're my big dolls."

Mr. Devon was a gentleman of the old school. He controlled himself admirably, bowed and said, "So be it."

Six weeks after our return a large box arrived. In it was the doll, just as he had described her, and two enema bags. The accompanying note said, "For a darling little girl. Hope you enjoy the enclosed *three* objects. With lots of love from Carl Devon."

107

Jimmy and I were a bit surprised. Karen was not. With the beautiful simplicity of a child's faith she said, "I knew he'd send them. He said he would."

That trip had been satisfactory in every way. Dr. B was pleased that Karen had started in kindergarten and he was also pleased with the work we had done with her. He told us to continue the table therapy and ordered parallel bars for her. This was a delightful command since it was the first active walking approach.

We had been a triumphant trio as we set out for home. Karen, like many a lonely child, had an imaginary playmate in the person of her Mouse. Up until the time that Rory was born, Mouse had been her constant companion. When we were undressing her we had to wait while she transferred Mouse from one hand to the other. She took shim (so called by Marie because she said she didn't know whether it was a she or a him) to the table, and placed it in the basin during her bath. But now she didn't play with Mouse any more except when she was away from Rory. He still accompanied us on all our trips.

Karen grew weary of sitting for a long time, so on the bus, from the railroad terminal in Jersey City to Columbus Circle, Jimmy would stand her between his legs, or she would hold on to the seat ahead. This trip, she sat for about half an hour talking to and playing with Mouse. Her clear high treble carried as far as the driver and benign passengers looked at her and supposed she was playing with a small stuffed animal. When she grew weary of sitting, Jimmy stood her up in the usual position. In the seat ahead of us was a beautifully groomed young woman. She was reading a book and even in her attitude of repose she was poised. Before either Jimmy or I knew what was happening, Karen leaned over and ran her finger across the woman's neck and up into her hair, at the same time calling loud and clear, "Oops, there goes my mouse." I was not present at the San Francisco earthquake, nor the Great Fire in Chicago,

108

but I have been to a few hotly contested World Series (and in Brooklyn). Never have I witnessed such pandemonium. Men and women screeched and leapt upon their seats. The bus lurched madly, and Karen, exhilarated beyond measure at this participation in her game, sporadically screamed, "There he goes—under the seat!" or "He's running up the back of your coat!" or "Can't you feel him on your foot?" The bus screamed to a stop. Jimmy clapped his hand over Karen's mouth and I dragged her into my lap. Our faces were flaming.

"She doesn't have a mouse—" I started.

"I do so," Karen yelled. I gave Jimmy a look which threatened mayhem if he allowed her to utter another word.

"It's a game." I labored on hopefully looking from one frozen face to another. I remembered very little of what else I said. Slowly the pretzeled passengers unwound, the erect and rigid ones unbound. The driver was standing arms akimbo less than a foot from me. His invectives were pithy and colorful. I pointed to Karen. "There's a child here."

"Child, hell, a she-devil." I never saw a man so mad. The passengers nodded. He had apparently aptly voiced a communion of sentiment.

The night after our return Gloria called and asked if she could come down and talk to us. She was very upset. The gist of the sad story that unfolded was that it was no longer possible for her mother to maintain their home. She was ill, and Gloria was not thinking of herself but of her younger sister. We sat up most of the night and the next day Gloria went to see an aunt by marriage who would be glad to have Jeanne come and live with her.

A long time ago we had given our hearts to Gloria, so it remained but to welcome her into our home. She listened unbelievingly as Jimmy pointed out that, if she cared for us as we did for her, she could bring us all great happiness by becoming one of our family. On

109

February 24, two days after Rory's birthday, she adopted us.

Gloria was maturing rapidly at fifteen and was judicious far beyond her years. She was already fulfilling the promise of beauty, both physically and spiritually, and we thanked God for sending us this lovely daughter. True, we were gypped out of the two o'clock bottle, colic, and the first tooth this time, but we were still young.

Every member of the family became a better and happier person after her advent. The girls were inordinately pleased with their new sister; Rory crowed in glee when she was there each morning and Jimmy and I were proud indeed. I think Jimmy summed it up very well when he said, "To him who hath, it shall be given."

When we returned home from each trip South to see Dr. B, we felt a stronger determination to do anything and everything we could on the total C.P. problem.

The fifty-eight cases on file represented quite a lot of information. We had developed a questionnaire which we sent to every lead we got and every parent who contacted us. One particularly alarming fact—the average number of doctors consulted by each parent was fourteen. But the whole file was alarming: an oft-reiterated report of incorrect diagnosis, faulty prognosis, children growing up confined to bed, ninety-nine out of a hundred receiving no treatment or education, an appreciable number improperly confined to mental institutions because they could not be taken care of at home, others hidden in attics. One child was found kept in a box in the cellar of his home. Children and parents doomed by society— because it didn't know, care or accept. Here was no question of blame, but rather an urgent need to deliver parents and their children, and the public at large, from the dark womb of ignorance. But how?

One evening, Jimmy and I were reading. It was about nine o'clock when the telephone rang. I answered it. "Is

110

this Mrs. Killilea who is interested in cerebral palsy?"

"Yes, it is," I answered apprehensively. The voice was frantic.

"My brother just tried to commit suicide. He's thirty-three. He has cerebral palsy. He's strong and I'm here alone with him and my baby. What shall I do?"

"What's your name?" I tried to speak calmly, fighting my own panic as well as hers. "Give me your address." She gave it. "Where is your brother now?"

"I've tied him to the bed, but he's getting loose."

"Go back to him. Try to be calm. Talk to him and we'll get you help." I tried to sound confident. Nine o'clock at night. Whom to call? Suddenly I thought—the commissioner of health—he would know what to do. Providentially his home phone was listed and as providentially he was in.

"I'll take care of it—don't worry." I hung up and started to cry. I couldn't stop. We've got to do something—but what? Round and round. At breakfast the next morning we started all over again. "I'm going to call Dr. B," I decided. "I'll tell him what we know. I'll tell him this story. I'll also tell him of the public-spirited citizens we have interested. He'll tell us what to do."

At nine o'clock sharp, I put through the call. "What shall we do?" I asked when I finished giving him the story in its entirety. "What can we do that such things need not happen in the future?"

"Mrs. Killilea," he answered, "the story you have just told me is far from an isolated case. The only way I know to halt such tragedies is to provide a solution of the problem. This means a broad program which will require large sums for support. My suggestion, after hearing of the interest you have aroused, is to organize a parents' group and bring into that group everyone you can interest."

"How?" I blurted.

"There is such a group in your state, in Rochester, I believe. I'll send you the man's name and address and also tell him to write to you. I know he'll do anything he can to help you get started."

In March I received a letter from Ralph Amdursky.

Dear Mrs. Killilea:

I, too, am interested in cerebral palsy and have been for about three years. My three-year-old son is one of the spastic group.

It is true that we have a well-organized parents' group here in Rochester. There are others in Buffalo, Ithaca, Elmira, Binghamton and Albany.

Our Rochester group was started when I contacted a local radio commentator. . . . Publicity is very important, for that is the only means of informing the public. . . .

I am enclosing a photostat of an article that appeared in the local papers. Many others have appeared, but this is the type that really arouses public interest.

I would like to refer you to an article that I wrote which will appear in the May issue of *Pageant* Magazine. It will appear on the newsstands on or about April 15. It is the story of cerebral palsy from the parent's point of view and asks *for a nation-wide foundation for cerebral palsy.*

The several cities mentioned will eventually form a New York State Cerebral Palsy Association. With that goal in mind, you might be able to arouse enough interest in your community to start a local group.

I am attaching a list of names of parents and interested persons in New York City. I will be happy to give you any information you request or assist in any way that I can.

Please keep me posted on your progress.

Sincerely,
Ralph Amdursky

We were immensely encouraged by this letter. Now we knew not only what to do but that others had done it successfully. I took the letter to Dr. Holla and we decided to call a meeting in about two weeks. Hugh Robertson put regular announcements in the papers, the radio plugged it, we sent invitations to the fifty whose names we had. Dr. Holla arranged for a meeting room in White Plains, the county seat. He asked us how many chairs we wished set up and we told him twenty and to have ten in the hall, just in case. The night before, Jimmy and I slept not at all. There was a job to be done, others had done it, but we couldn't do it alone. Suppose nobody came!

The meeting was scheduled for eight-fifteen o'clock. We arrived at seven-thirty o'clock and there were six or eight people there ahead of us. I had made a copy of Ralph Amdursky's letter, and a friend of mine mimeographed a hundred copies. Dr. Holla arrived at eight o'clock and the twenty chairs were filled. We set up the others. They were soon filled and still people kept coming. They stood around the room and overflowed into the corridor. We asked them to register and the final tally was 117. Robby sent over a reporter and the next day, in all the Macy papers, there appeared a write-up of the two-hour meeting, with the report that an organization had been started.

A few days later a reporter from the New York *Sun*, one Harvey Call, came to see me. I don't know whether it was because he considered the interview a "story," or whether it was because he felt the need, but he went back to his desk and wrote a wonderful piece—two columns. This was the first time C.P. had been featured by a New York paper and the response was large, and not confined to New York. We heard from parents in many other states.

In April, Albert Felmet, president of the Cerebral Palsy Association of Buffalo, wrote and suggested that the existing groups meet in Syracuse in June for the purpose of forming a New York State Cerebral Palsy Association. Jimmy couldn't get away and I planned to go with Shirley and Arthur Larchan from New York City and Frances Giden. How I happened to find Frances Giden was providential.

We had heard from a mother in Long Island and I had made a date to meet her for luncheon at a restaurant on 42nd Street. The lunch lasted into teatime. A cute young thing had taken the table next to ours and it was soon apparent that she was eavesdropping. "So much the better," my companion remarked. "One more person to hear about C.P." Finally the girl stood up and came over to our table.

"I hope you will forgive my intrusion and my eavesdropping," she said, "but I am much interested in cerebral palsy. I am studying at Columbia for my Master's and have selected C.P., as you call it, as the subject of my thesis. I am greatly discouraged both by the paucity of material and the few people who know anything about it."

"We know just how you feel," I remarked and briefed the story of our search as typical. "I have some material I should be glad to send you. Perhaps you could help us and tell us if you have met anyone with a knowledge and interest that could be of assistance."

"There is one person I feel you must see," she answered. "She is a C.P. herself and is a lawyer. She works at the Federation of the Handicapped. I'll tell you her story and you can decide."

We assented eagerly, and ordered our fourth pot of coffee. She continued, "Miss Giden is a C.P. of the ataxia group. She has poor balance and some involuntary motion. She started school when she was eight. She had to go to a private school since public schools will not accept a child who cannot walk. She had poor manual coordination and no speech, but she was highly intelligent. The story of the united family struggle to train and educate Frances and the story of her own struggle is too

114

long to tell here. Suffice to say it was successful and at the age of fifteen she entered Hunter College. She carried a heavy schedule which included calculus. Remember, everything had to be done by memory since she could not write. Because of her speech involvement she could not pronounce words—she could, however, articulate letters so she perforce must spell out the answer to all questions.

"She graduated from Hunter with honors and went to Fordham to study law. She was editor-in-chief of the *Fordham Law Review* for two years. She again graduated with honors and subsequently passed her bar examinations and the endorsements which would qualify her as a lawyer practicing in the Federal Courts. In this latter, she was the youngest woman ever to qualify." She stopped speaking.

We two others sat silent. We could not express what the story of this valiant girl meant to us, as mothers. Hope in the future became certainty. If Frances could do it—so could Karen and Val. The mother from Long Island had an appointment and left, and the young girl left with her. I went to the telephone, called the house to check with Mother Killilea that all the kids were still in one piece, and then called Miss Giden's office on 57th Street. The phone was answered immediately and I knew it must be Miss Giden because I had great difficulty understanding her. She asked me to come over.

I got off the elevator at the third floor and inquired for Miss Giden's office of a beautiful young redhead I met in the hall. Her reply really threw me. "I am Miss Giden." She spoke slowly, with conscious effort, and it was hard for me to understand her. She preceded me down the corridor, walking in flat-heeled shoes, with difficulty (like someone who's intoxicated, I thought). Her desk was a monumental pile of papers and books. The calendar beside the phone said April 18, 1946. We sat down. I couldn't help staring at her. A complexion *could* look like a peach. Her hair was naturally curly, cropped quite short, and it was the deep red of South

American mahogany, in which fire slumbered and leapt as the light touched it. Her eyes were brown and the lashes black and thick. Her eyebrows were peaked and would have made her appear haughty, if it were not for the fine humorous mouth, well set over a determined chin. I put her age at twenty-three—at least seventeen years younger than I had expected she would be.

We had a long talk and I enjoyed it immensely, though I had to struggle to understand her. It was also an instructive talk, for she had worked for some time in the field of the handicapped.

The phone was conveniently quiet during dinner that evening and I gave the family a full report. When I had finished Marie observed, "If Frances could do all these things, so can Karen."

After Marie and Karen and Rory had been tucked away, and I had the dishes washed and the clothes dampened for tomorrow's ironing, Jimmy and Gloria and I sat talking in the living room.

Jimmy commented, "Do you realize, hon, that since we've become involved in this work, we don't have time for our friends—a social life is a thing of the past."

"Morf and Anne Downes called the other day and asked me to remind you that they still live only four blocks from here and you haven't gotten together in eight months." This from Gloria with, I thought, a slight shade of rebuke in her voice.

"I know," I said regretfully, "they've even given up trying to get us on the phone. I guess they're sick and tired of getting a busy signal. Even Mother has taken to writing letters. That's how bad it is."

We reminisced for a while about the fun we used to have at our buffet suppers and how, on week-ends, lots of people would drop in starting at noon on Saturday and until late Sunday evening. "Gee, I'd love to see Bill and Floss, and Fred and Althea and the Healeys, and—"

"Karen's calling," I interrupted and went in to see which line of the Lilliput Litany was being used. "Mom,

116

I'm thirsty." "Mom, I have to go to the bathroom." All in all there are thirteen lines. Tonight it was the second. As I put her back to bed she said, "You know, Mom, you've *made* a lot of good friends too; there's Judge Bleakley and Al Felmet and Mr. Fanning and Robby and Jim and Ralph and Ben and Jack—" She paused for breath.

The Men in My Daughter's Life, I thought. "You should have been asleep hours ago." I spoke severely.

"O.K., Mom Pom, I'll go to sleep right away."

I loosened one of the ankle straps on her braces and covered her.

"But you wouldn't have met any of them if I didn't have C.P." She smiled up at me. "I think you should tell me 'Thank You.' "

Chapter 11

On June 10, 1946, sixteen of us formed the New
York State Cerebral Palsy Association, Inc. Al Felmet of
Buffalo was elected president. As the C.P. effort grew
rapidly and as Karen's program expanded, the days' activities had to be pounded and compressed like fodder
in a silo.

Karen's limitations must be acknowledged, at least on
a temporary basis, and handled accordingly. This called
for considerable ingenuity on our part. The simplest routine acts, which we take for granted, presented individual
problems.

Karen's spasticity gave her an over-all rigidity. Sitting
was at first impossible. Even when it became possible it
was difficult because of the lack of balance coupled with
the struggle to bend at the waist and to bend her knees.
Even when she learned to bend at the waist she had to
remember consciously to relax her knees since a stiff-
legged position would upset her backward. This difficulty
alone limited play and complicated eating, bathing and
dressing. For years, when we took her to the beach, we
had to dig a hole for her to sit in and build a backrest so
she wouldn't topple over.

Her arms, hands, feet and fingers were equally stiff so
that grasping and holding required intensive training
and any assisting device that we could concoct. In addition she had to contend with overflow motion. For example: When Karen spoke, or used her hands, or grew
excited, parts of the body that are not normally involved
in these situations received impulses, so that her feet
would stiffen, her toes curl under, her fingers knot, her
knees straighten out rigidly in front of her. This meant

that while she had to learn to use one series of muscles, she had, at the same time, to learn to hold quiet another series. It made me think of a game we used to play as kids, when we tried (unsuccessfully most of the time) to pat the top of our heads with an up-and-down motion with one hand, and massage our stomachs at the same time in a rotary motion with the other hand.

More important than the physiotherapy was the occupational therapy, which meant simply training her to the simple acts of self-help. Simple for normal people, that is. This was a job for the whole family, for each one of us had to learn to watch her struggle and it took a lot of self-discipline on our part to develop the patience necessary to let her do things for herself in spite of the effort it required and the time it took. This was harder for Jimmy and Marie than it was for Gloria and me. It was also hard for Rory, who at an incredibly early age found pleasure in doing anything and everything for Karen.

When the time came for her to feed herself, Jimmy bought a suction mat and put it under her dish and cup. Even so, I should like to have a nickel for every cup of milk I wiped up and every meal I swept from the floor only to prepare another. We bought a tin spoon and bent the handle in a big loop so she could hold and control it more easily. We could feed her in twenty minutes with no mess or trouble. For a long time, her own efforts required an hour to an hour and a half per meal. It wasn't long before all the household pets accompanied Karen to table, knowing full well that they would dine royally on what she spilled. Nothing made me so mad as to see those four-legged opportunists relishing lamb chop that had jumped off her spoon or a poached egg, bathed in butter, that somehow skidded off the plate and onto the floor. Her movements were so jerky and uncontrolled that it was several years before we allowed her to use a fork. We were afraid she'd put out one of her eyes.

We practiced long, dreary hours on an outsize saddle

119

shoe, fastened to a board. It had very heavy laces of a bright color and holes as big as a dime. We punched holes in hundreds of Christmas cards (they were pretty and interesting) and had her string them together to festoon her room. It wasn't a large room and visitors frequently looked a little dazed when they observed the overflow draping the living room cornices or the shower stall in July. Thus she was learning to lace her own shoes.

Her arms and trunk were so stiff that dressing her had always been a problem and we had to hunt for dresses that opened all the way down below her waist, for belts that could be sewn in at the seams on the side. Loose, they rode up to her chin. To get her arms in without tearing lining or seams, coats and jackets had to be bought a size larger than was required for a good fit.

When I felt it was time for her to begin learning to dress herself we started with a shirt. But before I could teach her I had to find out how I put on a shirt. When did I crook my elbow? How did I hold it to start with? What motions did I use to spread the bottom and hold it open? What precise movements did I make when inserting my head into the opening? How did I hold it down at the bottom while pushing my hands up and in?

Try it sometime. You will be delighted to find how clever and supple you are.

It took hours of analysis, hours of instruction, hours of supervised practice, and hardest of all, hours of watching and *not* helping while she struggled by herself. As in most C.P. efforts, it went on day after day, week after week, month after month, and yes, year after year. When I could do it for her in less than five minutes from the skin out, there were days when I thought I should go mad as I forced myself to sit by and limit my help to verbal directions. There was always the temptation to rationalize on the basis that there were diapers,

120

dishes, beds, cleaning, ironing, correspondence, tele-phoning, *ad repellum*, and I needed every minute.

I had to laugh when I thought of how I used to stew during the winter months over the time-consuming nui-sance of getting little Marie in and out of snowsuits and galoshes. It doesn't stack up, in nuisance value or time consumption, to dressing a youngster who can neither stand nor sit securely during the operation, whose whole body resists movement at joints, and who is cased in heavy cumbersome braces.

Karen's first efforts at brushing her own teeth required frequent sterilizations of the brush, and several brushes, because the brush was difficult for her to hold and she dropped it several times during the operation. Jimmy solved this by heating the plastic handle until he could bend it and by putting a nail in the wall behind the basin to which he attached one end of a piece of string; the other end he tied to the toothbrush. Now, when Karen dropped it, it fell only about ten inches and she could pull it back up. Even the ten-inch fall took three or four minutes to recover but—in one more activity—she was independent.

Not being able to stand or sit on the floor at play, Karen had been kneeling. This was stopped completely since we were told it would cause deformity. Because of her poor balance a proper kneeling position was im-possible. And owing to the tremendous pull of the ad-ductors, the muscles that pull the legs together, a kneeling position such as she was able to assume would further pull the femur out of the hip socket. As a result, her already limited play activity was curtailed to a heart-breaking degree. She had to sit at a specially constructed table, in a specially constructed chair ($85—C.O.D.) or stand at the standing table Jim Dempsey had made. There were few play activities that she could experience while gripping parallel bars.

Her total play area, therefore, was three feet square,

and this at the age when she should be pushing a doll carriage around the yard, playing tag, climbing trees, learning to skate and skip rope, and chasing from one plaything to another. Jimmy arranged a sandbox and a specially built stool with a back, which gave her some diversion.

It was an ever-present and seemingly hopeless task to see that she had diversion, fun and play activity on her intellectual level; to fetch and carry for her, and at the same time not overindulge, not pamper, not spoil. I could map out a six-year course of required study to fit parents for their role with a C.P. youngster. But, lacking this, God seems to endow us with a special brand of common sense and all we have to do is develop the courage and patience to apply it!

Karen's hair is fine and straight and she wore it in plaits. A shampoo was a major undertaking and required our combined efforts. She wasn't steady or flexible enough to stand over the basin, so it had to be done in the tub. Four hands never seemed enough to support her rigid form, keep her from sliding, hold the spray, cover her eyes with a cloth, apply the soap and rub. It was a forty-five-minute operation, if we were efficient.

Karen took a certain drug for about a year and a half. One of its side effects I have reason to remember vividly. Whatever else it was supposed to do (and didn't), it did make it necessary for her to go see Mrs. Murphy every half hour day and night. Though still small for her age, she was a considerable weight and size, and stiff withal. Added to that were the braces, which had now been extended so that she was braced from neck to foot. It was like carrying a forty-pound plank. After a while it became impossible for me to lift her from a standing position. I had to get down on one knee and start from there.

Jimmy and I took turns at night. After this had been going on for some months, I remember that we decided the most desirable thing in life would be to go to bed

122

and know that you did not have to get up till morning.

I wondered for a while if this whole performance could be some kind of a subconscious desire for some extra attention. But when the drug was discontinued, so were the trips.

Many times when someone has had the opportunity to watch Karen as she proudly flaunts her independence, he has remarked, "Where did you get your patience? I know I'd break down and help her." To this question there is only one answer: Every parent of a cerebral-palsied child lives with the thought, What will she do if something happens to us? And even if we live a long time, should a child be unable to seek a life of his own, away from home, because he cannot perform simple acts of self-help? We expect all children will grow up loving their parents, but the time may come when she will not enjoy living with them. Should she be forced to, by a selfishness that kept her dependent? Would the time come when the child's love for her parents would turn to resentment or even hate? We believe it is possible.

Thence springs an indestructible determination that, as soon as possible, regardless of cost, you will help your child to her rightful independence in bathing, dressing, eating, writing—all the talents of self-help. If, when Karen is mature, she lives with us, it will be because she wants to, not because she has to.

John had been right when he told us it would be difficult, discouraging and heartbreaking. How right, we couldn't know until we lived it. But he had also been right on the compensations, and unless one has been lucky enough to live through such happiness as ours, he could not understand.

Looking back on this period of our life is like sitting on a mountainside and watching the valley stretched below. As the clouds glide in swift procession through the sky, you can see, on the earth, alternate patterns of

123

somber strips and brilliant swaths. Our own family life and our life in the field of C.P. was just such a constant shifting from dark to light.

At home, there was the dark of the daily struggle against fatigue and discouragement, and the increasingly difficult struggle to meet our bills. Karen remarked one day, "Mom Pom, you get a lot of letters with windows in them." We had eight doctors of different specialties on our list to say nothing of prescriptions and equipment. And always there was the dark of worrying over giving the other three children their rightful share of our time, thoughts and efforts. Though Rory was a wonderful companion for her, Karen had many lonely moments.

Invariably when we thought that the clouds must be stationary and the dark permanent, some providential puff would move the clouds along and the pattern would again shift to light. All things being a matter of proportion, when things are very dark a small ray looks very bright.

There was the incident of the judge, the martini and the tooth. Jimmy had a pivot tooth about which he was inordinately sensitive. Somehow Karen got hold of it. She probably bribed Rory to commit the larcenous act.

One afternoon, a distinguished jurist, a former Supreme Court justice, came to call. He had read the article in the *Sun* and he wished to help. His name was Charles Harwood. I had arranged some lovely bouquets (a clever device which keeps all but the real snoopers from noticing fingerprints on the woodwork or dust under the chairs) and splurged on a bottle of gin.

We had a wonderful two-hour talk about the progress of the C.P. field of endeavor and he brought the discussion to a close by presenting our local association with a check for a thousand dollars, by far the largest contribution we had received to date.

He asked to meet the children (I would have managed that anyway). I rounded them up and brought Karen in and sat her on the couch beside him. Jimmy came in with a tray of martinis and we relaxed in excellent humor. Gloria and Marie were poised and gracious, Rory was subdued and charming, and Karen sparkled and chattered delightfully.

Jimmy poured the drinks and we raised our glasses in the usual toast. I was looking at the judge as he brought his glass to his lips. His former position as a jurist must have inured him to shock, but he gasped and gaped at the lovely fluid. I bent forward for a closer look, not knowing what to expect, and Karen, beside him, exploded with laughter.

I did a double-take.

There, nestled at the bottom of the glass, like a pearl on the ocean floor, was Jimmy's tooth! Fortunately Judge Harwood's sixty years had served to whet his sense of humor and he put his arm around her and laughed until the tears ran down his cheeks. It took two more martinis before any of us were properly revived. The judge was so captivated by Karen he asked her what she would like for her birthday. She demonstrated her objectivity about things medical, delivered a second and more sustained shock by blandly replying, "I should like a scalpel."

Of all our children, Karen provided the most surprises.

I arrived home one night about ten-thirty o'clock from a rather strenuous speaking engagement. She called to me and I went in to say good night. "Mother, something terrible happened today."

"What was it?" I braced myself to think, over my fatigue.

"The Russians walked out."

The worst of all was a phone call Jimmy took one Sunday morning. The man was incoherent and it took some time for Jimmy to understand what had happened. They had a twelve-year-old daughter—a badly involved tension athetoid. She had never had any treatment and was completely helpless and speechless. The mother had

125

been ill but had not been able to go to bed or hospital because there was no one to look after the child. They had applied to agency after agency, public and private, and had been turned down. The nature of the mother's illness caused her constant pain and last night the poor woman had given up in the face of her insurmountable difficulties. She had attempted to kill her child and herself.

Broken homes, suicides, alcoholics, psychotics—the effects of the unmet cerebral palsy problem were like an octopus, enveloping entire families in futile struggle and destroying the family as such. We came to recognize C.P. as a social problem and, like all social problems, we felt it should be the concern of each and every member of the community. The families on relief because of the funds expended in searching for an answer; the effects on the siblings when the C.P. child received exclusive love and attention from the parents, or when they themselves were overprotected because the parents lived in fear of an accident or illness that might cause C.P.; the family that was evicted because the other tenants in the house objected to a C.P. associating with their children —all these tragedies rooted in the public's ignorance of the true nature, needs, and solutions. Many cerebral-palsied men and women, capable of working, denied employment because of an uninformed public.

There were times when the enormity of the under-taking all but drained our courage. At such times we would stop and review what we, the parents—for the most part, a lot of little people—banded together, had already accomplished. We would consider that no matter how much we wished to help all C.P.'s there was One Who desired their welfare even more than we. We knew our efforts would be successful for "God is never outdone in generosity."

It put hope for the world in our hearts when Bob Sherburne, the grocer, waited for his bill that we might have the ready cash to visit a group upstate, to help

126

them get started. We rejoiced when a young soda jerker told us about his month at camp. "There was a kid up there that the others stayed away from. I saw that movie you showed at school, so I knew he had C.P. I told the other kids all about it and after that everything was all right."

It was a bright spot for many of us when Frances Giden acquired sufficient stability to graduate to Cuban heels. We took heart from her accomplishments.

We were delighted when Karen's emotional adjustment was evidenced by a remark to her friend Patty. The little girl arrived at the house after a trip to the orthodontist. She was sporting large braces on both upper and lower teeth. Karen studied her critically and remarked, "We're twins—you have braces on your teeth and I have braces on my legs."

We needed our swaths of light, because more and more we became a part of the darker patterns of other people's lives. It was not a rare experience to receive a call from a frantic parent in the middle of the night. "My child is having a convulsion. Whom shall I call? What shall I do in the meantime?"

It was immeasurably discouraging when we received a call from Mrs. C. Her son was a C.P., eighteen years old. He had slight difficulty in walking and talking. He couldn't write or print but was most efficient on an electric typewriter. He had graduated from high school with honors and had won a scholarship to a Western university. It had been a long and hard struggle for both, since her husband had died when the boy was a baby. But they had won; she could send J. to college; the struggle was over. The day J. arrived at the university, he had called her and said he was returning home immediately. He told his mother that when he walked into the registrar's office he had been rejected. They were sorry. They had not known he was a C.P. He had gone to the president of the university, who had said he would take the matter up with the registrar. J. had confidently

127

returned a few hours later and the registrar told him that it had been discussed—they were all very sorry—but he couldn't stay.

After experiences like this, we were heartened by the rapid growth of organizations all over the country. Growth both in numbers and in strength. In our county we were engaged in the complex preliminaries necessary to the establishment of a clinic. A number of the complexities were due to the fact that the clinic was to be run entirely by a private organization. Our efforts would have failed if it had not been for a large number of good Samaritans. For centuries, travelers on the road of life had seen the C.P. by the side of the road and "had passed by." Human nature has not changed and there are still those who, in current parlance, refer to the Samaritan as a "sucker."

Kay and Jim Jones were prize suckers or Samaritans, depending on your point of view. They had four children and, like most of us in the neighborhood, could afford no help. When I had to be away from home during the day, Kay would bring her children to my house and run things until my return. She fed, washed and cooked for seven youngsters and talked to the parents who phoned. Back home, she frequently had to do her own house work at night. On more than one occasion, Jim helped her wash on Sunday so she would be free to come up to our house on Monday.

C.P. got a series of boosts from Dora and Al McCann, the "McCanns at Home" radio program. They asked me to appear on their program and we totaled up twelve hundred replies. A curious aftermath of the initial broadcast was a letter I received a year later. It read, "Since I heard you on the McCann Show, I have had a baby boy. He has C.P. Can you help me?" Another couple phoned us from Pennsylvania. They told Jimmy that their eight-year-old C.P. daughter could walk unaided though she was most unstable. They despaired of her ever attempting to walk up and down stairs alone.

"What do you and your wife do when she is walking?" Jimmy asked him.

"We stay right behind her every minute. We don't let her walk unless we can be right there. We're so afraid she'll fall and hurt herself."

"Don't you think," Jimmy asked, "—and remember I'm not a professional in any sense of the word—that some of Eileen's instability may be caused by fear which you have transmitted to her? Why don't you try putting a football helmet on her to guard against head injury and let her solo?"

The girl's father said that he would try it—they were at the point where they would try anything. Three months later we received a special delivery letter in which he reported that the day before Eileen had walked up and down stairs, as confidently as you please, and that the whole walking picture was much improved. On the surface, a little thing; but the implications—physical, psychological, emotional—for the entire family are inestimable. Each such incident served to increase the determination of our group to establish a clinic as soon as practicable. Many parents and children must receive the help they needed now.

In this undertaking, I contacted a number of state officials. The majority were sympathetic and helpful; a few were very difficult. I still blanch when I recall the remark of one, a doctor at that: "It's a waste of money. The best you can teach these kids is a few tricks."

"But, Doctor," I protested and went into a detailed account of what was being done all over the country; I cited Karen's progress as an example.

"Are you a doctor?" he asked.

"No," I replied.

"Then you don't know anything about it. I am a doctor and I know."

I was thoroughly disgusted and very angry. "I may not be a doctor," I retorted sharply, "but my thinking is entirely formed by doctors who have sufficient humility to accept the findings of those expert in the field. It is a virtue you should cultivate, for your own good as well as others'." I strode out with an almost irresistible desire to slam the door behind me.

At one of the many meetings an official inquired, "Why don't you parents relax and stick to your knitting and let the state handle this?"

I patiently explained that we believed the primary responsibility for all children lay with the parents not the state; that we wished only co-operation between public and private agencies, that the job was too big for either to fully accomplish alone.

At this particular meeting there were present a number of people, most of them unknown to me. As the meeting progressed I became aware of a gentleman at the far end of the table who was giving me concentrated attention. As I addressed a remark to him, he winked at me. I'm quick on the trigger and I winked back, though I was mildly shocked. This performance was repeated a number of times and, as important as my presentation was, I began to wish to get away as quickly and as unobtrusively as possible. It took a determined effort of will not to glance toward his end of the table for the duration of the meeting. As soon as it was consistent with good judgement, I fled. The following day I called the friend who had arranged the meeting for me and told him about this embarrassing occurrence. Quite unsympathetically he bellowed with laughter and to my chagrin explained that the gentleman in question had a ticl

Chapter 12

OUR WESTCHESTER COUNTY GROUP had incorporated, received our Extension of Powers & Dispensary License (some undertaking this!). We were raising money, looking for suitable space which we could have rent-free, interviewing personnel, setting up records and ordering the innumerable items of equipment (therapy tables, skis, chairs, mirrors, sandbags, metronomes, parallel bars, standing tables, steps, mattresses, linens, etc.). Our head therapist, Miss Margaret Burns, was superbly trained and ideally suited for the work by experience, character, and personality. How ideally suited we could not know till time passed and we saw the wonders that she wrought. I expect to initiate the first move toward her canonization.

One afternoon when Gloria arrived from school she asked if she could borrow some of my large photographs of C.P. children. I was puzzled by the request but assented on the condition that she would return them a week from Sunday, when I needed them to illustrate a talk. Several days later I was in the Village and there in a store window was one of my photographs with a poster announcing a cake sale—under the auspices of Rye High School—the proceeds to go to the cerebral palsy clinic. As I walked down the main street I saw that almost every shop carried a picture and a poster. I was deeply moved and additionally touched when I found out that the girls were baking the cakes and cookies themselves.

The sale was held on Saturday. They opened for business at ten o'clock in the morning and sold the last cake about a quarter to six. It was a proud delegation that presented us with a check for thirty-six dollars and we were proud to receive it.

Teen-age Samaritans are worth their weight in gold. High-school sororities and fraternities came to our house, evenings or over week-ends, and addressed, stamped and sealed envelopes, folded thousands of sheets and ran errands. This interest acquires considerable significance when you stop to think that they are the parents, administrators, doctors, therapists, teachers, social workers, legislators, employers, of tomorrow.

Thanks to our press coverage we received many requests from service clubs, women's organizations, church groups, to speak to them on cerebral palsy. Nana took over when I went out to give a talk. One day I returned home rather upset. I had been scheduled to address a group at one o'clock, immediately following their business meeting. It was an annual meeting and the business dragged on and on. I was a little short on sleep and I was tired. Figures have always bored me (a defense mechanism, I suspect) and the financial report was endless. I became suddenly aware of a blow on the ankle and, from a great distance, I heard someone repeat, "Mrs. Killilea, Mrs. Killilea," and realized I had been hearing it for some time. I jerked erect and then almost collapsed for 110 pairs of eyes were focused expectantly on the "guest speaker" and the "speaker" was just waking up.

"We'll send Karen next time," said Mother, when I told her, "she can handle any situation. I put her out to play this afternoon," she continued, pouring me a cup of tea, that panacea for all ills. "She was beautifully groomed when I left her and when I went out an hour later, she was positively filthy. 'Just look at yourself,' I commanded, 'I'll bet you're the dirtiest child in Rye.'"

"What did she say?" I was curious, for Karen's replies were never dull.

"She studied me quite seriously," Mother said, "and this was her answer: 'Nana, don't you know God made dirt for kids to play in? Sister Rosalie told us so.'" As a matter of fact, our life was now governed by "Sister Rosalie says . . ."

Karen blossomed in the fertile soil of schooling. Her personality developed beautifully as a result of the socialization and competition. She was a pretty important person when she kissed her baby brother good-by each morning with an ever so casual "Karen has to go to school now, but I'll be home soon. Be a good boy." They adored each other and Rory always cried when she left. But even this could not mar the joy with which she set out each day.

The months sped by. Summer was late in arriving, but when it came, it blew in like a blast from a furnace. Like any family living in proximity to a beach, we were conscious of an almost sacred obligation to take the children swimming every day. This year each trip was a major undertaking. Gloria was working, and without Marie I never could have managed. The procedure was set up in six steps.

Step Number One—Preparation.

The amount of equipment which had to be assembled would have satisfied Amundsen. To wit: 1 large blanket, 4 towels, 3 pails, 3 shovels, 2 balsam life preservers, 1 bottle sun tan lotion, 3 hats, 3 beach robes, 1 beach umbrella, 2 boats (1 sail, 1 motor), 1 box Kleenex, sunglasses, 1 thermos of fruit juice, paper cups.

Nana had bought a twin stroller so that I could wheel Karen and Rory together. Once assembled the equipment then had to be packed in and around children in said stroller.

Step Number Two—Outward Bound (in two parts).

(a) From House to Park. A quarter-mile trip almost all uphill and heavy pushing all the way.

(b) From Park to Beach. This called for a careful unloading and stacking job. It was 25 yards from the

Park to the beach-gate. We then had to negotiate three flights of stairs to the sand and then some 30 yards to the spot best suited to the varied requirements of our age spread. The scrupulous unloading and stacking was to the end that no more than three round trips would be required from Park to spot on Sand.

These steps accomplished, I would collapse on the blanket, wanting nothing so much as ten minutes of suspended animation in the sun. My darlings didn't understand this and immediately set up a chant: "Mom Pom, hurry." "Take off my shoes." "Put on my life belt." "Let's make a castle." "Fix my boat's sail." "I'm thirsty." Now it was time for:

Step Number Three—Participation.

Finally I'd have all three of them launched, then they'd start with "Hey Mom, watch this—betcha you can't do it," "Look at me," "Watch, I'm a submarine"— each of my pets convinced that he or she had devised some totally new aquatic accomplishment. I was really busy. Marie liked me to race with her and Karen had to be supported much of the time. As for Rory, he had to be watched like a hawk, since he would walk into the water and keep on walking, as though he expected that when he got over his depth the waters would part or at least recede, to provide a depth permanently suited to his stature. He was three and a half before he realized that, though most things in life adjust to the convenience of a little boy, the tide does not.

After an hour and a half, it was time to go home. "Come on children, time to leave."

"Oh, Mommy, *no*." "Please!" "One more dip!" "You didn't finish my castle." I was at first quiet and gentle, then not so quiet, and finally on occasion not always gentle. A firm slap on a wet bottom doesn't hurt much but from the mother's point of view the accompanying sharp noise is valuable in producing the desired result.

Now for Step Number Four—Collecting.

134

This involved not only gathering together all that we had brought, but also returning sundry articles that had come into the children's possession from their playmates. And there was always one lost shoe. I've never yet lost two shoes, nor I think three, but I've yet to leave a beach without first having to scratch and dig like a terrier for one missing piece of footwear.

Step Number Five—Homeward Bound (in three parts).

(a) From the Sand to the Park. By this time the sand is scorching and not only Karen, but Rory too, has to be carried. So, whereas the trip out took three installments, the trip back to the Park takes four. The gear then has to be reloaded and Marie goes to work on Rory and I go to work on Karen, eliminating enough sand so that they may sit comfortably on the way home. It's roughly a half hour before we're ready for part (b).

(b) The journey Home presents a hazard I did not have to face on the way out. The refreshment stand is open. Along with the other benefits, the water gives people an appetite. My children were no exception. As we drew abreast of the stand, they began, "Mommy, I'm SO-o-o hungry." "Can we have a hot dog?" "Just this once?" "It won't spoil my dinner." "An ice cream cone maybe, huh?" "C'mon, Mom, please!" "Don't they smell scrumptious?" I ran this course every day, never varied my cruel negative reply, and yet, right up to September 12, they persisted in the blithe hope that Mom would relent.

(c) Last Lap Home. At this stage, even convent-bred ladies sweat, if they don't swear. The sun has reached its zenith: The quarter mile has become a half mile, flies and mosquitoes hover in ambush and confine their assault to those parts of the anatomy which you cannot reach to scratch, they zoom in like P-38s with hypodermic needles; your offspring are itchy, hot, tired, hungry and cranky.

At last you're home. But is this the end? Perish the thought. There is still

Step Number Six—Repatriation.

It is best described tersely. Leave Marie to watch carriage so it doesn't tip over backward; dash to kitchen to start lunch; dash to bathroom to turn on tub; race outside to unload gear; run around to the back yard to hang wet towels, blanket and robes on line so they will *surely* be dry for tomorrow; back to the front to pick up children and carry to bathroom; strip off suits, place children in tub; remove all sand from all creases. Leave Marie to help and watch little ones and hurry down to kitchen to check dinner. Return to bathroom; remove children from tub, towel, dress and carry down to kitchen.

With commendable devotion, sometime during the afternoon when I was trying to catch up with washing or cleaning, Jimmy would call and brightly inquire, "Did you get the kids to the beach today?" I never hung up on him, but I lived with the firm conviction that someday, something would snap, and I would.

I'm a grown woman, supposedly mature in my reasoning. I know that summer always follows spring. I wonder why I get so excited when I see the first robin.

During this summer, I experimented with giving Karen her physiotherapy on the beach. It didn't work.

I found that the cold water increased her spasticity, making already stiff muscles that much stiffer (temporarily). I found that more than twenty minutes of sun had much the same (temporary) effect.

I then tried doing her therapy immediately after her nap and so learned something interesting, and today still inexplicable. Instead of being relaxed and "soft" immediately after sleep, as one might reasonably expect, our daughter is more spastic and it is necessary to allow one full hour to elapse from the time of waking to the start of any therapy.

136

John had warned us that there would be days when the grind would seem unsupportable. And there were. Days when it took a physical effort to force myself to the foot of the table to do therapy; when I thought I should tear my hair over the daily, and apparently hopeless, task of teaching Karen to button a button; when I thought "One more trip upstairs and I shall just sit on the top step and never move again."

In addition there was always financial worry. Braces were expensive ($280—sent only C.O.D.). Shoes were expensive, and there was the added cost of the necessary work on them so they would fit the braces. There was frequent change in equipment.

Such a day was August 23, 1946.

My body was tired, my mind was tired. Karen had hit a plateau where she had stuck for three weeks. We had been to the beach and it was 4:00 p.m. before I started her physiotherapy. I asked the Lord to help me, for I knew I should never get through the session any other way. An hour later, when it was finished, we sat down to our button-board. I had come to hate the sight of the darn thing and would gladly have used it for kindling. It was made of two pieces of material attached to vertical edges of wood and fastened in the center with three huge buttons. Every day I pasted a new picture on the board under the cloth to provide incentive. "Today there's a picture of a beautiful animal," I prompted Karen. "He has short horns. Can you guess what it is?"

"Let's find it, I don't want to guess," she said, and started on the buttons. I always held back till the going got too tough and she began to feel frustrated. Today, I sat back and watched with only a small part of my attention on the detested board.

The minutes passed and suddenly I snapped back fast as Karen yelled, "I did it, Mommy, I did it—all by myself."

I grabbed her and hugged her and started to cry.

"I thought you'd be happy." Her elation ebbed as she saw my tears.

"I am, darling. I'm happier than I thought I could be. It's because I'm so happy I'm crying."

"You're silly," she laughed and grew more excited. "Wait till we tell Daddy and Nana and Dr. John and Burnzie. Let's call them right away." I grabbed her up and ran with her to the phone. As I called Jimmy's number, she said hopefully, "Do you think he will cry too?"

"Men don't cry, but he'll surely want to."

Miraculously, I wasn't tired any longer.

The compensations were indeed great.

A few days later, Karen had her first experience with grief. It was a sad, sad day for all of us when our beloved spaniel died. The whole family mourned, Jimmy and I particularly, for Potsy had been a part of our life for many years. She had even accompanied us on our honeymoon (since we couldn't afford to farm her out).

In an ill-advised attempt to console the children, Jimmy promised, "We'll get you another dog."

"I don't want another dog," Marie wailed. "Never, never, never!"—crescendo. Rory didn't understand but he joined in the spirit of the moment and wailed, "Neber, neber, neber."

Frank Bruckner, a friend of ours who raised Irish setters, heard of the tragedy and one Saturday afternoon arrived unexpectedly with a five-month-old mahogany setter pup. Such is the constancy of the human heart— the children loved him instantly. Karen's parallel bars were set up in the living room and, as this young excited creature gamboled crazily around the room, Jimmy leaped to steady tables and lamps. I stood close to Karen that she should not be mowed down. My solicitude was unnecessary, for when he came to her, he skidded to a stop. He licked her ear, face and knee, then raced away for further investigation. He tore through the house and plunged back into the living room at intervals. Each time he returned, he stopped short at the bars, greeting Karen gently, and then turning, leaped all over Marie. Scatter rugs flew, we lost one lamp and the children shrieked in high glee. Everybody was happy, though the adults were a trifle skeptical as to the wisdom of adding a beast this size to the existing menagerie. We had a dog again, but what we did not know until later was that Karen had acquired a guardian.

Shortly after the hound joined our animal kingdom, we made one of our regular visits to Dr. B. It was September and the beauty of the trip south was enhanced by the first blush of fall colors. The visit proved to be a momentous occasion, for Dr. B made two startling additions to Karen's curriculum. Each addition was to bring about a vast change in the lives of all of us.

After examining Karen, he expressed his pleasure at her improvement and told us that she was now ready for a tricycle and skis. Both a big forward step toward crutch-walking.

The skis were two flat pieces of wood about five inches wide and thirty inches long (the length determined by the height of the child). About four inches from the front there was a hole into which fitted, upright, a pole about as high as the child's head. In the center of the ski was built a harness, which laced around the shoe and held the foot secure.

For the first time, then, our daughter would move around beyond the limited confines of the seven-foot parallel bars. It was her first real freedom.

The tricycle, however, was the more important by far. Not because it taught reciprocal motion in a way that was real fun, not because it was a means of locomotion, not because it was a vehicle which would take her to

139

new experiences—but because, as she succinctly expressed it, "Just like the other kids, Daddy."

Excited beyond measure we had asked Dr. B just how soon we could expect Karen to graduate to crutches. His answer was surprising. "I don't know," he said slowly. "I've seen upward of fifty thousand cerebral palsied in my life and I don't believe I've ever seen two exactly alike."

We bought a regular tricycle with a broad base and large tires. Jimmy made the seat extra large and built a piece up the back so Karen could be tied to it and wouldn't topple off. She still had a long row to hoe on acquiring balance. Harnesses, similiar to those on the skis, were made on the pedals, since she did not have the power or the control to keep her feet in position.

We had bought the tricycle and Jimmy had fixed it up about a week before the skis arrived. (Made to order —$60.) By this time our abode resembled nothing so much as a cross between a zoo and a gymnasium. The nursery was a small room and could accommodate no more than the necessary furniture. The living room, being by far the largest room in the house, held the majority of the contraptions, including the seven-foot parallel bars. It was irritating, but also amusing, to watch guests weave a tortuous path as they entered and dodged and twisted across the room. Anyone glancing in the window at them would have decided they'd all been tippling. The kitchen was the second largest room and took the overflow.

For a while, I seriously considered that my safety and sanity could only be protected by dressing for the part like a goalie when I was in the kitchen. It wasn't only the pile of sandbags which always came unpiled as one shuffled past with a steaming kettle, or the movable mirror which, no matter how carefully I anchored it, behaved as though it should be exorcised, or the standing table and special chairs, but now Rory had reached the age where he was careening around in a Taylor Tot, in an inspired portrayal of a whirling dervish. Any kitchen activity was never a solo performance, but conducted with a full and vociferous cast, at least two of my own little ones and no less than two of somebody else's.

So, though we joyfully welcomed any new equipment for Karen, we made sure that our insurance and hospitalization was paid up to date.

We kept the one set of bars in the house and Jimmy built another set for the yard. As Karen grew accustomed to her braces, she was able to walk with some rapidity the length of the bars.

When she became more independent both on bars and skis, and while her balance was still faulty, it was inevitable that she would fall. We decided to guard against hurt and fear by teaching her *how* to fall. We resurrected an old mattress and started lessons in the art of falling. We took turns demonstrating, making our points as we fell. We did this for several weeks, before we started her at it.

It was a great game, with Jimmy and me shoving each other. And to make it even more fun, we included Gloria, Marie, Rory, and any other youngster that happened in at the time. What child doesn't like to shove? By the time we felt Karen was ready for participation in this game, she was thoroughly in the spirit of the sport and thought no more of the falling than she did of the accompanying shouts. We endeavored to teach her how to roll and take the force of the fall on the shoulder and how to keep her head up. Our various antics had earned us a rather dubious reputation. "If life is dull," it was said, "just stop in at the Killileas'."

All this speeded up Karen's walking, since she was unhampered by the fear of falling. "Just like Raggedy Ann," she'd shout after she'd plopped. She was a much

141

happier child in her new freedom, limited as it was, and we noticed that with the start of formal schooling there was the anticipated upsurge in physical improvement.

Chapter 13

WE HAD LONG SINCE given up an occasional cleaning woman or laundress and I was doing these things
myself. With Karen's program, housework, and C.P. activity, considerable responsibility devolved on Marie and
Gloria and it was good for them. Watching Karen's
daily struggle to accomplish the simple acts that we take
for granted was good for them too, and at an early age
they understood the meaning of compassion.

Karen loved music, and we continued to develop her
sense of rhythm and tone. We had a combination radio
and phonograph; at six, she requested the *Nutcracker
Suite* and at seven the score of *La Traviata* and "Atchi-
son, Topeka & Santa Fe."

Each night after dinner, the family would assemble
in the living room for fifteen minutes of music. Karen
was placed in her parallel bars and we would dance.
One night, Marie and I were acting out the "Parade of
the Wooden Soldiers" and Karen was "dancing" too,
swaying her body and stiffly jerking her legs. Suddenly
Marie stopped and ran from the room. I waited for her
to come back, and when she didn't, I went looking for
her. She was lying on my bed, sobbing as if her heart
were broken.

"Whatever is the matter—are you hurt?" I was dreadfully upset. In all her nine years, I'd never heard her
cry like this. I bent over her, looking for I knew not what.

She reached up and grabbed me and pulled me down
beside her. Satisfied that the cause was not physical, I
let her cry herself out. Her sobs were choking and deep

143

and it was some little while before they began to subside. She turned her tearstained face to mine and her words pierced my heart. "It hurts so to watch her." The tears flowed afresh. "If only I could give her my legs."

Although still tiny for her age, Karen had grown during the summer and had gained eight pounds. Carrying her grew daily more difficult, what with the added weight and rigidity of braces.

It was Friday, September 6, 1946. I had just started upstairs with Karen when I stumbled and only by the greatest good luck kept from falling. Considerably shaken, I sat down on the stairs holding her in my lap. "My, she's heavy," I thought. "I wonder why I noticed it so suddenly?" Then I realized that for the last three weeks Jimmy had been home on vacation and, counting week-ends, it had been almost a month since I had lifted her.

As I sat there on the dim stairway, a horrible knowledge came to me. It squeezed my heart with a steady grinding pressure.

I hugged Karen close—"Mom, you're hurting me." I relaxed my hold and leaned against the wall, cradling her in my arms. All the successes and happiness of the past year were blotted out by recognition—recognition that the most important factor in her growth had been placed beyond our reach, and my tears fell heavy and hot on her upturned face and her body shook with my sobs.

She was frightened. She'd never seen me cry before and this was the abandoned grief of the hopeless.

"Mommy, are you hurt? Please don't cry. Oh, Mommy, what's wrong, what hurts?" Her arm squeezed around me and she pushed her face hard against my shoulder.

Finally I could speak. "I hurt my ankle." Again the sobs tore through me. I fought with all my might for control. "It doesn't hurt as much now; it will be better in a few minutes." To myself—Dear God, how am I going to tell her—that she cannot go back to school? It will break her heart and her daddy's too.

I dried my eyes and steadied her while I stood up. "Come on, kitten, it's time for your nap." I bent and lifted her and started upstairs again. I washed her and settled her in bed. Back in our room I sat in my rocker. Last year it was increasingly hard for Sister Rosalie and this year Sister Cyra would find it impossible. If it is so difficult for me to lift and carry, when I've been doing it almost daily for six years, it just would not be possible for a nun with a large class, demanding not only her strength but her time and attention.

I got down on my knees and asked God to help me handle this so that Karen would have the least possible hurt.

She woke up at the same time as Rory and after I had dressed them I suggested that we take the big box of blocks and slats and build a great big farm. A little later Sandy came in and we played the phonograph and made up some funny dances and all the time I was wondering, When will be the right time?

I started their baths about five-thirty, and while I was busy soaping her, I said casually, "You know, Wren, you've grown a lot this summer. You're much taller and plumper than you were last year. You're really too heavy for Sister Cyra to lift or carry, so this year you're going to stay home and help me with Rory. You can teach him all the things you learned. He's old enough now, and we'll have a teacher come to the house for a while." I didn't pause but kept talking as I continued with her bath. "You and I will keep on working hard until you can do enough for yourself to go back to school. Sister isn't so strong as Mommy and if she tried to help you and take care of all those other children too, she'd get sick and we wouldn't want that."

Her lips quivered and the tears ran in a thick stream over her freckles. Still matter-of-fact, I rinsed her, lifted her out and sat her on my lap with a towel around her. "I know how badly you feel and I'm terribly sorry"—I said this softly while I dried her—"but it will be fun for us to run the house together." I slipped her nightie over her head. "It won't be easy but try to be a good sport."

"I'll try," she said in a small voice. That was all she said.

One of the darkest hours was the day school opened. I had laid Marie's clothes out the night before. She was excited and had to be coaxed through her breakfast. Then she had to be persuaded to take the time to brush her teeth, and she squirmed and wriggled so, it took twice the usual time to braid her hair. Finally she was ready—starched and prim. As the final hair ribbon was tied she dashed to the door, stopped short and dashed back and kissed us all, Rory, Karen and me, the cats, the rabbits, and the dog.

"Good-by, good-by," she sang as she raced down the hill.

I stood at the door holding Karen and we watched Marie until she was out of sight. The other youngsters trooped by in happy vocal groups, their bright dresses and jackets a colorful, shifting pattern in the warm sunshine. In exuberant abandon, they swung their lunch boxes and book bags.

"Mom Pom"—Karen twisted to face me, her lovely gray eyes filled with tears—"do you think I will ever go back to school?"

"I think so, dear," I replied gently and lightly. "That's one of the things we're working for."

"I should be going this year with Sandy and Ruth Anne." She spoke wistfully, more to herself than to me.

There was an immediate need for distraction and application for both of us.

"Come on, Wren." I turned away and we sat at the kitchen table. I took out my hankie. "Dry your tears before you flood the kitchen." I guided her hand till her cheeks were dry.

146

"Let's fix something special for Daddy's dinner."

I put her in her special chair which is about seven inches higher than a regular chair and has a wide foot-rest. (A regular highchair would have been ideal but you don't put a six-year-old in a highchair.) I moved her close to the table and tied on her apron which was just like mine. I put the scarf around her waist securing her to the chair.

From the pantry I took a bowl and a can of tomatoes, which I opened and put on the table in front of her. "I want you to help me make a meat loaf."

With considerable difficulty, and using both hands, she lifted the can and dumped the tomatoes in the bowl. She didn't spill much. I chopped some onions, mixed them with the tomatoes, added some seasoning and gave her the box of breadcrumbs.

Rory was a big help. He had to have a box too (empty). He turned it over the bowl for a while and then started kicking it around the floor. Soon tiring of this he began chinning himself on the table all the while shouting "Kawen, give Wowy gig o' mug," which translates into "drink of milk."

With these distractions on top of motor difficulty, it required a real effort for Karen to hold the box of bread-crumbs, raise it, turn it over and shake, and at the same time control the direction of the flow. She did well and didn't spill more than 50 per cent in her lap, on the table and floor. I laughed as I told her, "This will make walking around the kitchen doubly hazardous."

"What does 'hazardous' mean, Mom Pom?"

"It means dangerous."

"Hazardous"—she spoke the word as though savoring its flavor. "Climbing trees can be hazardous." I nodded. She smiled, pleased with another addition to her vocabulary.

I wasn't exaggerating when I said walking around our kitchen was hazardous. Because of the profusion of cats, dogs, rabbits, a turtle, a Taylor Tot, balls—the members of our household had acquired a peculiar shuffling gait. The normal step, which requires lifting the foot and then bringing it down on the floor, too often resulted in a wrenched back or a twisted ankle, as the foot came down, not on the solid floor, but on some squirming animal or treacherous toy. Slithering over a floor made slippery by breadcrumbs, I began to feel like Mary Pickford in *Through the Back Door*. I had to think back a good many years before I captured the theme.

"Karen, I've a wonderful story to tell you," I began. "Once Upon a Time . . ."

As I recited the delightful tale I got out the broom and set to work cleaning up the mess of our culinary caprice. The floor was so skiddy at times my story was interrupted as I fought for balance, utilizing the broom as a ski pole. The floor done, I poured a cup of coffee and sat down and finished the story. Karen laughed and laughed. "I'll bet she did look just like you. What a good story." I handed her a washcloth and she wiped her hands.

"Again. More," said my son who enjoyed the fun even if he didn't understand the words.

"Some other time," I answered, grabbing for him as he plunged both hands up to the wrist in the mixture.

Karen said, "Turn the radio on, Mom Pom, and we'll play our game while you're having your coffee." I flicked the switch, tuned to WQXR and waited for the music. (This station is unique in that it broadcasts many hours of classical music each day.) We would listen to a selection and then take turns giving each other the picture the music made. It was lots of fun and I enjoyed it as much as Karen. It was also educational and had helped to develop in her a catholic taste in music. Most important, she learned how to listen. She also came to recognize composers and could pick out the various orchestral instruments. She had been born with a wonderful sense of rhythm and early acquired perfect pitch.

I watched her with enjoyment as the sparkling *Nut-cracker Suite* leapt into the room and snatched her away. She has such a fluid face, it's intriguing—you never know what is going to happen to it.

The music had temporarily removed her from the morning's hurt, and as I sipped my coffee, I did a little inventory on our daughter. Motor difficulties, aplenty—and extensive hurts, heartaches, physical discomfort and pain, frustration and loneliness—and on the other side of the ledger—clear speech, assuredly a vital personality and a keen mind. But how were we going to fill and train the mind? I watched her.

The nickname "Wren" we had given her a long time ago. It suited her to a T. She was like these enchanting creatures, tiny, pert, friendly and not at all shy. Her voice was clear and sweet and she was just as gregarious as they. Of necessity, she had been much with adults, and as a consequence was thoroughly at ease in their company. She made friends readily, regardless of age, and this helped to diminish somewhat the loneliness incumbent on any exceptional child.

After her therapy, I decided to dispense with such inconsequentials as beds, vacuuming, ironing. I decided that Karen should have an outing and as much distraction as I could supply.

"If you will help me put on Rory's sweater, I'll take you both to the Village."

"Oh good," she chirruped happily, and then to her brother, "Come here, son."

He stamped his feet in excited approval. "Huwwy, huwwy, Kawen, help Mommy."

I drove along the main street and parked in front of Mr. Balfe's jewelry store. On more than one occasion I've sought solace in his shop for my own bruised spirit, and a visit to him was always a tonic to Karen. He thoroughly enjoyed her company, and always had a story

149

for her about one of the objects in his shop. Rory behaved better here than anywhere else. He loved Mr. Balfe, followed him like a lamb, and listened wide-eyed to his stories.

Theodore Balfe is a fine human being and a talented craftsman. Short, but broadly built, dark-complexioned, black hair, and eyes that are sad with the knowledge of much human misery, yet alight with compassion and hope. He has a special kinship for clocks. Like a physician, he handles them with deft gentleness; his skilled touch restores the fine voices of the grandfathers, and heals the delicate worn mechanism of the very old, which have come to him from all over the world. He rejuvenates the aged cuckoos, and that day he invited us to enjoy the perky wooden birds and their sweet proclamations. The children's eyes shone with delight.

Slightly stooped, he walked to his workroom in the back of the shop, and we followed. He paused in front of his bench and beckoned us. Reverently he lifted an old pocket watch and removed it from its outside case. I propped Karen on the edge of the bench and he put down the watch for a moment and lifted Rory and sat him beside her.

They bent forward intently as he picked up the watch. "This is very, very old," he said, "and has to be wound with a key."

Karen turned to me and whispered, "Here comes a story."

Mr. Balfe went on. "Now this watch has a very interesting history. Once Upon a Time, many, many, many years ago, in 1791 to be exact, there lived in England a watchmaker named Humel. One day, a wealthy lady came into his shop. He knew she was wealthy, because when he heard the doorbell tinkle, he looked up and saw a beautiful coach with four white horses. Also, this lady was dressed in rich blue velvet and heavy furs, and diamonds sparkled in her ears and around her throat. She smiled and spoke to him in a soft voice. 'I would like you to make a watch for my son who is going on a long, long, journey . . .' "

Chapter 14

OUR PROGRAM CALLED FOR us to use the skis twice a
day. I worked with Karen on them in the morning when
the therapy was over, and Jimmy did it at night. Her
daily program in toto now ran to about four hours. The
skis were the toughest part of the workout. We would
place Karen's feet in the harnesses and her hands on the
poles, set in front of each ski, then we would place our
own feet on the backs of the skis and teach her the walking pattern by pushing first one forward, then the other.
Karen was small but no flyweight, and with the braces—
this was some load to push.

Our thirteen-by-fifteen-foot rug was rather lost in the
middle of the living room and left a wide margin of un-
covered wood. This we sprinkled liberally with cornmeal
to reduce the friction and make it easier to push wood
over wood.

It was only after months and months of work that
Karen had the power, as well as the know-know, to push
her feet alternately forward without assistance.

When Jimmy undressed for his stint-on-skis, he was
a vision of loveliness in skivvy shirt and shorts. His
socked and gartered leg always had a look of indecency
with the rest of his habiliment. Summer or winter, he
worked up a good sweat, so he tied a handkerchief
around his head to keep the perspiration from dripping
on his dainty daughter.

Karen's braces were full length and were attached to
a pelvic band to keep her legs abducted (apart). She
wore night braces also, which had a spreader bar about
eight inches long to hold the legs even farther apart at
night. We were told that this was absolutely necessary

152

as she had developed partial dislocation of her hips. This had been caused by the tremendous pull of the muscles on the inside of the leg which caused a "scissor gait" and pulled the head of the femur out of the hip socket. The braces were to hold the femur in good position. To date, there was no surgical remedy for this and our effort was to prevent complete dislocation.

In addition, the braces held the foot at a right angle to the leg. This was to stretch a tight hamstring and heel cord. We were trying to prevent deformities.

The pull on the muscles was painful, and it was only after many months that Karen was conditioned to the point where she could keep them on for five or six hours each night. This conditioning was a hell for all of us.

We can only guess at what Karen went through during these months. Bed, normally the blessed haven of a child's weary body, was a different proposition for her.

Did she dread the hour of retiring? Did she think about it during the day? Did she ever compare our bed-time with her own? For us, it offered physical comfort, relaxation, and the pleasant twisting and turning until we found the best position for delicious sleep. For her, it meant physical discomfort, additional tautness rather than relaxation, immobility, frequent pain and sleep only when exhaustion overcame her. What did she think about during those first wakeful, lonely hours of the night?

The first step (as in everything else) was to get the child to assume the responsibility for its own improvement. For five dragging months, we never left the house at night. As each evening wore on, and her muscle pull increased, Karen wanted the spreader bar removed and the joint, locking the knees, and hence the legs into a straight position, unlocked. Added to the discomfort of the steady pull, was the discomfort of having to lie immobile on her back. Each time she called to us for relief, she had to be *encouraged* (never told) to hold out a little longer.

153

Many a night there were ten or fifteen calls from her, before we removed the braces. We'd been told that every extra minute was important. We'd work in the office, occasionally play cards, all the while tensed for the next summons.

Finally we took our questionings to our friend and mentor, Dr. Catherine Amatruda of Yale. Although we were aware of the physical benefits that could accrue, we were deeply disturbed over the emotional hazards attendant on this procedure. She saw Karen several times, consulted with Dr. B and, on the basis of considering the "whole" child, the night braces were discontinued.

(Just as sure as God made little apples, Canasta was developed by parents trying to educate their child, and themselves, to night braces.)

In the era of this endeavor, there were days when I was so tired that I felt as though there were an iron band around my head, and it was at that time that I developed my first real case of nerves. I was irritable, unjust, and jumped at the slightest noise. A decided "cross" to my family.

One afternoon, Karen was in her standing table feeding her doll, Rory was crawling around on the floor chasing a new gray and white Angora kitten, I was sitting in my rocker mending the bedroom curtains and wondering if they'd hold up another laundering. For the past two weeks the main topic of family conversation had been the choice of a name for the new kitten. Each of the three older children had definite ideas on the choice of an appellation and daily the debate grew more heated. Karen and I were rehashing all the suggestions when Marie came in from school. She immediately plunged into the discussion and it soon degenerated into an unholy Irish row—the issue apparently to be settled on the basis of lung power. I kept still as long as I could, then I shouted:

154

"Cut it out!" I sounded like a fishwife. "You're taking all the joy out of having the kitten by your bickering. I've had just enough, and this could go on till Tip's Eve. It's going to be settled now, for once and for all and by *me*."

I struggled hard to control my unreasonable anger. I put the curtains aside and went over to pick up the kitten, taking his tail out of Rory's mouth as I did so. In a somber voice, reflecting the gravity of the occasion, I said, "I christen thee Anonymous"—they were quiet and puzzled—"and thou shalt be called Nonny from this day forth."

"That's kinda cute, Mom Pom," said Karen, always the little diplomat. Marie nodded. I went on to explain what the word meant and the battle ended. Marie went over and sat on the floor beside Rory. All three of them regarded me with surprised hurt.

I left the room and went to my desk in the office. When I had first started working in the field of C.P., my mother had been at the house for the week-end. Before she left she handed me an ordinary 3 x 5 card. It was limp and frayed from much handling. It had typing on both sides and the print was smudged. "Keep it," she said. "Whether in your handling of Karen, or your work in C.P., it will help you."

I went over to the desk and stood in front of the card which was pasted at eye level with a piece of Scotch tape. I read the front of the card slowly and then realized that I didn't have to turn it over. I had used it so often, I knew it by heart.

Lord, make me an instrument of Thy peace, where there is hatred, let me sow love; where there is injury, pardon; where there is doubt, faith; where there is despair, hope; where there is darkness, light; and where there is sadness, joy.

155

And the second paragraph, I had underscored.

> O Divine Master, grant that I may seek not so
> much to be consoled as to console; to be under-
> stood, as to understand; to be loved, as to love;
> for it is in giving that we receive, it is in
> pardoning that we are pardoned, and it is in
> dying, that we are born to eternal life.

In spite of the difficulties of our personal situation, we
took heart from the establishment and growth of C.P. as-
sociations throughout New York State. In addition Shirley Larschan was developing most important contacts
with parents in all parts of the country. She stimulated
many of them to action and advised and guided them
on preliminary steps of organization and program.

We had a complete bibliography of writings extant on
the subject and an excellent film which we showed to
gatherings of every description throughout the state.
The value of this film could never be overestimated. It
was an accurate and artistic portrayal of the problem and
the existing methods of handling it. It showed all the
different types of involvements and also showed, most
vividly, the happiness and progress of youngsters who receive treatment and education. At this time, there were
facilities for only one out of every one hundred C.P.'s. No
matter how fatigued we might be we were always spurred
on by the need of the ninety-nine out of each hundred
who had nothing.

Karen's lack of education haunted us and at this junc-
ture the movement itself brought us a direct personal
benefit. For the New York State C.P. Association, Frances Giden had assumed the tremendous task of making a
digest of all the existing Laws of the State that related
to the physically handicapped. (Incidentally, this digest
has subsequently been used by the State Bill Drafting
Department.) The digest was distributed widely and we,
like many others found that the superintendent of schools

156

could send a home-teacher to a physically handicapped child and that the city would bear the cost 50-50 with the state.

We went to see our superintendent and he made arrangements to send a teacher to the house for one hour, three days a week. Little as it was, we were glad to have even this much, since we knew from previous experience that Karen's physical program moved ahead faster when coupled with the educational, and vice versa.

We didn't talk about Karen's educational program when we were with other parents because so many could not get even this much. Many of their children were arbitrarily disqualified because they couldn't get an average I.Q. rating from the standard psychometric tests. There is no state law requiring such a test but generally it is demanded as though such a law existed.

The hideous injustice of this procedure is sickening. How can one apply standard tests to a child who

1. Has not had experience, which, for all persons, is the basic growth factor;
2. Has presently little or poor motor control;
3. Has slight or severe, single or multiple sensory involvements.

We constantly sought a remedy for this appalling situation which deprived so many of education, and eventually we found a few doctors and educators who had made strides in developing valid testing methods for handicapped children. On one occasion, when I voiced a plea for the education of the handicapped, a leading state official retorted, "It would be a waste of the state's money. They'll never get jobs." Although he flaunted a number of degrees, apparently he had never encountered Descartes, who said, "I think, therefore I am."

We were frequently discouraged and not a little frightened as we found that many of our "learned" men felt the same way. Although a survey had been made of the

157

handicapped in industry, which should have impressed even the most prejudiced, it seemed to denote a philosophy of absolute materialism on the part of men charged with the responsibility of government.

It was particularly shattering when a state commissioner inquired, "What's the sense of spending money teaching them anything if they can't sell what they learn? It costs too much. It's not worth it to them or to us."

When I reported this conversation to Jimmy, he exploded. "For God's sake! Don't they know it's far more costly for everybody to go on supporting people who could be supporting themselves as well as contributing their share in taxes? And doesn't this commissioner know, or worse doesn't he care, that 'Education is an end in itself'?"

"Knowledge for knowledge's sake," I muttered. "I guess we're out of step with the times."

"With such people entrusted with the affairs of government, I take a very dim view of the future."

"Jimmy, do you realize that this attitude demands strong and militant action from citizen groups like ours?"

"I darn well do," said he, with more feeling than syntax. "Well, thank God our superintendent is a sensible man, because I'd battle this right to the Governor's Mansion, if I had to."

A week later Karen's teacher arrived. In a small community like Rye, there is a limited selection of teachers. This first one, sent to Karen, came for two months then fortunately resigned from the job before I threw her out on her ear. She was dull, disinterested, resentful, and antagonistic. We were glad to see the last of her. We were pessimistic over her successor, in fact thoroughly discouraged about the whole business.

Our worry was wasted (as worry usually is) since the new incumbent was precisely what I would have specified if I could have had a teacher made to order. Mary Robards was the school psychologist and she had had many years' experience in remedial reading. She, like Burnzie, had a vocation for her work. It was no easy task for her since the only time she could come was at the end of a full day, during which she covered assignments in three schools. It was far from the best time for Karen either, since by five or six in the afternoon, she too was tired. More tired than the average child since for Karen to walk across the room required the same amount of effort and concentration as it would for one of us to cover a greater distance on a tight-rope.

In these hours Karen had the undivided attention of her teacher, but she did not have the socialization and competition that are so much a part of a child's schooling. Her spastic hands complicated things further; her left-handedness was an additional difficulty. On top of all this was the situation which made her read "was" for "saw." Mary was faced with a challenge which would have floored a less hardy and determined soul. Karen's sitting balance was far from perfect and I learned how important posture is to study and concentration.

Specifically, Karen could not hold a book, turn a page, direct or control a pencil or crayon. The finger-painting, which had been a part of our occupational therapy for some time, had improved her manual dexterity somewhat, and at Mary's suggestion we bought outsize coloring books and outsize crayons and chalk. (You can buy chalk as big around as the best Corona-Corona.) Mary had the unusual opportunity of working with Burnzie, one of the best physiotherapists ever to come down the pike.

She was family by now and interested in this phase of Karen's development. She has a genius for invention, and to help solve the problems of handling books she purchased for us a wooden cook-book stand to support the book and suggested a clothespin to hold the pages.

In spite of the little time we had from Burnzie and Mary, they were a good team and we soon saw the results of their combined efforts.

We kept our own charts and graphs in addition to

159

those kept professionally. With the recommencement of Karen's education there came a spurt in her physical progress. We observed that in all endeavors, at irregular intervals, we reach a "plateau"—that futile period of time, lasting days, sometimes weeks or even months, when the child stays at the same level of learning. We also have periods of regression. One of the things that interested us was the fact that the physical graph and the mental graph kept apace. They spurted together, leveled off together, and dropped together. I know of no extensive or conclusive research on this and hope that if such research has been done it will be brought to light; if not, that it will soon be undertaken.

Having a home-teacher had given Karen standing with her group. It also provided diversion, filled many empty hours, and she reveled in the undivided attention. The days Mary did not come she was dejected. Her progress was slow—so slow, that to my untrained observation there were long periods when I could see no progress at all. She had a short attention span, and this presented the biggest hurdle. But as the months went by, great things were accomplished.

One afternoon, when the semester was drawing to a close, Mary and I sat over a cup of coffee. Helping herself to a second spoonful of sugar, she confided, "I had my doubts about this assignment. Not because of the child but because I had no way of knowing what the maternal attitude would be. Your attitude, for good or ill, would affect all our efforts. Our introduction satisfied me or I would not have taken the job."

"It didn't satisfy me," I confessed. "You weren't exactly warm and the only time you spoke was to ask a silly question."

"Not so silly," said Mary. "It was your answer that decided me."

"I don't even remember it."

"I asked you," Mary said, " 'What do you expect Karen to accomplish and over what period of time?' "

"So you did, and I still think it was silly."

"You replied," Mary stirred her coffee, ignoring my comments, "'How could I possibly know? That's a question only Karen's teacher could possibly answer.' Then I knew," Mary laughed, "that I should have no trouble with Mama."

"Oh. As long as we're going in for true confessions," I said, "a well-known child-guidance center observed Karen over a period of three years. They gave her the standard psychometric tests and stated positively that her I.Q. was between 75 and 85."

Mary hooted. "Standard tests for a child with extremely limited experience and severe motor disabilities." She switched around in her chair. "120 to 140 would be my guess."

Before I could reply, Marie came bursting in from school. "Hi, Mom. Hi, Mary," she caroled, brushing a kiss across the top of our heads. She danced over to the icebox and after thoughtful consideration selected an orange and brought it over to the table.

"I have a favor to ask, Mommy." She started to peel her orange.

"What is it, hon? You look unusually serious."

"Can I borrow the movie on C.P.?"

"May I," I corrected automatically. "Whatever for?" I couldn't have been more surprised if she'd asked to take the car for the evening.

"I want to take it to school and have Sister show it to the kids. They're always showing what they call 'Educational Films.'"

I got a nice warm feeling all over. "That's a wonderful idea. Of course you may borrow it, but I think I had better speak to Sister first. Whatever prompted such an idea?" I was pleased but immensely curious.

"Well, after all," she answered, wiping some juice from her chin, then looking at me with grave intentness, "you're not so young any more and when you die someone will have to do the work."

161

Mary covered a snicker with a cough. I collapsed slowly against the back of my chair. I was thirty-two and though I felt a little seamy some days, salespeople still addressed me as "Miss." (Maybe there was more to this selling business than I thought.) I put my hand to my cheek. Maybe it was time to get my first facial. I touched my hair. Maybe if I rebudgeted carefully for a week or two or three, I might be able to manage a permanent. "Your interest is laudable," I mumbled, "though I don't know how you came up with correct conclusions when they are based on a faulty premise."

"Huh?"

"Never mind. Your interest makes me very happy. I'll bet all you kids will always help."

Jimmy was suitably impressed with her idea and gratifyingly amused at her reason. "You look younger than you did when we were married and you're certainly prettier—though you were pretty enough then."

In the end I was glad the whole thing had come up.

Sister was pleased with the idea and wisely observed, "You know, Mrs. Killilea, if we could educate all the children today, there would be no job of public education tomorrow." I thought of the potential teachers in her class and the training necessary to qualify anyone to teach the cerebral palsied. It not only takes skill, but since many C.P.'s have visual, oral or auditory difficulties as well as motor difficulties, specialized training is a must. And here in the field of teaching we had the same lack of trained personnel that we had in the medical and therapeutic.

Chapter 15

KAREN GREW SLOWLY, but Gloria, Marie, and Rory seemed to get bigger every day—and incidentally, so did the Irish setter. By this time he had become a very important member of the family. His period of orientation was strenuous and, if it had not been for Karen, I think I should have conceded him to be the superior "Mick" and shipped him back whence he had come.

When he came to us, he was a badly disciplined young male and large enough that his every exuberant movement was a threat. Ash trays, lamps, books, vases, even the fire screen, fell before the onslaught of this red demon. He had been registered with the American Kennel Club as Tam O'Shanter of Knightscroft. At the end of two weeks we applied to have him re-registered under a more appropriate title—Shanty Irish. The American Kennel Club was horrified—he was of Champion Stock; but we were adamant and "Shanty Irish" he became.

The strain of molding this recalcitrant creature to domesticity was such that I became desperate. I finally appealed to Jimmy. "I've trained a lot of dogs in my day but never have I had to cope with anything like this."

"I don't think it's because he's stupid," Jimmy said.

"Oh he's not stupid"—I was growing heated—"if anything, he's too darn smart."

"That might explain it," my loving spouse answered viciously.

"Well, if you don't have him psychoanalyzed, before long you'll have to do the job on me."

"I guess we'd better get rid of him. There are too many important things that need your attention." (This is

known as negative selling.) And then very casually—
"How is he with Karen?"

"Don't be cute. You know full well how he is with
Karen. All right, I'll struggle on." (What woman doesn't
relish the role of martyr?)

The dog was certainly smart. He did everything his
cunning canine mind could concoct to enrich Karen's
life. If she had a ball and dropped it, he fetched it. He
was company for her. Setters are supposed to stray, but
this hound never strayed more than a few feet from her
side. And he guarded her, not belligerently but effectively.

One morning I had placed her parallel bars in the sun
at the base of the bank in the front yard. As I made the
beds in the nursery I glanced appreciatively at the pair.
A few minutes later I saw Shanty move away from her
and this was so unusual I went to the door to see why.
Running along the top of the bank was a wire-haired
terrier (he reminded me of my French Professor at Mt. St.
Vincent). Shanty went up and introduced himself to the
terrier in the quaint way dogs have. The pup turned and
headed curiously for Karen and her bars and Shanty
watched from the top of the bank. The newcomer was
about five feet from her when he barked, and then Shanty
took off. He charged down the bank, a red and raucous
bolt of wrath. The terrier was almost to Karen when the
bolt struck him. He wasn't bitten or even snapped at, but
he was hurled twenty feet by the impact of Shanty's
head against his side.

A few days after this episode, a gentleman came to
fetch me to speak at the Rotary Club luncheon. Karen
and Shanty were out front when he arrived. "This is my
daughter Karen," I introduced them.

"How do you do," she acknowledged, and turning to
the dog she added gravely, "and this is Shanty, my
guardian angel."

This date with the Rotary Club of Port Chester was a
return engagement. They wanted a progress report on the

work throughout the state. I told about a recent trip upstate to the second birthday meeting of the Ithaca group: how a year ago there had been thirty at the annual dinner and this year there had been over four hundred. It was no longer just a parents' group—the mayor was the guest of honor. He was flanked by civic leaders, lawyers, dentists, a few bankers, the local baker, schoolteachers, several policemen, salesmen, a plumber, an architect, parents of C.P's and public-spirited citizens. A fine cross section of a typical American community.

I told them of a significant incident which had occurred on the way home. As my train sped south, I was mulling over the events of the previous evening, and reflecting how the mixed assembly demonstrated incontrovertibly that cerebral palsy is no respecter of race, creed, or color, financial, social or intellectual standing. I was pretty buoyed up by the affair, and I must have been sitting there smirking, because the conductor came over and remarked, "It's good to see someone looking happy for a change."

"I am happy," I said, and not being one to overlook an opportunity, I told him a little about C.P. and why I was happy. There was only one other passenger in the car and the conductor settled himself in the seat beside me. He was a little gray man with thick glasses, neat as a pin and quick in his movements and speech. He asked a lot of questions.

"I'll show you something pretty. You're lucky; I couldn't do this if we had a crowd." He rose and turned off the lights in the car. "Now watch out the window." We were traveling through the mountains, beside a river. There had been a heavy snow and, staring through the pane, I could see the fir trees humped, like pickers, beneath their load. The moon glittered on ice chunks piled against the shore.

"Watch the clearings," my companion whispered, "watch closely." In a few moments I saw a figure glide

165

across the whiteness. Now there were more clearings and more figures. With a thrill I realized that they were deer feeding.

"There's a stretch of about twenty-five miles along here," he said, "where they come to feed when the snow is on the ground. I've been on this run for eighteen years and I still get a kick out of it."

I kept my face turned to the beauty outside. Behind me, my friend was speaking again, quietly. "I've been thinking about all the things you told me. I've got an older brother. The only way he can get around is on a wooden platform we made him. We always just accepted him as crippled. His body moves a lot, he can't help it. My mother said that when he was little he fell on the back of his head. His talk ain't so good neither. Now I know. He has cerebral palsy, just like those people you were telling me about."

Chapter 16

RORY WAS ADORABLE. Everybody said so. Sturdy, and in spite of his rotundity, quick. He was sweet and gentle, and at the same time he had a propensity for the kind of mischief that makes messes. Marie was maturing so rapidly she was fast catching up with Gloria.

How closely I watched Rory, not even Jimmy knew. How closely Jimmy watched I can only surmise. We hadn't properly applauded the wonder when Marie first grabbed a rattle, splashed in the tub, knocked the spoon from my hand, humped up on her knees, crawled and—that most wondrous moment of all—pulled herself to a standing position in the playpen. But with Rory, each miracle of movement was devoutly relished.

It was Christmas again and a happier season than we had known in many years. We had Christmas dinner as usual the Sunday before so we would be free of such mundane matters as cooking and cleaning up which would take some time away from the children. We strode through mounds of tissue paper, stepped carefully across the littered floors, to dress and undress dolls, experiment with toy instruments, xylophone, drum and a sax; and best of all, we played with Rory's trains and football. The cutest sight of the day was our son, who was not quite two, toddling around with a list to starboard, as he lugged behind him a baseball bat, a present from Nana. "It's not a bit too early," she pontificated when Jimmy snickered. She also presented Rory with a picture of the Cincinnati team, a duplicate of which hangs in Cooperstown. Five minutes after he got it, he walked on it.

All in all, this Christmas was a little more violent than usual. The trouble had started the night before, when

167

Tam O'Shanter of Knightscroft had flirted, unknowingly, with death. Over the years I had cherished five boxes of ornaments that Daddy had bought in F.A.O. Schwarz for my first Christmas. No ornaments like them have been made for a long time. The design and workmanship is priceless. Tiny silver bugles, hand-painted fragile balls laced round with cobwebby strands, lovely bells, each with a different note, ruddy laughing children waving from two-inch sleds. These are always hung the last thing on Christmas Eve and with appropriate ceremony.

At 3:00 a.m., with the last one hung, we went down to the kitchen for coffee. Before going to bed we went back to the living room to make sure that all the lights were working and to admire our masterpiece of decoration. Mother and I sank exhausted on the couch and Jimmy switched on the lights. I stared in disbelief. Our Hound of Satan was crouched under the tree with a number of the precious ornaments lying broken around him. I approached him menacingly and stopped in horror. He was *eating* one and had, on the evidence, *eaten* others. He lay with his head between his paws, his ears flat to his head, his eyes rolled up in quivering guilt and clinging to his chops and feathers were remnants of "angelhair" and silver thread. I didn't dare touch him for I was so mad that if I had I would have killed him.

The following morning the youngsters roused us at five-twenty and before eight o'clock their friends began to arrive to view the loot. Marie seemed listless as the day wore on but I charged it off to too much excitement and too little sleep. In the afternoon, she seemed reluctant to go up and down stairs and when I commented on it, she said her legs hurt.

She perked up a bit the day after Christmas but continued to complain of pains in her legs. I kept her in bed and checked her temperature for the next few days and found it running about a degree above normal. Friday I took her to John and, after examining her, he sent us to the hospital for some blood tests. I didn't like it but I wasn't particularly worried. She was tall, plump, rosy and strong and had a good appetite. The next morning he called.

"Did you find anything?" I asked him.

"Run up here to the office around four o'clock, if you can."

"That won't be any problem. Jimmy's home today."

I got to the office a few minutes early, and while I waited for John to complete the pulverization of a couple of infants, I tried to enjoy the "Postscripts" in the *Saturday Evening Post*. But with each passing minute a feeling of foreboding grew into the all too familiar sense of suffocation.

"Come in, Marie," John called from the doorway. Reluctantly I crossed the room and walked down the hall to his office. I closed the door behind me and sat down beside his desk. His phone rang and while he was inquiring about symptoms and prescribing I noticed that he was wearing a beautiful maroon and gray striped tie, that there was a new photograph of the boys on the desk, that the latest *American Journal of Pediatrics* had four markers sticking out, and that my mouth had a well-remembered dryness.

"Well, what did you find, John?" He looked at the blur my wet palm had left on the glass top of the desk.

"Not enough to warrant all of that," he chided me gently, "but Marie is going to have to stay in bed for a little while. She has rheumatic fever."

January and February were bleak.

Nine is a particularly difficult age at which to be a bed patient. It was very hard for Marie because she had never been one to sit and play but, like her mother, was a real tomboy. Because she was such a good sport about the whole miserable mess, we were all doubly anxious to help her. Gloria discovered that Marie was clever with her hands. She bought her some pipe cleaners and crepe paper and a stapling machine and glue. It was all very hush-hush. Some ten days after these curious purchases

169

Marie asked Gloria to summon the family. When we were all assembled they made quite a business of unveiling a large tray to the melody of Strauss's "Vienna Woods."

"It's a work of art!" Jimmy gasped in amazed admiration. I was too surprised to speak. On the tray were two circular pieces of mirror about eight inches in diameter. She had arranged, in clever groupings on each piece, six ballet dancers. They stood delicately poised in various postures of the dance. So this was what she had done with the pipe cleaners! The crepe paper was their costuming, gay and charming. There were men in tights and women in short fluted skirts of every hue. There were even minute laced ballet shoes.

Encouraged by the applause won by her first production, she made all the baskets for Rory's birthday party on the twenty-second of February. Each was red, white and blue and she braided handles and attached a tiny hatchet and two cherries. Absorbed in such detailed creative effort, she chafed less at her confinement. Sometimes she'd ask me to put Karen's standing table beside her bed so Karen could "help" her. They were sweet with each other.

Karen used her right hand very little and we tried all kinds of devices to get her to use it more. The two loved to finger-paint together, and Burnzie suggested that we draw a line down the paper over which Karen's left hand must not go. In the beginning we put it close to the right-hand edge of the paper and, over a period of many months, gradually moved the line farther to the left. In order to get a full picture on the page she had to use both hands.

We brought the neighborhood in on this. We'd invite four or five youngsters at a time to enter a contest. Marie would proctor and I would hustle dripping sheets from bathroom to bedroom. At the end of a noisy wet afternoon we would award prizes for: The Best, The Most Colorful, The Most Dramatic, The Best Stroking, etc.

The awards had to be made without my knowing who did which picture. They could do as many as they liked in the allotted time and sometimes there would be twenty to judge at the end of the afternoon. Of course they had to be "hung" for the judging and the walls and doors of the kitchen would be covered. So would the children. There was the Good Work Prize merited by the child who most frequently found Karen straying over her line. So correction came from someone other than me and was in the nature of a game. Red was the favorite color. The paint washed off, but unfailingly when the time for judging came and I re-entered the room I was appalled, for it usually looked like the Massacre of the Innocents.

Jimmy and I had continued success in doing Karen's therapy. We were luckier than many parents. With no treatment centers, clinics or private therapists available to the majority of C.P.'s, it was a case of the parents giving the therapy or no therapy being given. The main block in this arrangement was the difficult task of transferring from the parent-child relationship to the teacher-pupil relationship and back again. Jimmy and I had been able to handle this transition effectively, but many parents, through no fault of their own, could not. A solution of sorts was used in a number of cases. Mrs. A and Mrs. B had cerebral-palsy children, but neither could give therapy to her own child; so Mrs. A was instructed in the therapy needed by Mrs. B's child, and Mrs. B was instructed in the therapy needed by Mrs. A's child; and the personal transition was unnecessary.

Because we had been successful with the therapy, we assumed that we would have equal success in helping Karen with her school work. But it didn't work out that way at all. In this endeavor we were totally unable to effect the transition to the teacher-pupil relationship. Mary Robards had discovered Karen's quirk of reading backward—"was" for "saw." She told us that if and when Karen learned to write it would complicate the procedure considerably. I struggled on for weeks and Mary did everything she could think of to help, but to no avail.

Jimmy decided that he would have a try at it. It didn't make sense to his logical male mind that Karen would behave one way with Mary and a completely different way with us.

He tried, oh Lord how he tried! He would first carefully set the stage. His grandfather had had a little Morris chair, a replica of his own, made for Jimmy some thirty years ago. He would get Karen all set in this, with the back raised to just the right angle. He would put a sand-bag on her feet, to counteract overflow motion, and then move a small, special table ($27—and the guy gave us a break at that) in front of her. He sat on the ottoman be-side her and set to work.

His results were no different from mine. The virtues which Karen exhibited in working with Mary, were just nonexistent with us. Gone were the attention, the in-terest, the co-operation, the eagerness to attend to the matter at hand. She squirmed and prattled and whistled. She looked right at Jimmy and didn't hear a word he said. When the going got rough, he divested himself of coat and tie. Ordinarily he has a talent for teaching any-body anything, but when he tried to teach Karen, this talent vanished like a politician's promise. His voice—deep, rich and resonant—never grew impatient or angry or sharp, but there was an increasing crouch to his broad shoulders; and as his frustration grew acute, he ran his fingers through his hair with increasing momentum, re-leasing the waves, usually so carefully subjugated. I knew when he had reached the end of his rope, when he started pulling at the lobe of his ear, a habit he has in time of ex-treme agitation. Finally he too gave up.

One night he carried Marie to the sofa in front of the fire. Outside, the fog was slick and slimy and it seemed to seep in and chill even the warmth of lamplight. A roar-ing blaze of locust logs sought to repel the intruder and was balm to the spirit. Shanty was stretched out on the hearth, the cats between his feet, his rich, red coat flame-like in the glow. The brass lamps and jug poured their gleaming warmth into dim corners, and from the draperies drawn against the night the firelight plucked the richness of the damask. Above the mantel, Raphael's "Madonna of the Chair" was illumined softly, and Mother and Child seemed to smile in benediction. Shadows tiptoed up the walls and then flung themselves in rapturous dance against the high ceiling.

A chatelaine content, I turned to Marie and could not help a stir of admiration, she looked so regal in her red robe against the gold of the couch. The flames had captured her lovely eyes, her face was flushed and the short tendrils, that would not stay caught in braids, curled around her face and the nape of her neck. Jimmy lay on his back on the floor, his head on Shanty's shoulder, his fingers absently twisting the silky "feathers." The muted gray of his slacks and sweater, the blue of his sport shirt, accented the beautiful blue of his eyes. He was watching Marie too and had a look of proud contentment.

Gloria sat tailor fashion against the couch and her hair gleamed as she bent her head over her knitting. Jimmy's Argyles in the making made bright diamonds of color against her dark skirt.

Without taking her eyes from the fire Marie said, "Daddy, there's not much for me to do in bed. Why not let me try to help Karen with her school work?"

Jimmy glanced at me. "What do you think, Mother?"

"I think it's a swell idea," I replied swiftly. "I think Marie may succeed where we have failed."

"I'd try to be very patient," Marie said.

"I'm sure of that," Jimmy told her.

"And she's using some of the books I had in school."

Right away I thought of how good this would be for Marie. She would get considerable satisfaction if she could help where we couldn't, and besides that, it

173

would give her a feeling of usefulness—a feeling she very much needed at this point. "You can start tomorrow morning."

"What do you think, Glor?" Marie asked her.

"I know you can help her a lot." She put down her knitting and went over and sat on the arm of the couch. "You can make a game of it. Play school. And some afternoons, I think it would be a good idea to invite Kathy and some of the others in to play too."

"And then Mommy could give them a tea party."

"It sounds better and better," I said, lighting a cigarette, pleased with the picture as it was shaping up.

Jimmy rolled over on his stomach, lazily picked up the poker and pushed a log into position. The wood gave a couple of sharp cracks and the sparks swirled like a flock of fireflies. "It's pretty nice when your children help you figure out your problems," he said complacently.

"Glo, get me a pad and a pencil, please," Marie asked. "I think it would be good to make up a daily report card."

When Gloria had returned with the articles, she said, "I'll buy a box of those colored stars with the glue on the back and you can use those the way they do in school."

"Oh, swell!" Marie was getting more enthusiastic as her idea developed. I glanced at Jimmy's watch and was shocked at the lateness of the hour.

"Time for bed, young lady, and don't you ever tell Dr. John I let you stay up this late." I went in to get her bed ready and Jimmy got up to carry her in. After she'd been bathed and brushed and her prayers were said, I kissed her and said more gratefully than she knew, "Thank you for coming to our house."

When I got back to the living room, Jimmy had put on some records, Glo had gone to get ready for bed.

"May I have this dance?"—he was very formal. I dropped a deep curtsy (shades of Mt. St. Vincent's—Mrs. Seraphine Fowler).

"You may, sir." We danced while the fire burned down, doing the "Merry Widow Waltz" for the first time in a

174

long while. We were both a bit rusty but it didn't matter. We did the polka too and that finished us.

"Sweetheart, I hate to say this," my loving husband panted as he sank to the floor, "but we're getting old."

"You are, dear,"—I tried to speak without gasping—"I feel as fresh as a daisy."

"I believe it. Last year's daisy."

Chapter 17

MARIE'S WORK WITH KAREN proved really helpful. It was far from a real teaching session, but Karen responded and Mary was pleased since she had stressed the importance of Karen doing reading twice a day. Marie had none of the difficulty that Jimmy and I had had and she was deliciously self-satisfied with her results. Considering everything, I think it did as much for her as it did for Karen.

I had routinized and organized our daily schedule so that in the past year I had been able to visit a number of cities throughout the state to work with them on organization and program, show the film, and speak to groups. I was an expert in the field of cerebral palsy for two reasons. First, there were very few who had had as much experience at this time; and second, those who did could not get away from their jobs or homes. That made me the winner of invitations by default.

Flying was a great boon as a time-saver and made possible trips I could not otherwise have taken because the distance would have kept me away too long. In April, I had a two-day trip planned. I would fly to Syracuse for a meeting. From there I would go to Ithaca for the group's birthday dinner meeting, and from there to Utica where Maurice Sheehan was doing a wonderful job in getting an organization under way.

Most of the time I depended on Matt or Marion Taylor, both writers, to chauffeur me to planes, trains and buses. I never thought of them as working people, but rather as individuals engaged in an occupation that demanded no more than the occasional satisfaction of the urge to create, through the simple and pleasant expedient of addressing themselves sporadically to an intelligent machine with forty-eight keys, while sitting in a comfortable chair in a lovely study where the sun shone warmly on the paper, and wisteria vines whispered at the windows; and the fragrant smell of brewing coffee floated in from the adjacent kitchen. No commuting. No nine to five o'clock. No braving the elements in pursuit of a tardy bus, taking one to a train that was never late. What a life! They can have it!!

Matt drove me to Newark, waved a cheery farewell, and I settled myself for the trip, got out some papers and a pencil and prepared to do some work. The passengers were the usual assortment, which seems to be a good cross section of any American community. The young, the old, the blatantly successful, the eager, the sophisticated, and always a few who look scared. Across from me was a handsome woman in her fifties, beautifully tailored, and a young lady obviously her daughter. They were so nonchalant I wondered if this was their first trip. They had enough reading material to do them on a nonstop flight to Johannesburg.

Shortly the plane took off. In a matter of seconds I began to feel horrible. We were still over the field and just beginning to climb. Our altitude must have been about eight hundred feet at the most. I felt hollow and infinitely tired. My head rolled with the motion of the plane though it was resting on the seat. My pencil slipped from my fingers because I hadn't the power to hold it. My arms slipped to my sides and I couldn't raise them. The stewardess stopped when she noticed that I hadn't undone my safety belt.

"Are you all right?" She looked at me intently. Thank Heaven, I had no feeling of nausea. I thought she was worried about that so I tried to reassure her. It took a superhuman effort and a long time to gather the strength to say "yes." She was a sweet little thing, a very pert bru-

177

nette, and the uniform might have been designed specially for her. She passed from passenger to passenger dispensing all the refinements of air travel and stopped frequently at my seat. The two women across the aisle had begun to take an interest in me and troubled little to conceal it.

My weakness became so extreme that with what little mental alertness I had, I tried to prepare myself for death. No one could feel like this and live to tell it. Of that I was sure. The stewardess brought me some spirits of ammonia and it helped some, so I could partially control the head that was fastened to my neck.

The trip was fifty-five minutes. We had had to climb over the clouds and when my head had rolled toward the window it had seemed as though we were flying over valleys and mountains of snow. After half an hour there was no doubt in my mind that I had been mistaken. Not mountains of snow were we heading into, but the Pearly Gates—just as I had seen them in pictures.

At long, long last, the trip was over. We circled the Syracuse airfield and came in for a perfect landing. I had been unable to fasten my safety belt and I was unable to unfasten it because my hands just wouldn't work. I had to wait on the good offices of the stewardess which further intrigued the two ladies across the aisle. The stewardess had to help me to my feet. My legs behaved as if they were boneless and I stumbled because I couldn't tell just where my feet were. The ladies were whispering and watching. As I leaned heavily on the stewardess and staggered to the door, I realized that I had attracted the attention of some of the other passengers.

Ben Di Young was waiting and as the stewardess and I started down the ramp, she more than half carrying me, mite that she was, Ben ran forward with a look of alarm. Our faltering progress had slowed up those behind us, and, morbidly curious, they stood in a cluster and watched me transferred from the stewardess to Ben. He asked her a quick question and she answered, but her an-

wer was lost in the strong voice of the Tailored Woman
who addressed herself with indignant virtue to the as-
emblage.

"There is nothing more revolting than a drunken
woman—and at this hour of the morning—"

In two hours I had recovered sufficiently to relish the
humor of the situation. Except for the usual agony of
nervousness, by meeting time I felt fine. When I got up
to speak I told the audience of my experience and the
disgust and scorn of the witnesses. They were vastly
amused, and when the laughter had died down, I
pointed out that, temporarily, I had been ataxic—ataxia
being one of the five types of cerebral palsy; and that
the misunderstanding, disgust and scorn leveled at me,
was the everyday experience of C.P.'s.

The room had grown very quiet. The after-dinner shifting of chairs and clink of china was stilled.

"I'm going to tell you about a friend of mine." I
paused to look from one side of the room to the other,
from the first row to the last. They wanted to hear about
Frances Giden, there was no doubt of it. I told them of
her original handicaps, of her ceaseless twenty-three-
year struggle and her victory over handicaps which would
have defeated a less valiant spirit.

"Two years ago Frances and I had a dinner date," I
went on. "At that time her gait was still noticeably unsteady (just like mine in the plane). We went to a Broadway restaurant that was more than half empty when we
arrived. I noticed the Capitaine watching us closely as we
approached. Holding a menu in front of him like a bar-
rier, he came up to us, glaring in righteous wrath at what
he assumed to be a case of intoxication. With implac-
able finality he said, 'The tables are all reserved.'

"I looked pointedly at the dozens of empty tables and
turned to give him a thorough tongue lashing. Frances
took my arm and said urgently, 'Please.' Her whole attitude pleaded with me to be still.

"Reluctantly I held my tongue and, responding to the

179

firm pressure on my arm, I turned with her and we left."
My audience stared at me with shocked hurt as the full
realization of the indignity struck home. I continued
quietly, "My anger made me physically sick. We went
out into the street and turned uptown, walking slowly.
A half a block farther on, I stopped and stood in the
middle of the sidewalk. The crowd jostled and pushed
and mumbled but I couldn't move. Like a bolt of light-
ning I had been struck with the awareness— This is
what is in store for my Karen.

"Frances waited silently beside me. My face must have
blazed as I turned to her for she said softly, 'You have
no right to be angry. He doesn't know about C.P. You
have no right to blame him for that.' She paused to let
that sink in, then took my arm and we began walking.
We crossed 53rd Street and she went on with deliberate
emphasis, 'Six years, ago, *you* didn't know about C.P.' I
had no reply.

" 'This is the best example you can have of the need
for public education,' she said. 'Aside from this kind of
misunderstanding and hurt, which so many are exposed
to, there is another much more important consideration.
You speak of your ultimate aim as the training and education of all C.P.'s. That's where you're wrong. The final
goal must be that the trained and educated C.P. may
take his rightful place in society and industry.' I looked
at her, staggered by her objectivity. Her face was serene.

" 'You have a big job ahead of you,' she continued,
'and public education is the most important part of it, so
that Karen and all the other Karens of today, and the
Karens yet unborn, will be accorded the full measure of
human dignity—tomorrow.' "

Jimmy and I held that all phases of a child's growth
should be considered simultaneously: spiritual, educational, social, psychological, and physical.
When Karen was still very young, we had begun taking

180

her with us to church. The uncompromising pews helped her sitting balance. She was doing what the other children did on Sunday, she mingled with people after the service, so the benefits were physical, psychological and social, as well as spiritual. Because she was unable to attend regular classes of religious instruction, Father O'Brien came regularly to the house to instruct her.

I well remember his first visit. I had settled Karen in her special chair beside the couch and then excused myself. With great stealth I settled on the stairs to eavesdrop. They had been chatting about half an hour when I heard Karen ask, "Father, why does your pipe keep going out?"

"Because I forget to draw on it, I guess."

"Then I wonder," said my child seriously, "if you should be my teacher. That doesn't seem very smart." I almost rolled down the stairs. I couldn't say anything—I wasn't supposed to be listening.

With relief, I heard a delighted burst of laughter from Father O'Brien. "You're so right," he laughed. "But let's give me a try anyway."

The lesson continued, and at the end of an hour he said, "That's enough for today. I'll come back the day after tomorrow. I want to tell your mother I find you a very smart young lady." I came in on cue and smiled down on her with maternal pride.

"May I ask a question before you go?" Karen said.

"Of course."

Tapping the arms of her chair for emphasis, she asked, "Tell me, Father, just where is my soul?"

He looked startled and momentarily stunned. He pulled himself together and answered, "That will be the subject for our lesson on Wednesday."

At dinner that night I told Jimmy, Gloria and Marie about Karen's theological bent. Jimmy didn't enjoy the story as much as I had anticipated. As a matter of fact I realized that I hadn't told it with my usual verve.

"What's the matter, honey?" I asked him. "Don't you feel well?"

"I feel punk."

"That's funny, so do I." I shivered. "I'm hot one minute and cold the next."

"You both look dreadful," Glo observed. "Go on upstairs, Marie and I will clean up."

Jimmy came around the table and took my hand. "Boy, oh, boy!" I looked at him closely. "You've got a good temp. Your hand is burning." We sort of helped each other upstairs, two people in their early thirties who looked as though old age had galloped up on them and caught them unawares.

Before we could go to bed and enjoy our illness, we had 280 notices that had to be in the mail by six o'clock in the morning. I sat at the typewriter and the machine swayed and blurred, and I alternately sweated and shook. Jimmy signed, folded and stamped what I had written. We finished about one-thirty in the morning. He had been chewing sulfa pills like so many candy mints, and when the last piece was done he capitulated to what turned out to be a vicious virus.

It would be suicide for me to go out and I was faced with the problem of getting the stuff to the post office. "What to do?" I didn't have the heart to rout any of our long-suffering friends out of bed and taxis had closed up shop. Possibly from the fever, I had a sudden idea, at once brilliant and simple. I was a taxpayer, wasn't I? I was. Were not the blue-coated figures that patrolled our streets there to help as well as protect? They were. Weren't they a grand bunch of men? Always kind, courteous and helpful? They were. Wouldn't they welcome an opportunity for service to C.P.? Of course they would. Vastly encouraged by my answers, I groped my way to the phone. The floor slanted and heaved like a Jersey Shore Bird in a high sea. Fuzzily I gave the number. My head hurt and was so heavy.

"Sergeant Burke speaking."

"Sergeant, I'm in trouble and need your help"—and I recited my piteous plight. I must have sounded as bad as I felt.

"Stop stewing," he said. "You know all the boys have radios in their cars. I'll send out a call immediately and the car nearest you will pick them up and take them to the post office."

"That's wonderful," I said in a weak voice. "I don't know how to thank you."

"That's all right. Anything for the kids. Just leave them at the door, take a hot lemonade, a couple of aspirins, go to bed and forget about it. We'll see to everything."

"You'll get your crown in Heaven," I promised vaguely and hung up.

Once Karen's religious instruction was under way, she assumed the role of instructor to Rory. These lessons were usually conducted after they went to bed at night. Jimmy, Gloria, Marie, and I would sit in the hallway outside the nursery door and listen, always with a handkerchief ready to clamp over our mouth to stifle the laugh that was sure to be provoked.

She started off by telling him about Heaven. "Heaven is so beautiful you can't imagine," she said in the hushed tone adopted when she was supposed to be sleeping. "You only go to Heaven if you're very, very *good*. Nobody in Heaven is ever tired, hurt, sick or lonesome. When you get to Heaven, God will give you anything you want. Nobody cries in Heaven. Nobody is crippled."

Rory ignored the last two statements and fastened on the one before. "Can I have ice cream?"

"If you want it."

"Wory is a berry, berry good boy."

"Of course, very *bad* people go to Hell. In Hell everybody is lonesome and sad and it's hot—"

183

"Burny hot?"

"Hotter than Mommy's iron. Of course, you can't go to Heaven until you die. Mommy and Daddy will go to Heaven." And then we were startled to hear her cogitation. "I wonder whether Mommy or Daddy will die first." Marie almost strangled.

During these evening seminars, Karen told Rory that he was God's child. That God just loaned children to parents until it was time for them to go back home to Heaven. This, repeated often over a year, made quite an impression because he subsequently came to speak of having been carried down by an angel. Because Heaven was the Ideal Home and he had come from there, when we gave him a distasteful command, he would say, "They didn't make me do that in Heaven." Or when forbidden something—"When I was in Heaven, God let me do it."

Karen learned the Ten Commandments and the word "adultery" was interpreted to her as "immodesty." One Sunday, late in April, I heard her yelling in the front yard. Rory was yelling too, and I rushed out to see which one was bleeding. As I charged through the front door, Karen screamed, "Rory is committing adultery. I told him to stop and he won't. He's got his pants off."

For weeks, every time I put an apple on the table, we were told the story of Adam and Eve. Finally in desperation I said, "Remember, Eve was made from Adam's rib." For a long time after that, every time she had a bath, I listened to the story of Adam and Eve; so I didn't gain much.

Just before Her First Communion Day I said, "Now, Karen, you're sure you understand what a mortal sin is?"

"Oh, yes. And suicide's a mortal sin—unless you're sick in the head."

After her first Confession, wishing to help her, I joined her at the altar rail, whence the priest had carried her

184

after hearing her Confession in the sacristy. When he left, I said, "What is your penance? I'll help you."

"That," replied my child, "is between God and me."

We didn't have to make quite so many trips south now that we had Burnzie in the county. She had a genius for simultaneously correcting and encouraging both mother and child, and could extract the last ounce of effort from both. No clergyman ever had a truer vocation for the healing of the soul than has this girl for the healing of the body. A person of great personal goodness and faith, she believes in the dignity and personal worth of all men, made in the image and likeness of God. She loves her crippled children and, as she dedicates her life to eliminating the crippling conditions of the body, so she is also dedicated to the prevention of any consequent crippling of mind or spirit.

I have watched Burnzie handle hundreds of youngsters; I have seen her succeed where others have failed; I have seen her kindle a spark where some thought there was none; and I have seen the little faces of her brood shine in loving acknowledgment of a delightful partnership.

Burnzie, always interested in the "whole" child, encouraged Karen to talk about her playmates, her games, her religious instruction. It was a proud day for Karen when she announced to Burnzie, "Father O'Brien says I am ready to make my First Holy Communion."

Burnzie bent over and kissed her and said, "I'm proud of you and hope you will ask me to be there."

"Oh, you'll be there," replied Karen, "because I want you to be the one to help me to the altar rail."

Burnzie's eyes filled with tears and in a whisper she said, "I'll consider it an honor."

The appointed day was May 11, 1947. It dawned bright and warm. The Mass was scheduled for eight o'clock.

We were up early, and as we prepared the family for church, Jimmy and I noticed that the usual confusion and noise was lacking. Even Rory seemed to realize that this was a day of special significance and modified his behavior accordingly. John, recognizing the full worth of the occasion for each member of the family, had given Marie permission to get up for a few hours so that she too might be present at the Mass.

When the last flick had been given to Karen's sash, and the final buff to her shoes and braces, Glo and Marie supported her and I stepped back to survey the total effect. She was a picture of innocent loveliness in her dress of fine white organdy with its foamy lace ruching at the throat. Her lovely hair, hanging in braids over her shoulders, gleamed under the delicate white veil which floated in gentle folds to her waist. Her eyes glowed with a sweet joy I had never seen before.

Beside me, Jimmy spoke in a hushed voice, "She looks like an angel." He picked her up and carried her to the car.

Burnzie was waiting for us at the church and the five of us followed Jimmy as he carried Karen to the first pew on the left in front of Our Lady's altar. Thirty-five other white-robed little ones took their places in the pews around us, and, as we waited for Mass to begin, Karen leaned to Jimmy and said, "Daddy, I wish it was right away, now, for me to hold the Baby Jesus in my heart."

The little sacristy bell tinkled and we rose as the priest walked to the foot of the altar. Looking to the tabernacle he spoke, "I will go unto the altar of God . . ."

And the acolytes responded, "Unto God Who giveth joy to my youth."

"Our help is in the name of the Lord."

"Who made Heaven and earth."

The tall figure of the priest bowed low, his garments swaying about him. "I confess to Almighty God—and to you, brethren, that I have sinned"—he straightened,

186

went slowly up the steps and to the right side of the altar. With measured majesty, the Mass continued.

"*Kyrie eleison—Christe eleison.*" (Lord have mercy, Christ have mercy.)

In the center of the altar the priest intoned and the choir seized his words and flung them skyward with full-throated joy, "*Gloria in excelsis Deo. Et in terra pax hominibus bonae voluntatis. Laudamus te. Benedicimus te. Adoramus te. Glorificamus te.*" (Glory be to God on high. And on earth peace to men of good will. We praise thee. We bless thee. We adore thee. We glorify thee.)

Deliberately the priest moved to the left side of the altar and we stood for the Gospel, the recorded Word of God, the Son: "Amen, Amen, I say to you, if you ask the Father anything in my Name, He will give it to you."

Bowed once more before the tabernacle, the priest, choir, congregation, acolytes professed, "*Credo in unum Deum, Patrem omnipotentem . . .*" (I believe in one God, the Father almighty . . .)

The second part of the Mass began: the reverent preparation for the incomprehensible Act of Transubstantiation, The Creator of Heaven and Earth descending physically to the altar under the appearance of bread and wine. And, as if that were not enough, again the shiny music of the bells lightened the air and announced that He was ready to be received by our lips.

"*Domine, non sum dignus . . .*" (Lord, I am not worthy . . .)

Jimmy lifted Karen into the aisle and Burnzie stepped behind her, held her forearms. Haltingly, laboriously, Karen inched forward. It took several minutes before she reached the altar rail. Burnzie lifted her to the top step and stood behind her supporting her.

Karen folded her hands and slowly raised her face. We watched the priest approach, saw her lips part as he placed the Sacred Host on her tongue. Burnzie waited a moment, then lifted her down and they started back to the pew. Jimmy was holding my hand in his. As Karen came toward us, her face was pale, her eyes closed. She wore an expression of such rapture as to transcend the mortal.

She was with her God.

Chapter 18

JUNE BROUGHT US ANOTHER DAY of pride and happiness. Gloria graduated from high school. The preparations for the great day had been a tonic for Marie. She was at the age when clothes become important, and "fittings" were all done at her bedside. Karen's delight was equal to Marie's.

We were all together in Marie's room one day; Gloria was trying on her dress, I was hemming a slip, Karen was directing, and Rory was making noisy snowballs from a pile of tissue paper.

"It won't be long until you're getting me ready to graduate," said Karen, looking up at me bright-eyed.

"It will be all too soon," Gloria said, "but it is still a few years off." She turned slowly so I could check the hem.

"It won't be as long as you think," Karen said. "I'm Phi Beta Kappa, you know." (Mary Robards had once said so.)

We howled and Gloria said, "Isn't that just like her, always upstaging me."

Gloria looked lovely. Her white tulle dress was a masterpiece of feminine daintiness. Her shiny curls were drawn in a cluster on the nape of her neck. Her eyes sparkled and a natural flush colored her cheeks. She wore red roses at her waist and on her arms the lace mitts I had worn for my wedding.

I took her hand and led her in to Jimmy.

He stared and, dipping deeply from the waist, he said, "Your servant, lady. You are ravishingly beautiful." She

189

crimsoned with pleasure, dropped him a curtsy, turned and walked regally from the room.

He grinned at me. "You're pretty proud of your daughter."

"No prouder than you are," I answered.

"You know something—if Gloria were homely, people would still find her lovely because she carries herself like a queen."

Just two days after graduation, Gloria announced, "I am now a career woman."

"Lord help us," groaned Jimmy.

"Hush," I told him, and to her—"What do you mean?"

"I am now a secretary in the office of Barber and McCullough, attorneys at law. I start Monday. Isn't it wonderful?"

"Well, you couldn't have picked a nicer boss," Jimmy said, still a little dazed. Frank McCullough was our state assemblyman and we had been friends for years. It was he who had labored through the legal intricacies of our local incorporation and guided us through the legalistic mazes of establishing our organization and clinic. He, too, did it just for "the kids."

Jimmy said, "Honey, I think you should take a couple of weeks' vacation first. You've been working pretty hard the last nine months, what with school and helping Marie so much on C.P."

"I've been a liability too long," she answered with a new definiteness. "Besides I might get rusty. Anyhow, it's all settled. I told Mr. McCullough I'd be there on Monday."

Jimmy had a glint of proud amusement in his eye.

"What will your job consist of?" I asked.

"That's the wonderful part of it," she answered. "I'll get a chance to do everything. Of course, not at first. But there's a lovely woman in the office and I'm to help her. She said she thought I'd learn quickly. Her name is Mrs.

190

Foster and she's beautiful and seems very sweet. You'll like her."

"What will you do at first?" Jimmy asked with only slight emphasis on the last word.

"First, I'll learn the files" (she was oblivious to the emphasis), "and they said they'd start giving me dictation right away. Boy, was I glad for the stenographic experience I've had here on C.P. I think that impressed them." She laughed.

"So much the better," I said, glad that she'd gotten something tangible from her hours in the office.

"And I'll work on all kinds of legal documents. Bonds and deeds and mortgages . . ." Her voice trailed off. She was lost in a vision of *This indenture, dated the———day of———between the party of the first and the party of the second part.*

Whenever we became absorbed in our own happiness, Providence unfailingly stepped in with a reminder. A few days later I received a letter from the father of a twenty-six-year-old lad with C.P.

> I pray that the dream you hold for all C.P.'s may come true. For I have dreamed that dream too, Marie. And I have watched a little boy, who was proud and gay and forever laughing, grow into a man of twenty-six, whose pride has turned to bitterness and hate, and whose dignity is now a cringing servility to any hireling who will bring him a cup of water; who will move his wheel chair from drafts, and who will put his food into his mouth.
>
> So keep your faith, my dear, and the dream will become a reality and we who have labored for all C.P.'s shall know the love of God that comes only to those who love and serve God's creatures.

Ordinarily I love the hot weather and thrive on it, but this summer was different. The heat meant several sponge baths for Marie during the day, to keep her comfortable. It also meant taking off Karen's braces and putting them back on (a twenty-minute operation) at least twice a day, so I could tub her. Of course, every time she was tubbed, Rory had to be tubbed too.

This summer was tough for Marie, not only because of the heat, but because in the past she had spent several hours each day on the beach from June to September. Her confinement also confined Karen and Rory, since I couldn't leave her to take them to the beach or anywhere else. Jimmy tried to alleviate this situation by taking the little ones for an early evening dip when he came home.

The heat wrought some curious changes. It made our stairs longer and steeper and the endless bed trays heavier. It made Karen and Rory heavier too and pushed my weight down to an unattractive 100 pounds. Rory was at the Age of Exploration, and most of the time I felt like a pursuit plane operating on two spark plugs. It took a superhuman effort to lift Karen up on the table for therapy. By the time I was done with exercises and had her braces back on, I had to slide her off the table because I couldn't lift.

Jimmy was miserable, worrying over me and Marie and Karen and trying to earn a living at the same time. Our medical bills began to look like the National Debt (a frightening figure even in 1947). Jimmy had moved up to a splendid position in his company with commensurate salary and responsibility, and under normal conditions our income would have been more than adequate. But in our circumstances it was a bitter struggle. Karen's medical expenses ran an average of $2,300 a year (she had been on a drug for a year and a half that cost us $1.00 a day), and Marie's illness this year on top of it had us on a spot.

One evening in July, Jimmy came home and announced that he had a job with the United Surgical

Supplies which he would handle in the evening and on week-ends. I protested violently but he paid me no heed, and the second week in July he started. The girls took over his evening therapy and Jimmy and I scarcely saw each other.

He commuted to New York, leaving Rye at seven-twenty in the morning. He put in a full day's work and arrived home at six-thirty. He had a hurried dinner and left the house at seven-fifteen. Rarely did he return before eleven o'clock or eleven-thirty and then he had studying to do, to learn the line, and orders to write. These were days when waking up in the morning was a disagreeable business.

Hour after hour, day after day, month after month—passive exercises on the table, using our hands, working toward the day when Karen's brain would assume this task of transmitting orders to the muscles. When the communication route was established, the exercises would be "active" rather than "passive."

> Gallopy trot
> To the Blacksmith's shop
> To shoe the horse
> To shoe the mare
> And let the wee baby colt
> Go bare.

Each time the exercise was completed, we would stand with our hands at our sides and say, "All right, Wren, come on now, you do it."

It was August 23, a day so hot it made you think that if Purgatory was anything like this, you'd better watch your P's and Q's. By the time I had Karen's braces off and placed her on the table, I was soaking wet. "Here we go, Snickle-britches!"

"Gee, it's awful hot, Mommy." Her hair was damp and the perspiration lay heavy on her upper lip. "I don't suppose it would be good to skip our exercises just this once, 'cuz it is so hot?" Her voice was wistful, almost pleading.

"It's beastly," I concurred. "As a matter of fact I don't think I can remember another day as hot as this one." I pushed her wet hair off her forehead. "Suppose Mom gives you a nice sponge bath, right here on the table, and then we'll talk some more about it."

"O.K."

I sponged her all over and then daubed her with my cherished Charbert, a regular Christmas gift from my beloved Jim Meighan.

"Isn't that Jim's toilet water?" she asked.

"It is; nothing but the best for my sweetheart."

"I miss him. I haven't seen him in a long time." (It was just five days.) "He's my best beau."

"How about Daddy?"

"That's different."

"If we're hot, here in the country, imagine how hot Daddy is in the city. But when you're working for something important, like taking care of your family, I guess you don't mind so much." I sat on the corner of the table beside her and lit a cigarette. "Of course, therapy is working for something important too. I suppose when Daddy comes home tonight, he'll say to me, 'Marie, Karen and I are the two hardest workers in the family, so I think she and I ought to go down to the beach for a dip. I hope the rest of you won't mind.' And I'll say, 'Of course not, we don't mind. You've both earned it. Maybe you two hard workers would like to take a picnic supper just for the two of you.' But I couldn't say this, if you don't work."

Thoughtfully she replied, with only a small sigh, "A picnic would be fun. O.K. let's start."

We did exercises for back, neck, ankles, toes, and five different ones for legs. "Gallopy trot" she liked the best so I always left that till last. Fifty times we went through this training for reciprocal motion. I pushed first one foot up to the buttocks and then as I brought it

194

down straight, pushed the other up. One hour and five minutes later we were finished.

I dropped into a chair and said, routinely, "Now, sweetheart, let's see you do it." With little interest I sat looking at her feet.

And then a miracle happened.

Very slowly, the left knee began to bend and the left heel to slide. I didn't dare move. Slowly up-up-up, till it stopped a whole three inches above its starting point. It started down. I stiffened. No second-class miracle—this, for as the left foot started down the right foot started up in true reciprocal motion. The full cycle completed, Karen cried, "I did it, Mom, I did it. All by myself!"

"I saw you, I saw you!" I cried in turn. "All by yourself. I can't believe it, I just can't believe it." I picked her up and held her close to my heart. My happiness was overshadowed by a feeling of awe. I don't think there was any blasphemy in my thought: I feel a little bit like God.

It was too hot to sit close for long. I took her out on the back lawn and we lay under the pine tree. I sprawled on my back nibbling a pine needle. "I guess I can do anything if I work hard enough," Karen observed with deep wonder. "With God's help," I amended. "Let's say thank you."

Lying side by side, looking up the dark well of green to the bits of blue above, we said it together, "Thank you, God, for everything."

Later that afternoon, while still in somewhat of a trance, I was called upon to handle one of the toughest situations that is ever faced by parents of a handicapped child.

For some time I had been preparing myself, as well as Karen, for this inevitable situation. It was still oppressively hot and she was helping me in the kitchen. I was trying to concoct an enticing salad for dinner and she was breaking off celery leaves for me to chop. She had

195

been singing contentedly and broke off in the middle of a bar. Looking at me squarely, she asked, "Mom Pom, why did God make me a cripple?"

"Here it is," I thought, "and I'm not ready after all." I breathed a swift prayer for guidance. I fully realized how much depended on my answer. I dried my hands and sat at the table beside her.

"I think, Karen, because God loves you better than most people," I answered slowly. "He didn't pick Gloria or Marie or Rory to be C.P.; He picked you. You have suffered already and you will suffer more. Not only will your body be hurt at times, but your mind and your heart. It takes a very special person to handle hurt." I moved closer to her. "Karen, whom do you think God loved more than anyone else in the world?"

She pondered. "His mother, I guess."

"You're right, darling. He loved His mother more than anyone else, and yet He allowed her to suffer more than anyone else. Suffering, sweetheart, is a sign of God's special love. That's why you're crippled and we are not. He just loves you more, that's all."

"It's hard, but I'm really lucky. It's all right now I know."

Chapter 19

LABOR DAY, marking the close of summer and heralding the coming of fall, finally arrived. John stopped down in the afternoon and after a prolonged examination pronounced Marie well enough to get up a little each day. The cool weather came quickly and, all of a sudden, waking up in the morning began to be an agreeable business once again.

Early in November, when Marie was ten, she was well enough to stay with the Joneses, Ruth Fendler took Rory, and again we set out on our southern pilgrimage. By this time the trip was an important social event for Karen. Porters, conductors, stewards, bellhops, waitresses, all were glad to see her and took time to visit with her.

Karen had been seven the preceding August and for three and a half years we had been grinding daily toward the goal of independent walking. Each time we went to see Dr. B we asked ourselves, "Is it now?"

As usual, this question was uppermost in our minds when we greeted him that day. We gave our report on sitting balance, bar work, ski work, the victory of active reciprocal motion, self-help in feeding, washing, and dressing.

When he finished his examination of both Karen and her braces, he sat down with her on his lap. "You'll have to stay over an extra day," he said. "She's grown so, her braces need considerable adjustment." We groaned over the additional expense.

"We made arrangements for Marie and Rory in case we had to," Jimmy said. "Tell us, what do you think of Karen?"

"I want to tell you that Karen is one of the best patients I've ever had. What this child has done for herself is marvelous. I consider that she and she alone is responsible for such unusual progress. Her understanding, courage, determination—these are what have moved her ahead with such rapidity to where she is today." He smiled down on Karen. "You know, kitten, you're way ahead of schedule. You're ready for crutches."

She was measured before we left for home.

Each morning when we saw the mail truck, I grabbed Karen and raced to the door. How could it take so long to make a pair of crutches? A week went by. Two. We were fiercely impatient because Dr. B had told us not to have her attempt to walk on them for a month or two, but rather that she should work in the beginning only at acquiring balance and confidence. "About two months after she gets them, she will be able to take a few steps," he had said.

The long days we waited for the crutches we talked of little else.

"Will I truly be able to go way beyond my bars—any place I want?" Karen asked repeatedly.

"Absolutely," I confirmed. "You'll be free as a bird."

"Remember, Karen, the doctor said it was going to take time," I warned her, "probably several months."

"I bet I'll do it quicker than that," she said surely.

It was November 17, 1947. It was a day of shadows and the wind howled around the house like the lost souls of all time. I put Karen in her bars in the living room in front of the fire and placed some waltzes on the Victrola. "I'm going in to take my bath and dress. If anyone knocks at the door just sing out." I left her jiggling happily with Shanty curled up at her feet.

I creamed my face and relaxed into a steaming tub that was going to make me feel like a new and younger woman. I hoped. "I'll give myself a full twenty minutes," I vowed and sank deeper into the water. I had probably not been there a full five minutes when I heard Karen call, "There's someone at the door." I scrambled out, my thoughts decidedly unladylike, dabbed at my dripping form and slithered into a robe.

"Coming," I yelled, hoping my voice would carry to the far side of the door. Leaving moist prints I padded out, opened the door just a bit and poked my head around. "Package, Mrs. Killilea." I opened it wider and the driver pushed in a long cardboard box. Shanty darted out through the open door.

"Karen, they're here, they're here!" I slammed the door and frenziedly started tearing at the wrappings. They could have traveled by open dog sled from the Yukon without damage, so well wrapped were they. I threw the package on the couch and scampered off for a pair of scissors. It took a few minutes but finally I was down to the box. I took the box and placed it on the floor in front of Karen. Reverently I raised the lid. I looked at Karen. She was staring down, spellbound.

There in all their gleaming beauty were our crutches. "Isn't the wood beautiful," she said in a hushed voice.

Lifting her out of the bars, I sat her on the ottoman. My hands trembled as I lifted the crutches from their box. Wood or wings?

They weren't the standard crutch that fits under the armpit. They were shorter and came to just below the elbow, with a four-inch leather cuff for the forearm. To use these requires more weight placing on the legs and does not overdevelop the shoulders and upper arms.

I slipped her hands through the cuffs to the grips. "Now just sit there for a minute and get the feel of them."

She placed her hands firmly, sat for just a moment, and announced, "Now I want to stand with them. Dr. B said I should practice balance."

"O.K., let's go." I placed her on her feet. She swayed a little at first but in a few minutes was balancing well. We rested and did it again and again and again. We had always been warned to guard against overfatigue, so after the fifth time I suggested, "Let's not get too tired.

You've done beautifully and you'll want to show Daddy when he comes home. If you get too tired you won't do so well. I'm so proud, sweetheart."

I removed the crutches and placed them against the ottoman on either side of her. I was shivering, whether from evaporation or nervous excitement I couldn't tell. What I need is a brisk toweling, a warm sweater and slacks, I said to myself. Karen was sitting very still, her cheeks were scarlet and her eyes shone. "I'll be back in a jiffy," I said and went to my room.

I was half dressed when I happened to glance through my door into the living room. My heart stopped. Karen was not sitting on the ottoman. She had the crutches on and was walking toward me. One faltering step and another and another—I realized I was counting out loud. "Five, six— Dear Lord. she is apt to take a bad fall but if I go to her I'll make her think it isn't safe. I'll make her afraid. Seven, eight, nine, ten"— I wasn't breathing.

Her face was chalky, drawn with effort and strain. "Eleven, twelve—" I could see tiny drops of moisture on her forehead and upper lip. "Thirteen, fourteen—" She swayed and then steadied. A crutch moved forward slowly again, and a foot, and another— "Fifteen, sixteen, seventeen."

How far she might have gone I do not know, but my heart couldn't stand any more. I walked across to her slowly, stopped and moved forward again. Calm—calm —I reached her. She had stopped and was watching me closely, perhaps looking for uncertainty or fear. I smiled and stopped and took her and her blessed crutches into my arms. Then I went to pieces. I cried and cried and couldn't stop. Leaning back, she looked into my eyes, "Just like the button board," she shrieked. "You're happy, so happy you're crying."

"Better than the button board," I choked. I kissed her over and over, her eyes, her cheeks, her nose, her chin. Her face was wet from mine.

"Did you see me, did you see me?" Her voice rose and

shook as the full realization of what she had done swept over her. "Mom Pom, I can walk, I can walk all by myself."

Marie couldn't wait for school to be out the next day. She went from house to house telling all the children— "Be at our house at three-thirty, we have a big surprise for you. Leave your dog home today," she flung over her shoulder as she darted away to the next house.

I had called Kay Jones the night before and she bawled like a baby. Before she brought her youngsters up, she sat down and had a good talk with them. "Crutches may seem like a sign of trouble to you," she told them, "but to Karen they are the solution to many problems and heartaches."

Karen and I carefully set the stage. At three-thirty she was sitting on the ottoman a study in nonchalance, except for her eyes which glittered with barely suppressed excitement. The crutches were leaning beside her, covered with a doll's blanket. When fourteen young ones were assembled and Marie had shepherded them into a semblance of quiet, she took the center of the floor. With flawless timing, she waited for the babble to subside and then she said, "Karen has something to show you and you couldn't guess what it is." Kay eyed her brood menacingly, lest they spoil the punch line. Marie stepped aside and with a grand gesture pointed to the blanket.

Karen was, by this time, so excited her legs were sticking straight out in front of her and she would have tumbled backward except that she was bent double in glee. She seized the blanket and with a mighty effort tore it off. A gasp and a prolonged "Oh-o-o—" from the staring children. Then they raced across the room to surround her. "They're pretty." "Look at them shine." Sandy, cynical at ten, picked one up and smelled the leather cuff. "Real leather too. May I try them?" "May I?" "May I?" The clamor rose and filled the room and Karen sat grinning and chuckling and hugging herself in a near hysteria of joy.

"Take it easy, take it easy," Kay, Marie and I yelled together. When the chaos had been reduced to a state of confusion I said, "You can all have a turn but we have another surprise first." Karen clapped her hand to her mouth as is her wont in times of great emotional stress. "Are you ready, Karen?"

"Yes!" she shrieked.

Marie handed her the crutches and the children stood frozen while she fitted her arms in the cuffs. Anticipating their reaction she kept looking from one face to another. She moved to the edge of her seat, set the crutch tips about a foot ahead of her, bent over and then, slowly straightened up. Another prolonged "Oh-o-o—" which grew in volume as she took a step, and another, and another. Marie walked beside her, her head high with pride. Rory must have climbed out of his crib, for at this point, he came charging into the room yelling, "Kawan walking, Kawan walking." This released the others from their enthralled observance, and as Marie grabbed Karen, they swooped down upon her.

We left Marie as proctor and Kay and I went down to the kitchen and prepared a "cocktail party." The sunburst cocktail glasses filled with orange juice, and canapés of peanut butter and jelly. It was a gala affair.

As I watched Karen, surrounded by her fans, I thought maybe Carl Hubbell felt an equal measure of triumph when he struck out Ruth, Gehrig, Double X Foxx—but I doubted it.

Waking up in the morning was wonderful these days. Karen and I practiced early and late on the crutches and her progress was extremely rapid. I thought about little else. She must, of course, use the crutches properly right from the beginning, with the reciprocal motion we had rehearsed for so long. Burnzie put a pink ribbon on the left crutch and the right shoe, and a blue ribbon on the right crutch and the left shoe to help her establish the alternate use of arm and leg.

Many days the breakfast dishes were piled in the sink, the beds went unmade, and immediately after Marie left for school, Rory, Karen and I would get out the crutches and go into our routine. I would crouch about three feet in front of Karen. Rory would study my position and then with considerable difficulty, he'd hoist and jounce and wiggle his posterior until he had attained a reasonable facsimile of my posture. He had a lot of trouble, he was so fat, and as often as not he'd topple and that would make him mad and he'd yell in vexation and start all over again. Karen laughed so hard at his ridiculous antics that I'd have to prop her on her chair or she'd have taken a header. At last the three of us would be set and I'd say, "Blue crutch, blue foot—pink crutch, pink foot—blue crutch, blue foot." Rory would join the chant, "Boo cwutch, boo foot, pink cwutch, pink foot." Sometimes he'd ad lib, "Good Kawan—good, good. Kawan walking, Mummy." We acquired a certain amount of self-discipline after a while and could tolerate his attendance without complete disruption.

"Blue crutch, blue foot, pink crutch, pink foot." Ten, twenty, thirty, one hundred times a day. Tedious? Not on your life.

One day, at the end of the third week of our newfound happiness, Karen stopped to rest and inquire, "Aren't you ever going to do any more C.P. business, Mom Pom?"

"Of course," I answered without thinking.

"When?" she wanted to know. That brought me up short and made me think. I had been so wrapped up in our joy, that for three weeks I had given not a thought to the misery of many others. I experienced a nasty feeling of shame.

That night when Jimmy was through with his studying (there hadn't been any orders) I said to him, "Why didn't you jolt me out of it?"

"I thought it was good for you," he answered. "I wasn't going to break the spell. I knew it would end soon

203

enough. But to tell you the truth, it never occurred to me that your small daughter would be the one to bring it to your attention."

Friday I resumed my "C.P. business" and went into Yew Nork," as Rory called it. It was a deceptively mild day. I did a lot of chores the night before so I could leave the house early. I had a number of appointments lined up, from early morning until late afternoon. Mother was living in New York in the west thirties and I had planned to have dinner with her.

It had become increasingly obvious that eventually there must be a nation-wide organization exclusively for cerebral palsy if the total job for the total number was to be done. A necessary part of this concept was the need to study other national health agencies. In some instances these agencies' histories went back more than twenty years, and necessitated a tremendous amount of work. The work was all digging. In order to dig out the facts it was first necessary to dig out the people and groups best equipped to make the facts available. As in many efforts it sometimes meant going through five, ten, or even more contacts until I reached the person for the purpose.

Sitter cost ran high, so did traveling expenses, to say nothing of stockings. I acquired a repugnant intimacy with subways, bus routes, and the best walking routes. I also acquired an intimacy with the receptionists and furnishings of many offices, as well as literature most commonly to be found in them. I developed an antipathy for "modern" chairs and couches. As soon as I had found a comfortable position I started to slip and if I attempted to while away the waiting by smoking, it required some gymnastics to draw myself erect and then jackknife into a position that enabled me to reach the "modern" low table holding the ash tray. Ordinarily one would place the ash tray on the arm of the chair— but these chairs were svelte and, like the Venus de

Milo, considered doubly alluring for the lack of anything as utilitarian as arms.

At the end of a day spent traveling from one end of the city to the other, racing to keep appointments, and then waiting anywhere from fifteen minutes to three hours for the personage involved, I was often out on my feet. I developed an ability to anticipate such sequences, and once in a while, instead of hurrying home, would seek solace, comfort and nourishment from a dinner with Mother.

This particular day at six o'clock, I dragged a weary mind and body to Mother's apartment. It had been a discouraging day and the appointments not very productive. Verbalizing difficulties, problems, progress, and failure is an excellent medium for re-establishing perspective; and an interested, yet composed, listener like Mother is almost a guarantee.

After dinner we had a family chat, and about eight-thirty, Mother put me in a cab for Grand Central. I sank back to wallow in the unaccustomed luxury. We crossed Ninth Avenue and Eighth—I closed my eyes. Dimly, at first, I was aware that the cabbie was addressing me.

"Aren't you the lady who has a little girl with cerebral palsy?"

"Yes, I am," I answered, not immediately grasping any significance to his question.

"I was sure I recognized you."

"But how?" I was anxiously trying to recollect the face on the card behind the driver and tie it to something.

"Well"—he spoke eagerly, half turning toward the back seat—"about two years ago I was cruising past the Russell Sage Foundation on Twenty-Second Street about half-past eleven at night and you flagged me. I asked you what you were doing there so late and you told me you had been to a meeting with a lot of other parents because you were trying to do something for lots of kids with cerebral palsy." Suddenly I remembered the incident quite clearly, because my chauffeur had been genuinely interested and asked many questions. I recalled that he had had me explain what the condition was, and how many had it, how few knew about it or understood it, and consequently how little was done about it. He had been heartwarmingly sympathetic, and told me that he had four sons of his own, and then asked, "Is there anything I can do to help?"

"Is it your custom to say night prayers?" I had asked him.

"Yes, ma'am," he had assured me earnestly. "I was in the service for two years and I never went to sleep without getting down on my knees first." He reminisced, "Some of the boys laughed at first but after a while they stopped, and you know, after a while some of the other guys used to do it too. I've brought my kids up that way." He had stopped on Lexington Avenue before the terminal and turned to face me.

"In that case there is something you can do that would be most helpful," I had told him. "You can tell people about it and maybe you would ask your boys to pray with you and your wife for the success of our efforts."

"I sure will," he had said simply.

As the warm memory of this conversation came flooding back I smiled in the darkness. His eyes were ahead on the traffic and we stopped for a red light. He turned to me. "You know, lady, that's over two years ago and since that night the six of us have prayed for your work every single night."

Two weeks before Christmas we again headed south. The day broke clear and bright and sharply cold. We got under way about eight o'clock. Our car had no heater and considerably more ventilation than its maker had arranged for. We were pretty cold by the time we hit Columbus Circle. Here we parked the car and took a bus to the B. & O. terminal in Jersey City where we regularly boarded the "Marylander." We had the same feeling of kinship with this train and her staff as we did for the "Royal Blue" which brought us home.

The bus took us right up beside the train. The air was filled with the three-dimensional sounds peculiar to railroad stations and the steam coiled itself around the cars. We saw the familiar faces of the conductor and porter as they stood stamping their feet at the train steps. From the moment I stepped down from the bus I never took my eyes from their faces. In four years they had come to know our daughter and had a real interest in her progress. Behind me, Jimmy had handed Karen her crutches and I heard the tap tap as, for the first time, she walked from the bus to the train.

The porter was absently looking our way. It was some seconds before he recognized her and probably a minute before he grasped the significance of what he saw. His dark face appeared to tear apart with his grin and I heard a sound that was both exclamation and joyous laugh. He dug his elbow into the conductor's midriff and without taking his eyes off Karen he pointed to her and started over to us at a trot. He bent down and ever so carefully put his hands on her shoulders. "Little lady, little lady," he said over and over.

The conductor came up behind him blowing his nose and wiping his eyes and his voice was very hoarse.

"Look at my sweetheart—she's walking all by herself." Karen's March of Triumph had begun.

Settled in our seats a little later, Karen looked up at the conductor and commiseratingly remarked, "You have an awful cold."

Then it was time to go to the diner. She produced no less an effect there. Customers sat untended while our friends the waiters clustered round and then surrounded Karen—a guard of honor—as she went to our table. Throughout the trip, porters and trainmen from other cars came to call as the word spread, and Karen never did get to take her usual nap.

When we drew up in front of the Stratford Hotel it

was warmer than it had been in New York, but windy and raw. The porter greeted me as he came down the steps. He went around to the back of the cab to get our bags, then on ahead to wait on the other side of the revolving doors. Jimmy carried Karen up the steps and then turned the doors slowly so she could walk through. I shall never forget that porter's expression as Karen emerged in turn.

It's some thirty feet from the door to the desk, and the manager saw us coming. He was unashamed (or maybe unaware) of the tears on his cheeks, as he came out to Karen and kissed her. He summoned the housekeeper and the elevator girl, and there was great rejoicing. Karen evidenced a nice sense of theater. While her audience was still enthralled, she walked over to the elevator and balancing on her right crutch, raised the left and pressed the elevator button.

The next day, the March of Triumph continued, attended by the waitresses and the street cleaner we always passed on the way to the doctor's office. We were the first patients and the doctor was in his office when we arrived. As soon as we had Karen's things off, she started for his door. It's a double sliding door and moves soundlessly. We were watching her so intently we did not realize that the doors had opened and Dr. B was standing there. Slowly he came to meet her and, with ineffable sweetness and simplicity, he bent to her and said, "My kitten is walking."

Chapter 20

It was Christmas again, in this wonderful Year of Our Lord, one thousand nine hundred and forty-seven. Verily, "our cup runneth over."

Gloria was eighteen and lovely with her shiny look of charm and goodness, properly mature since she had become a career woman. Marie, at ten, was handsome. She was tall for her age and slender. Her shoulders were broad and Jimmy used to look at her and sigh, "What a halfback she would have made." Her hair had darkened and was now a deep chestnut; her eyes, large and dark, were heavily lashed. Her nose still tilted and her mouth was sweet. She was enough like her mother to require considerable discipline. She was witty, generous to a fault, quick-tempered, and forgiving. Like Gloria, she had had a great deal of responsibility and was poised beyond her years. Karen at seven looked like a pixie. Tiny for her age, ever so dainty and ever so feminine, she had freckles that clung throughout the winter, and a sudden and completely captivating smile. Rory, at two, was still perfectly round like those toys that roll and dip but always right themselves. He looked so much like Marie that we couldn't tell their baby pictures apart. He had developed delightful dimples and a pronounced cleft in his chin, like his Daddy's.

Shanty had long feathers, long ears, long legs and a long tail.

A week before Christmas, we had gone on the annual hunt for a tree. There was one major requirement. It must be the biggest tree on Hill Street. Fortunately our living room was eighteen by twenty-five with a fifteen-foot ceiling. It might have been designed especially for Christmas by virtue of its size and shape, studio ceiling, and the wide fieldstone chimney.

We drove from place to place, and each time we stopped the six of us lined up to inspect what they had to offer. We hadn't found anything to fill our demands when we drove by the Baptist Church in Port Chester. Rory let out a shout, "There's my tree!" and pointed to a majestic spruce growing to the left of the entrance. It was some thirty feet in height, broad and full, its lower branches brushing the ground.

"Stop, Daddy, stop," he yelled. "I want it." I tried to explain that we couldn't have it. That the only trees we could buy were those that had been cut for Christmas. "Cut it," he demanded. I explained some more. He was hungry and tired and disappointed. He began to cry. He used up Daddy's large handkerchief and mine, and no one had another. The wind howled.

It got colder and colder, and after the seventh unfruitful stop I began to wonder why we did this every year. The next time we stopped, I knew. There was our tree, leaning against the fence in solitary glory, waiting for us. I ran over and tried to hold it straight. "Here it is," I called to the children. Its smell was strong and sharp and it had double needles. It was so big and heavy, I couldn't hold it upright without help. The four children accepted it instantly but Jimmy clapped his hand to his forehead. "It's far too big," he said.

"No, Daddy, no," they yelled together.

"I couldn't even get it home on the car." He sounded frightened.

A little man, looking appropriately like a gnome, with a permanent crystal drop on the end of his nose had come up to us, and very sweetly he said, "That's all right, kiddies, I'll send it down by truck tomorrow." They screamed in gloating triumph.

"It won't fit in the living room," Jimmy protested vehemently.

"I'll cut off a couple of feet," said the children's friend.

210

"Oh, don't do that." I turned and smiled at him. "I'll just cut a small hole in the floor." I beckoned Jimmy to come hold the tree, watched when he grasped to be sure he didn't knock off a needle, and walked over to the man who was looking at me curiously. He transferred his gaze to Jimmy and back to me, shifted his weight and smiled tentatively. "And I know you'll give us a reasonable price." My voice had the lilt of complete confidence. "It's really too big for most people and I don't think anyone else would be willing to cut a hole in the floor. What do you think?" I asked him politely.

"Yes, ma'am, no, ma'am." He quoted a nice price, and retreated a few feet.

"We'll help you tie it so the branches won't be broken in delivery, and we're all very happy."

"Yes, ma'am."

Jimmy, speechless with I know not what emotion, carefully brought the tree to rest on the ground. Gloria herded the ecstatic young ones back into the car and we supervised till the last knot was tied and our tree was trussed for its trip. We gave the stunned man our name and address. As we drove off he pointed us out to some newcomers and made a vividly descriptive circular motion with his index finger pointed at his temple.

Two nights later Jimmy brought home a new stand and we set to work. It took the two of us, straining and panting, to carry the tree in the house. A tree must be placed to show its full glory. With some hesitancy, I remarked that the perfect spot was at present occupied by the piano. I didn't look at Jimmy when I said it, but walked over, moved a chair, and then turned to him. His expression of patient martyrdom reminded me of a picture that hung in the classroom when I was in 3B. It was a brown and white print of the Coliseum. Around the interior prowled six savage beasts looking hungrily toward the gates. Outside stood an assembly of doomed Christians.

With poor grace he moved the piano, after first shifting

211

two chairs, one table and the couch. Before setting the tree in the stand we decided to place it and turn it to get the best effect. With its branches unleashed it was difficult to get through to grasp the trunk. We struggled ten minutes to get it erect. I thought my back would break but I didn't dare complain. And then, oh horror! It didn't fit. Too wide, too tall, too everything. Gently we eased it to the floor. Gently we moved it across the room. Not at all gently Jimmy started moving the piano, the couch, the chairs, the table, back to their original positions.

"The middle wall opposite the fireplace is the only possible spot. We will have to move half of the furniture into the office, turn under the rug." My loved one was speaking in a monotone. He walked over and turned the thermostat down to 60.

Karen called and I went to take her to the bathroom. When I came back he had set up the stand and secured it to the floor with a few three-inch nails. "Here we go again," he barked at me. The unequal struggle was on. This time the tree had to be raised before it could be placed in the stand. Ten minutes, fifteen, twenty. My spouse broke the silence. "We'll have to have help." I nodded, dizzy from my efforts. "You call George—it was all your idea." George and Kavy had moved in across the street. We relied on them in all emergencies from a pound of butter to a sick child.

George came over promptly and as I opened the door to him he stopped and stared. I promised myself that if he laughed I would shoot him. Maybe he understood my expression or maybe his laughter died at the sight of Jimmy, who was sweating profusely and whose face, arms, hands and slacks were black with resin.

"It's a beautiful tree," he gasped and stripped for action. Finally we felt the base of the tree slip into its stand. Jimmy cautiously let go and slid under to tighten the clamps. And at that moment the stand gave away. It collapsed, disintegrated, vanished into nothingness.

I knew I was going to cry. My back ached, my arms and hands throbbed. Just then, Karen called for another trip. Very quickly I told Jimmy I'd take care of her, and when I finally got her back up on the bed, I lay down beside her. "Why do we look forward to Christmas?" I asked myself silently. It was a good question and I pondered it quite a while.

When I returned to the living room, the boys were seeking solace and strength from a tall glass of beer and the tree was up. I dropped to my knees to scrutinize what miracle of engineering had been wrought. The old stand was resurrected from the cellar, sturdy and strong (F.A.O. Schwarz—1916) and there were guy wires, five of them, from the tree to the baseboard. It was beautiful, so very beautiful I said, "What a pity, almost a sacrilege to trim it."

"The loveliest tree ever," said Jimmy and came over and kissed me.

"You're crazy," said George.

The children had the biggest tree on Hill Street.

Each year, we set up a crèche that my daddy had bought for my first Christmas. The figures are old and their colors dull, but every piece is a work of art. Mary looks young and proud. Joseph looks proud and, I think, a little worried. There are the figures of the shepherds and the small worn figures of the animals. And, in the manger, the figure of the Infant.

Before the children go to the tree and the presents for the material part of Christmas, they first go in to greet the newborn Savior.

As usual, our darlings were awake before dawn. Jimmy and I stood by the crib and waited for them. We love to watch their faces as they come toward us Christmas morning.

Rory came first, his eyes shining, his hair standing on end and half the back flap of his pajamas down. (Is there anything cuter than the south end of a little boy going north?) Then our girls, in their flowered robes, the younger ones with their braids hanging in sweet disorder over their shoulders, and Gloria, the blush of sleep still on her.

I'm afraid we watched Karen most that morning. Straight as a queen, crutches tapping decisively, though slowly, she walked with the others to the crib. She dropped her right crutch and, balancing precariously on the other, she stretched out her hand and ever so gently rested it on the foot of the Infant. Then, sweetly and distinctly, with the others, she sang:

Happy Birthday to You. Happy Birthday to You.
Happy Birthday, Baby Jesus, Happy Birthday to You.

High and clear their voices sounded through the dim room. Jimmy and I tried to sing too, but our voices were unsteady, and tears of happiness fell unnoticed. I could but whisper to the Baby, "Thank You, thank You."

The compensations are indeed great.

That same morning brought another great occasion. For five years now we had carried Karen into church. This morning she was to walk in for the first time. Jimmy let us out at the door. Marie carried her crutches and Gloria and I helped her up the steps and into the vestibule where we waited for him. He helped her fit her arms into the cuffs and we started up the aisle, Nana close at Karen's side.

It was not only happiness we felt that morning but a great and wonderful pride. Each slow step we took with her was in itself a full reward. And each slow step swept away forever all past discouragements, disappointments, hurts, and heartaches.

When Mass was over, we were delighted to find that our daughter must hold court. Neighbors, friends, and total strangers surrounded us to clasp our hands, to give a swift embrace, to congratulate, to praise. Men and women we had seen, but never spoken to, tried to speak and failed. There were some who, wordless, rested a hand in benediction on Karen's head and turned away and cried. One and all they shared our happiness and rejoiced with us.

Like a queen, accepting the plaudits of her subjects, Karen stood with simple dignity, while through the wide-flung doors of the church, spilled the liquid voice of the organ, raised in exultation.

Glory to God in the Highest!

Chapter 21

AROUND THE MIDDLE of January I took the four children to John Gundy for their regular checkup. It was just routine, since they had been collectively healthier than they had been in several years. As we waited our turn, I mentally reviewed some of our past problems.

Since the age of three, Marie had had a bad sinus condition. We had doctored extensively and expensively with an ENT specialist but had found only brief, temporary relief. The specialist had felt that many of her illnesses had their origin in the bad sinuses and he had advised, nay, urged us, to pull up stakes and move to Arizona. Our decision to stay had been a difficult one and was based on two considerations. First, necessary proximity to Dr. B. Second, Jimmy's lengthy and satisfactory relationship with the New York Telephone Company. He had had a number of offers of better positions but thinking of Karen's security and having a reasonable doubt of "peace in our time," he had decided not to make a change. A move to Arizona would necessitate such a change and we had reserved decision until John had returned after the war. He was an allergy specialist as well as a pediatrician. John had found Marie to be allergic and had treated her accordingly. She had improved rapidly, and although she was still under treatment we had been able to forget about Arizona. We got a break there, I thought gratefully.

It took John some time to work his way through my brood. He did all the routine things including booster shots and some tests. He didn't find a thing and said

216

they were a credit to us. I was always afraid that each examination would reveal something obscure and bad, so I was in a gala mood when we left. I decided Jimmy and I should celebrate. We should go out to dinner and the movies.

I asked Marie and Glo to take over with the little ones and spent a luxurious half hour in the tub. Another half hour on my hair and a make-up job, and a good twenty minutes deciding between my black crepe and a soft green wool. I chose the latter (I love any color as long as it's green), dug deep in my handkerchief case and extracted a fine linen square I had been saving for a special occasion and used my Charbert without stint.

I met Jimmy at the door and he greeted me with a delightfully vulgar whistle. He kissed the kids hello and good-by and we drove off feeling young and carefree. We splurged and ordered cocktails and then spaghetti with red wine. We went to a double feature and came home feeling like proper sports and quite buoyed up as one is apt to be by unwarranted extravagance.

Two days later, I was ironing in the kitchen when Marie came home from school. She took off her things and came over to me holding out her arm.

"Mommy, is my arm supposed to look like this?" Casually, I glanced at the extended forearm. About four inches above the wrist, there was a large swelling. John had given them all tuberculin tests, and I had absently checked arms at night never expecting to see anything. I must have stared, for with quick fear in her voice Marie asked, "Mommy, is anything wrong— you look so funny. . . . Hey, you're burning Karen's dress." I lifted the iron, put it on the stand, moved slowly around the table and sat down.

"Nothing's wrong that I know of—it's just—well— well, I'm sort of surprised—that's all." I tried to speak with maternal imperturbability. "Will you put Karen in her standing table and set her up with her finger-paints?

I'm going to sit and have a cup of coffee and be lazy for a few minutes."

"O.K., Mom." She got out the big flat roasting pan for the water, a couple of towels, and off she went.

I sat staring out the window at the sparrows hopping around on the crust of the snow. I didn't feel. I didn't think. Must call John—must call John. . . . The phrase kept passing in front of my eyes like the news sign on the Times building. The words slid along slowly. I had nothing to do with them and they had nothing to do with me. I felt a quick pain and looked down to see that I was holding a cigarette that I didn't remember lighting. It had burned down to my fingers. I wish Mother was here to brew me a pot of strong tea, I thought. My feet dragged and I walked to the phone. "Port Chester 8991." My voice came out funny and flat and it took a second effort to speak loud enough for the operator to hear me.

John answered and I described Marie's arm. "Bring her up in about an hour and I'll take a look at it," he said. "In the meantime don't stew, there's nothing conclusive about it."

"All right, I'll be there around four-thirty." I hung up and went back to the kitchen. I put the board away, rolled up the dampened clothes, scrubbed some potatoes for dinner. By the time I had set the table, I felt a little more alive, and Fear, which had been such a constant lodger, for ever so long, was again licking my limbs with an icy tongue.

I went upstairs and called Kavy and asked her to come over and stay with Karen and Rory. He had risen quietly from his nap and was trying to sail a cigar box in the basin. It took fifteen minutes to peel off his soaking pajamas, towel him, dress him and another ten to "put on my face" as he called it. I smeared the lipstick twice and had to do it over. My eyes looked very dark in the mirror and stared fixedly back at their own reflection. This will never do. I shook myself mentally. Some mother—you. Just seeing you looking like this will scare the child to death and there's probably nothing to be scared about.

Very soon Kavy came with her two in tow and kindly talked a running line of distracting inconsequentials until it was time for me to leave. Our tires were too smooth to trust on the icy roads so I took her car. There were trucks stuck on the Post Road hill and I had to detour through the Village and up Ridge Street and it was twenty-five minutes before we got to the office.

John studied the mark on Marie's arm and remarked casually, "Just to be sure, I think we'll get some X-rays." He called the hospital and through some fluke they were able to take us immediately. John said he would look at the plates at noon the next day and I said I'd stop at the office around one.

Ordinarily I would not have said anything to Jimmy until I had definite word one way or the other, but this time I was sure I knew what the verdict would be and I thought it would be easier if he moved up to it, rather than got it as a sudden slap. After I told him, we didn't talk about it—there really wasn't anything to talk about.

It was one-thirty in the morning and I was trying to lie still, so as not to disturb him, and fingering my rosary.

"Are you asleep?" he asked softly.

"Not yet," I answered.

"How about some double solitaire?"

"Let's get something to eat first." We went down to the kitchen and killed about an hour fussing with a supper we hardly touched, and cleaning up afterward.

"Might as well set the table for breakfast," he said. That took another ten minutes. We went back to our room and played cards until it was time to get up.

The next afternoon, at one-thirty on the dot, I took my customary place in the chair beside John's desk, very deliberately took a cigarette from my case, tapped it and lit it, to demonstrate how controlled I was. It was a creditable performance but no one was fooled.

"You know me, John, if it's bad, let's have it quick."

I had seen that look in his eyes when he had bad news for me before. I wouldn't want to be in his boots, I thought. What a rotten job doctoring is.

"I saw the plates," he said, "and had Dr. West look at them too. There is no question. Marie's left lung is affected."

Immediate and complete bed rest!

John called in a top T.B. man. He said Marie could stay at home, since children did not transmit the disease. No, he couldn't say how long it would be. He ordered the immediate family, grandmothers, grandfather, close friends, to be X-rayed to discover a possible source of infection. All were negative.

This confinement of Marie's was much worse than the rheumatic-fever deal because for a while she wasn't even allowed to sit up. But the first siege had at least partially conditioned her for the second. Us too. On the other hand, its coming so soon after her release from the first made it that much harder to bear.

Marie needed more of my time, Karen needed more of my time, Rory needed more of my time. Time. Time. Time. "Great Jumping Jupiter, were there really people in this world who had some left over?"

I had not realized how much responsibility Marie had assumed nor how many trips her sturdy legs had saved me. Nor what faithful chaperoning she had given Rory. I think for the first time I really appreciated our wonderful daughter.

Most of the occupations she had discovered or invented before were helpful now and her increasing absorption in books filled many hours. Contrarily enough, because she was so darn sweet about the whole thing, we felt for her the more.

220

It almost seems as though fate contrived to help us build character in all our youngsters at a very early age. Now, at two-going-on-three there were many little tasks for Rory. Always a sweet child, he grew even sweeter as he was needed to pick up something for Karen or fetch something for Marie, or run an errand for me. We were all elaborate in our thanks and praise and he began to fancy himself a Most Important Person indeed.

When I indulged in an unholy orgy of grousing over "bad luck," and when sympathetic friends deplored it with me, it was because none of us turned the page to see what followed. Many things have followed our "bad luck," and not the least is that all our children, at an early age, have had the opportunity to learn the joy of service. That they are better people for it goes without saying. That the world will be a little better place to live in because of it, is, I think, just as obvious. So much of the strife, dissension, unhappiness and unrest in the world today is due to the fact that too few hold any concept of service. There is authoritative support for this observation. Dr. William Menninger, in his book *You and Psychiatry,* speaks thus: *"A well adjusted* person is one who has learned that it is more blessed to give than to receive." Through our "troubles" our entire family had an opportunity to become "well adjusted."

In this age, so enlightened that even dogs have their psychiatrists, I suppose Shanty would be considered "well adjusted" also, for his life was one of constant service. There were times when his devotion to Karen caused him to be considerably annoyed with us. Before she had started on crutches, any walking she had done had been while holding on to a solid object. This he approved, though he stayed beside her always. As a matter of fact he took his position routinely on her left, and when she felt herself falling she would twist toward him and the fall was generally well broken by his body.

He did not approve of the crutches. They were mov-

221

able, unsteady, on the whole not to be trusted. When she first used them, he would lie in front of her and take hold of one of the tips in his teeth so she could not raise it. It took some time to break him of this, but, not to be thwarted in his role of protector, he substituted his paws for his teeth and so anchored the crutch. When we had broken him of this, his final protest was to lie across her path. She'd ask him to "Please move"; prod him in the side with a crutch and finally yell at him in frustrated fury. He'd lay back his ears, put his chin on the floor, roll his eyes, wag his tail, whimper, but move?—he would not. Finally he co-operated but he never condoned.

With Marie in bed I couldn't take Karen out much, and if it hadn't been for this four-legged, lumbering load of loyalty, she would have gotten out very little. He developed three distinct barks.

"She's fallen, but I'm not worried."

"There's someone strange around."

"*Danger.*"

No matter how I was attired or what I was doing when I heard the last I took off. One mild day in February, I was giving Marie a bed bath and Karen was out in the back yard. I heard bark number three. I dropped the cloth, skidded down the stair, through the dining room and kitchen and around back. Another little girl named Karen, and Elaine Gustavson were swinging on the tire. I could see that Karen had inched in close enough to warrant being hit by it as the swingers gained momentum. Shanty was standing between her and this black pendulum, barking in her face, and gently shouldering her backward. She was retreating, she had no choice, and she was furious. I patted the dog and praised him and explained to Karen what he was doing. It took her a little while to get over her mad and then she said, "He's awful smart, isn't he, Mom Pom? I guess after this I better take his advice."

A month or so later Johnny Griffen, thinking to give

222

Karen a treat, put her in his express wagon for a ride down the street. The hound objected so strenuously that, before I could get outside, Karen told Johnny, "Shanty's worried. You better ask my mother if it is all right."

Chapter 22

A COUPLE OF MONTHS before our regular trip to Dr. B,
we had to make a special trip because Karen's braces
needed adjusting. As she grew, these trips for adjustments
grew more and more frequent. It was awkward, because
it meant that Jimmy had to leave the office for a day or
two, and it was also darned expensive.

The adjustments necessary were more extensive than
any done before (and that much more costly). It was
two weeks before Karen got her braces back. Jimmy was
putting her to bed one night before they came and she
said to him, "I don't mean to be yappy, Dad, but it sure
feels good to go to bed without my braces. It's so comfortable."

His eyes filled when he told me this and he said, "I
wish to God the damn brace shop would burn down and
they'd never come back." Later on when we were settling
ourselves in bed he said, "I feel guilty every time I get
into bed and find it so comfortable."

The braces finally arrived on Thursday morning. Friday I had been working with Karen (and Rory) in the
living room and left them to go in and make the beds. I
heard Karen tap across the living room toward the library
which had been turned into an office. The rooms were
separated by double French doors and an inch-high
threshold. Rory ran in to help me turn the mattress, making the job doubly difficult, and he said, "Kawen's
talking." As I thumped and pushed, I listened, and I
could hear her. She was talking to herself, and after a
couple of minutes I tiptoed out in the hall. She was
standing at the threshold, exerting every possible ounce
of effort to raise her foot the necessary inch to cross it. I

was pleased that she was trying this on her own but worried over her disappointment when she failed. Her voice grew louder, more urgent. Her face was drawn tight with the strain of exertion and there were beads of perspiration on her head and lip. In a tone at once of demand and supplication she said, "Guardian Angel, won't you *please* help me. *Please, please.*"

She tightened her grip on the crutch bars and leaned farther forward. Her foot came up again slowly and to my complete amazement cleared the threshold with a speck to spare and slid over. I didn't move. She'd never make it with the other foot too. There just wasn't the balance or the strength. I wished she wouldn't try. "*Please,*" she said again. And the second foot went up slowly and over—and she didn't fall. She was grinning from ear to ear and, still unaware of my presence, she said, quite matter-of-factly, "Thank you. Thank you *very* much."

It was at times like this that I would be struck with the comparison of Karen's childhood to my own. My father had been a great athlete and he had had his daughters playing baseball and out on the tennis court when proper little ladies were wheeling doll carriages. It required as much concentration and physical effort for Karen to cross the threshold as it would have for me, at the same age, to pass my dad with a fast serve. For Karen to walk a block required the same amount of concentration and effort as it would for any of us to walk a tightrope suspended between two buildings, the same distance.

One of the hardest parts of being the parents of a C.P. child is to think up and encourage difficult activities that are necessary for self-help. To prod, yet never nag. To know when to call quits so that the child will not be frustrated. To keep different phases of development proportionately important. Until we parents learn otherwise, we are apt to overemphasize the importance of walking with consequent lack of appreciation of the all-important use of hands. When Karen was acquiring

225

dexterity with her crutches, we had to remind ourselves to allow an equal amount of time to developing her hands.

We placed our radio-phonograph in Marie's room on a table just the right height for Karen to reach from her chair. We started her off with unbreakable records, not so much to save expense as to remove the fear of breaking. I have noticed that children in general are most prone to smash things when Mama foolishly says, "Be careful. Don't drop it, it's breakable."

It took only a few months for Karen to learn that she could put records on and take them off without dropping them, and this confidence made it possible for her to handle regular records. Of course, she did break some, but not many more than anyone else. (She was to some extent handicapped by her environment since we are notoriously a "breaky" family and in the first ten years of marriage we went through four complete dinner sets.)

Placing the tips of the thumb and index finger together is a "fine" motion as distinguished from other finger activities that are "gross" motions. The human is the only creature capable of performing this particular "fine" motion. Placing the needle on the edge of the record required this motion and a precision that was excellent training. (So does pushing a button through a button hole.) Precision was also required in using a finger to push the different buttons for the radio stations and a lesser amount, but a good circular wrist motion, for turning the knobs. At first, Karen's inability to make one finger work without the others horning in on the job resulted in several buttons being pressed at once—with chaotic results and temper tantrums of impatience. Almost as important as being able to care for herself was being able to entertain herself, so we kept doggedly at it.

This particular radio-phonograph business gave us our first real problem with Marie. She resented having to wait four or five minutes for a change of records and rebelled openly. She had been so good about so much that we sometimes forgot her youth, and I think expected too much of her. It took some time and it was only after I had made many mistakes that Marie was straightened out.

During this miserable period, Jimmy and I realized fully, for the first time, that we had no way of knowing whether our many decisions were correct. There were no precedents. Only time will tell, and we were, and are, quite aware that if time proves us wrong there will then be nothing we can do about it.

We hope we have been right in our discipline of Karen. It was just what we had given the others in similar circumstances. A number of times she merited severe punishment. There was some deviltry that was beyond her because of her physical limitations, so she would devise some mischief particularly hellish and then direct Rory in its execution. Because she was so intelligent she knew she was persuading him to be bad also and this doubled the seriousness of the offense.

One night in the middle of March, Jimmy was at a meeting of the Dad's Club and I was typing in the office. I heard a suspicious noise from the nursery, the kind of a noise that makes you move quickly. I opened the door to find Rory balancing on the sill of the open window. Not the front window which is only three feet above the lawn, but the side window which looks over the base of a sharp slope at the side of the house. Distance from window to ground is about thirteen feet. As I walked slowly across the room, I could see with wonderful clarity the beautiful, irregular, jagged rocks below that made this spot such a lovely rock garden. I stopped a few feet short of our son. I wanted to look at Karen but didn't dare take my eyes from Rory. "Let's see what a good mountain climber you are," I said, "and how carefully you can climb down to the top of the radiator under the window." And to myself—"Then by gum I'll grab you." A few seconds later he had gone the necessary safe four inches and I moved in. I picked him up and without a word sat him on the bed beside Karen. Then I stepped

227

back and just looked at the two of them in silence. A minute of this was all he could take.

"No matter, Mommy. I'm a fireman." He smiled at me guilelessly.

Even in the dim light I could see Karen coloring. "Guilty," said her fixed eyes, the slight twitch of her mouth, *and* her silence.

"I just climbed and pushed the thing down," Rory went on conversationally. The clasps on our casement windows were a little complicated, far beyond him unless he was acting under instruction.

"Well?" I said directly to Karen.

In a very small voice she said, "I told him to."

"Don't you know that's dangerous?"

"Yes." In a smaller voice.

"You not only did wrong, but you influenced somebody else to do wrong. You've reached the age of reason. You know the difference between right and wrong."

"Yes, Mom Pom."

"A double wrong, a doubly hard spanking. The fact that he could have been hurt and wasn't has nothing to do with it."

"I'm sorry."

"She's sowwy," chirruped Rory.

"So am I," I said. "There's nothing hurts a mommy or daddy more than to have to punish."

"I will never do such a thing again." Karen was sure she spoke the truth.

"Haven't I expected you to watch over Rory? Haven't I told you that if he ever went near a window or climbed up on the furniture, you should call me?"

"Yes, you did."

"Les lou did," Rory echoed.

"Please don't spank me, Mom," Karen pleaded.

"I don't have any choice," I told her, feeling sick inside and wishing I were at the Dad's Club and Father were home. "When God gives us children, He gives us the job of teaching them to be good and He expects us to do

228

our job, no matter how distasteful it is for either of us. Believe me, it would be much nicer for me to turn around and walk out and forget the whole thing. But I can't. I'm going to spank you, Karen."

"Why did I do it?" she wailed.

"Don't spank Kawen," Rory wailed too on a rising note.

I lifted him into his crib, the wails growing louder, closed the window and dragged myself over to Karen. I turned her on her side and delivered four resounding thwacks on her bottom. She didn't cry much. She never did. Rory cried enough for both.

"Good night." I kissed them and went out closing the door behind me. I felt awful. In the living room I lay down on the couch. Rory stopped crying and must have fallen asleep immediately. Karen sobbed softly for a little while and then all was quiet. I picked up a magazine, riffled through the pages and then threw it on the floor. I got up, walked across the room and then went back and lay down. Some fifteen minutes later Karen called me softly. I got up and went in.

"I don't think I want to be a mommy," she said. "It must be so hard to spank your little girl. I feel so sorry for you." I lay down beside her and she put her arms around me and I stayed until she fell asleep.

I had barely recovered from this episode when I faced another and the slap was delivered even as Karen spoke the last word of the sentence which provoked it.

Five youngsters were playing "doctor" in the nursery. They had dolls and animals lying on the bed or rather "table" in a row. Empty medicine bottles of all shapes and sizes (our house had quantity as well as quality), were arrayed on the top of the doll's trunk which I discovered was covered with one of my imported guest towels. There was also a jam jar filled with cotton, Karen's two enema bags, a crayon stuck in a cream bottle as a thermometer and a stethoscope made out of an old leather leash. I was scrubbing the bathroom floor when I was called to help splint the panda's leg. Halfway through this intricate assignment, conducted under the surveillance of ten critical eyes, the telephone rang.

It was a new parent with the old problem and no solution, so it was some time before I started back to finish my job on the panda. I walked down the hall and heard Karen demanding somebody get something and I didn't at all like her tone. As I walked into the room she said in a tone of revolting complacency, "You have to do it for me—I'm crippled."

Mama struck.

Maybe it was good. Maybe it was bad. I still don't know. But the action was a simple reflex. Eight years old and capitalizing on her handicap! I knew from harsh personal experience the abundant misery that stems from such a trick and I reacted as I would if I saw a black-widow spider crawling toward her—I'd crush it instantly.

Later on that evening Jimmy and I talked with her about it, and when we were finished she understood that it was fundamentally dishonest and just as wrong as lying or cheating. I guess it was good it happened, for forewarned is forearmed, and from then on we were constantly on guard. We didn't wait for her to get sick with such an attitude but inoculated her against it and at intervals gave her booster shots.

Chapter 23

FOR THE PAST TWO WINTERS Karen had had a series of tonsillitis attacks and concurrent bad ears. The third week in March she came down with an attack of both and John decreed that as soon as it was safe she should have her tonsils out. It was not a matter of the sickness alone, but each one cut into her therapy program, and in this, continuity was all important.

Jimmy felt that she would be better off in the Children's Ward than in a private room and I agreed with him. Hospitals in general are not anxious to handle C.P.'s, and this one was no exception. We had no difficulty, therefore, in arranging that I should stay at the hospital for the three or four days of Karen's stay.

Jimmy drove us to the hospital at the stipulated ungodly six forty-five. We went up to the ward with Karen and undressed her, arranged her things in her stand and plugged in her little radio, a present from Nana. She went through all the nasty preliminary probings, peerings, prickings, and at seven forty-five we dressed her in a sterile gown, stockings that came up to her armpits and the white cap. Her cheeks were red and her eyes bright with nervousness. For all her apprehension she was docile and quiet and completely co-operative. Jimmy and I had a bad time of it when they placed her on the stretcher and started her down the corridor. She looked exactly like little Marie at that moment. She twisted her head sideways and clung to us with her eyes until she was wheeled around the corner to the elevator.

We had the best man to do the operation and the best man to give the anesthetic, so we were scared only on general principles. One thing that did concern us, how-

231

ever, was avoiding the harmful emotional jolts which such experiences mean to most children and which most doctors and hospitals blandly disregard.

We had explained the procedures and their purposes to Karen in bits and pieces some time before. We also told her that when she woke up she would have a sore throat, but we hoped that after this she wouldn't be sick with sore throats any more.

We knew we'd have some time to wait while she was upstairs so we drove to a diner for breakfast. We talked about the chances that the Pittsburgh Pirates had this year of ending up in the first division, about the beautiful lilac bush that Mother Killilea had planted for us that was giving up the ghost, about the trouble Jimmy was having with one of his accounts, about the number of orders for surgical supplies he had had in the last month, about everything but Karen. He smoked one cigarette after another, even between mouthfuls of ham and eggs, and we drank three cups of coffee apiece. I would judge that he looked at his watch on an average of every three minutes. When his hands were not occupied with fork, knife or spoon, he drummed his fingers on the table. Finally I said sharply, "Stop that—" and ashamed, added, "please."

"Stop what?" he innocently inquired, drumming away.

"That," I said, pointing.

"Oh. Oh, sure," he said. Then he laughed. "Stop that —please."

"Who, me? What?" I said blankly.

"That," he said, pointing. "You're swinging your leg like a pendulum gone berserk."

"I didn't realize—" I felt a little foolish.

"Let's go," he said.

Back at the hospital, we went right upstairs and a few minutes later they wheeled Karen in. Jimmy moved her from the stretcher to the bed. Her breathing seemed good, her pulse O.K., and her color was not too bad. Her freckles did stand out like wood shavings on snow. Her eyes were closed and looked as though they had been put in with a smutty finger. Jimmy looked at me. There was pain in his fine eyes. "Did you notice?" he asked. Without waiting for an answer he put his hands under the covers and gently moved her legs out a little and bent the knees a little. Her hands lay limp and flat on the bed.

There was no spasticity. She was still under the anesthesia and her muscles and joints were soft and fluid. It was the first time we had seen Karen with no rigidity.

The anesthetist came in with the surgeon and they reported that everything had gone very well. The surgeon laughed. "I hope she never starts drinking," he said. "Dr. G gave her a whole can of ether and she was still carrying on a bright conversation."

"Look what I got," said Dr. G. "I always look for loose teeth before we start because of the danger of their coming out and being inhaled. Sure enough, I found one. Here it is"—and he placed a tooth in the palm of my hand.

They checked everything there was to check and turned to go. The surgeon was a short man and his eyes were a little below mine. They twinkled up at me and he said, "She is certainly one wonderful youngster. You should be very proud of her." He patted Jimmy's arm. "Everything's perfect. Not a thing to worry about. See you later." And he bounced off.

Jimmy left after a little for the office and I sat in a rattan and canvas porch chair that had been thoughtfully placed at the foot of the bed. The ward was pleasantly noisy with the sounds of starched bustling, the squeak of rubber soles, the clink of enamel. There were eleven children of all ages, who were either ill enough to be quiescent or well enough to be rambunctious.

Karen was sick to her stomach as soon as she wakened. No more nor less than normal. I had a big ache as I watched the spasticity creep over her again. The nurses were not at all sure how to handle a C.P. and were glad to have me take over entirely. I did the routine things for her comfort and read until I was hoarse. The rattan chair I enjoyed until I found that no arrangements had been made for a cot at night, and none would be made.

Karen's postoperative discomfort was minimized by her absorption in all that went on about her. She loved being a part of so much activity and having so many people around. It was a problem to get her to take a nap. Before closing her eyes she'd insist, "Promise to wake me if anything important happens." "Anything important" had a broad definition: an enema, a transfusion, a dressing, a new admittance, a visit by a doctor (it didn't have to be hers).

On the afternoon of the third day, Rory came with Jimmy to pick us up. Rory was standing beside the car when Jimmy carried Karen out. He came charging across the driveway, his face bright with love. Although I had been gone exactly the same length of time, I detected a shade more attention to Karen. "Don't forget he was worried about her," Jimmy said to me under his breath. "I hope your nose isn't out of joint."

On the way home in the car the four of us sat in front and Rory kept his fat little arms around Karen's knees.

The lawns were showing a hint of green, the branches of bushes and trees were tinged by the freshening surge of sap. The day was overcast, threatening rain at any moment, and the sweet smell of spring hung in the air. About a mile from the hospital the clouds opened and the earth was deluged. Our old Ford did not provide the snug protection from the storm that one might reasonably expect. The roof leaked in several places and the rain ran almost as generously down and around the inside panes as it did the outside. For the driver, who this day was I, it meant a double job of concentration. Long since, the windshield wipers had failed to function and the horn had croaked its last. The headlights, needed to penetrate the gloom, were weak and vacillating. There were two floor boards missing just under the driver's legs. When we came to a puddle, it was no mean assignment to keep one's feet dry so they should not slip off the pedals. This required faultless timing. Just before the gush of water up through the floor, it was necessary to take a firm grip on the wheel, snatch the right foot off the accelerator and fling the legs wide and to the side till the puddle was passed. So far as the children were concerned, all of this added zest to driving that others missed. Poor things!

Glo had left the office early to prepare for Karen's homecoming. Jimmy and I were as surprised and pleased as Karen when we saw the nursery. Glo had festooned the room with yellow crepe paper which looked like streaks of sunshine against the deep green walls. She had arranged three bouquets of yellow daisies and had washed and ironed the doll's clothes, dressed their hair, and sat them in a prim row, waiting for their mistress.

Later that evening, after the little ones had been bedded down about an hour and a half, Jimmy went in to check Karen. Rory's crib was empty. He turned swiftly to Karen's bed and found her lying on her side with Rory close beside her, their arms around each other.

"Did you move him?" I asked when he told me.

"Not on your life," he answered.

That night, we left the doors open between our rooms but neither of them stirred during the night. Karen said Rory woke her at dawn the next morning, said, "Hello, sweetheart," and went back to sleep.

Chapter 24

THERE WAS NO JOY in the spring this year, for Mother
Killilea, who was still in her sixties, began to fail very
rapidly. She had high blood pressure and arterial sclerosis
and she faded into that gentle senility produced by this
combination. I had known and loved her for sixteen years
and in all that time I had never heard her complain
about anything. If she had a pain or an ache, no one
knew. If she was unhappy or upset, no one knew. She
lived only and always for her family with no thought
of self. They were all perfect in her eyes, including me.
She was not unselfish, but rather selfless, since she never
considered herself in the first instance. (Jimmy used to
say that our mothers were cut from the same pattern and
then it was thrown away.) By May she was living in a
pitiable depression. At the end of the month she had a
stroke which made her a helpless C.P. In June, God took
her home, and for her sake we were glad. The worst of our
grief was that our children would lose her gentle influence and example.

The year before, she had decided that Karen should do
some real honest to goodness gardening. Karen's braces
made it impossible for her to get down to work in the
garden, so Mother had put a window box on the side of
the hill, which Karen could stand beside. She had
planted perennials and with infinite patience had taught
Karen the difference between weeds and seedlings and
instructed her in the care of her plants. It was fine occupational therapy because it required many of the fine
finger motions. "Besides," Mother said, "to work the earth
is good for the soul."

Karen was terribly excited when her plants burgeoned

this year. It looked as though she had inherited Mother's green thumb and not my black one. Her garden gave her a continuing pride of accomplishment and she was jealous of her success to the point of resenting and denying all offers of advice or assistance. "But I know how," she'd say when we proffered either. "You can just leave me alone." Her words and tone were somewhat lacking in filial respect but her independence and confidence were too precious to tamper with.

One day early in July she was sitting in her tall chair in the kitchen, her feet on the shelflike rest. She was excitedly reporting on the morning's activity. "I found eleven Japanese beetles and squashed them all between my fingers." Rory shuddered. "I dropped two and they flew away, but one came back and I got him good." As always, when Karen was interested or excited about something, there was overflow motion in the feet and legs. She let out a sudden sharp yell, "My feet, oh, my feet."

I ran over to her and saw that somehow her feet had slipped backward off the rest and were caught behind it. I tried to move them up and out but with each second the muscle spasms increased and her legs became locked more securely.

There was a knock on the screen door and I looked up to see the man who collects for the Lighting Company. "Come in, come in," I yelled. "Come in quick."

He'd been on the job fourteen years and this unique reception held him rooted to the spot. He looked dazed and, I thought, quite stupid.

"Hurry," I yelled at him as Karen gave an agonized shriek. This seemed to release him from his shock and he flung open the door and landed beside her in three steps. Rory sat very still, almost as pale as Karen.

"I'll get a saw." I was out to the cellar and back and thrusting it at him. It was apparent that he was unnerved but he didn't get excited and went right to work. I put my arms around Karen from behind and held her and tried to soothe her but I don't think she either felt me or heard me. In a very few minutes he was through the inch and a half of wood on one side and he seized it and ripped it off. Karen's legs shot out in front of her stiff and rigid and the rest of her sagged. He caught her as she slid out of the chair. "Poor baby," he murmured as he picked her up. "We'd better lay her down," he said to me. He followed me upstairs and eased her down on my bed. Rory followed close at his heels with his hand on Karen's foot. I pulled the heating pad out of the bottom drawer and wrapped it around her legs. I don't have any idea why I did this, nor whether it was good or bad.

"I'm so glad you came." Karen looked up at the man and the tears ran sideways into her ears as she smiled at him. "Mom Pom just can't learn to saw any good at all."

"I can. I'm good," Rory said.

"I'm glad you came too," I told him. "The Lord only knows how long it would have taken me, if I could have done it at all."

"Just a lucky break," he said. "I'm sorry but I have to go now." I went to the door with him.

"Won't you have a cup of coffee or let me make you a pot of tea?"

"Thanks just the same, I'm behind schedule now. Good-by. She's a good kid." He started down the path. At the curb he stopped and turned. "This is awful—" he stammered, coloring slightly, "but I'm supposed to get a check for $33.75."

"Oh, but of course. I forgot."

I wrote the check and he left.

Rory and Karen together gave Jimmy a grisly account of the crisis. "All you had to do," he said to me with patient tolerance, "was take out two screws on one side and swing the thing out."

"Holy Smokes, how stupid can one dame be," I said.

"Lou not stoopid, Mommy," Rory consoled me.

"You're smart," Karen said, but it sounded a little forced.

238

On July 15, 1948, the work of many people, for a number of years, took tangible form. Frederick G. Schmidt, justice of the Supreme Court, affixed his signature to a significant document, a certificate of incorporation; and our United Cerebral Palsy Association was officially born. Now we had a volunteer, nonprofit organization, devoted exclusively to C.P.

There were other reasons why this summer was memorable, and they were supplied by our son.

It had started off with a bang as follows (reprinted in its entirety from the Port Chester *Daily Item*):

> The baseball season opened officially in Rye today, when a three-and-a-half-year-old hurler, with phenomenal force and accuracy, pegged one through Mr. Gillette's garage window.
>
> The alleged offender, who gave his name as Rory Killilea, was apprehended and immediately released.

Jimmy explained that restitution must be made. Rory nodded his head in complete agreement. "Just give me the money, Daddy, and I'll take it over."

"It must be your money," Jimmy explained. "We'll see if you have enough in your piggy bank."

"No, Daddy, no. That's circus money."

"It's not your money any more," Jimmy said. "You owe it to Mr. Gillette."

Rory chased after him into the nursery, protesting at the top of his lungs. Before he closed the door I heard Jimmy say, "Let's sit down and talk some more. I want you to understand."

A little later they came out and Jimmy whispered to me, "It's all set. . . . He is really smart for his age. He understands perfectly now." He left the room and Rory came over and looked up at me, his big eyes round and serious.

"I'm going to tell Mr. Gillette I'm sorry," he nodded

239

virtuously. "I can't give him Daddy's money. He gets mine from my bank."

"Good boy," I applauded.

"Then," he added happily, "when I come home *lou* can give me lours for my bank."

Jimmy was right. Rory was smart for his age.

Rory was also curious, gregarious and most imitative. The Village was laying pipes and putting in a real road in Vale Place. It was some time before I associated this with a strange odor on Rory's breath. I finally got hep when he dallied home from there each day for lunch and had little or no appetite. I began synchronizing his activity with the twelve o'clock whistle. No matter where he was or what he was doing, when the whistle sounded he took off for Vale Place. One day I left Karen in with Marie and followed him. In the best "pocket book" tradition, I kept a safe distance, and sought the concealment of hedges and trees. Peering around the corner of Scalzi's house I saw workmen settle on the running board of their truck or on the grass for lunch and watched them unwrap "wedgies." Now for the uninitiated (and they are to be pitied) a "wedgy" is a super sandwich. It is a whole loaf of Italian bread, cut lengthwise, and inside that are such wonders of gastronomical delight as to provoke even the most pallid appetite. Hot pastrami, or hot sausage, or meat balls, all highly seasoned and embellished with garlic, or peppers and onions, or peppers and eggs.

Rory had taken his place in a convivial group settled on the grass. He was talking at a great rate and watching unwrappings with a judicious eye. Having apparently come to a decision he got up and walked over and sat beside a middle-aged man who had an imposing meal spread out on his overalled lap. It was plain Rory didn't ask for anything. It was also plain that this had been going on long enough that it wasn't necessary. His gracious companion took his penknife and carefully cut off about a fifth of his "wedgy" and handed it to Rory. The time for talk had passed and with the others he silently fell to. He never attacked a carefully balanced dinner of lamb chops, baked potatoes swimming in butter, and fresh peas with the consummate relish he brought to this meal.

Our toaster had gone on the blink a year ago, and as my mother spent frequent week-ends with us, she finally wearied of the smoke screen we laid down each morning when attempting to make toast in the oven. Oven toast is delicious, but unless there is a certain concentrated attention on its preparation the result is charred hunks. Somehow, no one of us ever seemed able to provide concentrated attention for the necessary period. So Mother gave us a beautiful new automatic toaster. For three days it worked like a charm and then, on the fourth, it failed to eject the slices and delivered instead a suffocating wall of foul smoke. Jimmy quickly disconnected it and wrapping a towel around it, rushed it outside. I gaped at the table where it had rested. There was an undulating, sticky mass of black goo. I showed it to him.

"I guess they've forgotten how to make good simple products since the war," he opined. "All the insulation has melted."

"It stinks," said Rory succinctly.

"I'll find out where Mother got it and take it back."

Two days later Jimmy reported. "Did I feel like a complete fool. I read a fine lecture on Pride in Your Product when I left the toaster. When I went back today to get it, they informed me that there was only one thing wrong with it. It had never been intended for crayons." Karen found this so amusing that she laughed until she cried. Gloria and I did a good job of controlling our mirth until Jimmy took the matter up with Rory. That was too much, and although Papa got simply wild, we couldn't stop laughing. Rory had listened to his irate father with respectful attention and when Jimmy finished he said, "Son, do you understand?"

"Yes, Daddy," said Rory. "Now I understand why the crayons didn't pop up."

Karen's vocabulary grew apace (we all saw to that) and as Rory suddenly became a chatterbox, her vocabulary became his. He was never "hungry"; he was "rabenous." A thing wasn't "bad"; it was "rebolting." On more than one occasion, when Marie was convalescing, I sent him to "bisit" with her. There was always a laugh either in words or pronunciation. He still could not say a proper initial "y" and his "I love lou" was delicious. We missed a lot of these laughs since he wanted "pwivacy" for his "bisits."

One beastly hot day I was sitting in with Marie. Karen was playing under the trees with the little girl next door. I had left Rory with her. She called me and said that Gretchen had just seen Rory crossing Rye Beach Avenue. I went after him and hauled him home. I was good and mad for we were very strict about his crossing a cement road. Karen reproached him not at all gently and said angrily, "You know you shouldn't cross that road."

"I didn't cross the road."

Karen was shocked at this flagrant fib. "You did too."

"I did not."

"You did too."

"I did—"

"Hey, wait a minute," I yelled, interjecting myself into the monotonous dialogue. "If you didn't cross the road, Rory, maybe you will tell us how you got to the other side."

"A kind leprechaun came along and picked me up—and—and—I was on the other side."

His antics were so unpredictable both in their nature and timing that neither Karen nor Marie had nearly enough of my attention that summer. Jimmy tried to make it up to Karen by taking her to the beach evenings before he left to sell surgical supplies and Gloria spent much of her week-ends, and many of her evenings, playing games or cards with Marie. When Glo was out and

242

work had to be done, I'd take my typewriter into Marie's room.

A few of Rory's antics held a monetary penalty. Like picking up a neighbor's hose and turning it in their living room window to water their plants. They were away at the time and the damage went undetected till the following day. Of course we had the lovely little table refinished.

We bought a special kind of modeling clay for Karen and Marie to work with. Marie's figures were creditable and she taught Karen much. In the execution Karen was training both hands and fingers. Not a lesson; but as fun. And how could Rory know that the warm praise we heaped on them would not be his when he did likewise, fashioning figures on the hot radiator of George Langeloh's car? How could he know that the clay would melt and indelibly mar the lovely maroon sheen?

That summer was hot and long. Jimmy lost nine pounds and I worried about him constantly. Marie grew moody and irritable, I think mostly because no one could say how long her bed rest must last. Rory was finding the discipline incumbent on the awakening spirit of experiment and adventure a heavy yoke indeed. And Karen—Karen was entering into her own purgatory which was to last many, many months.

She had outgrown her braces and in June had gotten new ones. From the very beginning, they just weren't right. It was not possible to continue trips south for all the adjustments. Jimmy could not take the days away from the office, and the expense was prohibitive, coming as it did on top of some three hundred dollars for the new braces and shoes and the cost of Marie's illness. To boot, the mere cost of living was skyrocketing.

Had we been going into the business, we could not have investigated more completely the industry of brace-making. We learned more about metal, machines, leather and techniques of construction than I would ever have

243

believed possible. We also learned that the science of bracemaking was certainly not keeping pace with progress in the other sciences.

Lou Whiton, who had become a close friend in the past year—first through his interest in the C.P. movement, and then through his ever-growing love for Karen —became interested in this problem. When Jimmy couldn't get away and when the Ford was too feeble, Lou would leave his considerable business responsibilities and drive us on the ever-widening search.

We tried several shops in our vicinity (thirty-mile radius) but they made things worse. Finally we found a man in Brooklyn who had some experience with C.P. braces. All through the summer, we drove the seventy-mile round trip once a week. Forty of these miles were in the heavy traffic of New York City and Brooklyn. Within half an hour after we left home, the car would be like an oven. Crawling through traffic snarls, or just standing waiting for them to unravel, there was no breeze at all. Once arrived, Karen had anywhere from fifteen minutes to an hour in a tiny unventilated room on a second floor, where she lay on a table while the metal was bent or precise measurements made on three or four different parts. She went through having her braces taken off and put back on once, twice, or thrice, as the case might be. She never griped once. Not once.

In hot weather, even perfect braces provide a special brand of discomfort. She started with a heavy, high brown shoe with a steel plate in the sole. The brace fits into slots on each side of the shoe and the bar runs up both sides of each leg to the waist. There is an ankle strap around the shoe. There is a cup cuff of leather, three inches wide, just below the calf. Next come knee pads, four inches up and down, and six inches across. Next a four-by-eight-inch cuff on the thigh. Then the leg is free of all except metal up to the band at the waist. This rigid band is also made of metal, two and a half inches wide, is covered with leather, encircles three-fifths of the

244

waist and then fastens around the stomach with an inch-wide leather strap. Spinal splints of metal run from this band up the back to the shoulder blades and they are held in place by tying canvas straps around the shoulder under the armpit, where there is more leather padding. The braces weigh in all thirty pounds. From shoe to shoulder there were fourteen straps and fourteen buckles. It is pointless to elaborate on technical difficulties like internal rotation, weak gluteus maximus, etc., which the braces are designed to help or correct. Karen understood the purpose of each torturous centimeter and accepted.

Well-fitted braces shouldn't hurt. But we couldn't seem to get hers right and they did hurt. She also developed pressure sores. There were ugly and painful and were made worse by the perspiration which could not evaporate under the leather. She had them on ankles, the inside of her knees and her hips. Morning and night we patted the skin with benzoin to toughen it up, but the sores came anyway. Once the skin was broken we couldn't use the benzoin because it burned so. The braces also had a bad effect cosmetically. When Karen played in the water at the beach, of course the braces were off, and one fine day she broke my heart when she confided to me, "Mom Pom, I'm so embarrassed by these ugly, yellow, leather stains on my legs."

Two days after we returned from one of these hideous Brooklyn trips, Lou stopped at the house and saw that again we had gained nothing from the changes. "Good God," he exclaimed when we were alone, "this is a fine kettle of fish. It's criminal, that's what it is. That that child should work and suffer the way she has to reach a goal and we can't provide the mechanical aid to help her along."

"And she's just one," I reminded him. "There are thousands and thousands of other kids whose braces are worse."

"It's enough to make one retch every time he hears

245

the word 'progress.' " I loved Lou because he loved our daughter so much. "We need engineers, that's what we need," he exploded. "It's like building a bridge. One man decides that we must span a river, from which place and why. Others know how to use metals and chemicals to build, but, by Heaven, it takes an engineer to bridge the gap between the two. And that's just how I see this brace problem. There must be someone who understands what the doctor is trying to do and who can then tell the bracemaker how to do it. That's a job for an engineer. I'm an engineer. But I haven't used my knowledge in years so I can't help. We must find engineers who can and will. After all, the best brains should be available for such a task, for nothing."

At this writing, three years later, we're still looking for an answer to the brace problem and so are a lot of others. It had one salutary effect, however. Through frustration, bitterness and suffering, came the realization that the basic step in C.P. must be research. The brace problem was just one example. Why did doctors, almost to a man, devote their energies to lessening and controlling deformities, instead of investigating and working to eliminate the CAUSE? Is it true science that concerns itself with the treatment of symptoms and ignores the cause? Is the doctor *primarily* interested in finding a cream to conceal chicken pox blemishes and relieve the itching—or is he concerned with the infection that causes the blemishes? In their approach to cerebral palsy, many doctors are intellectually inconsistent.

Flashing through this somber summer, like spearing through dark water, were incidents of light and joy.

One Sunday late in May Nana came up to stay with Marie so we could take the other children to the beach for a picnic. There were no more than thirty people scattered across the quarter mile of sand. The tide was low and where the sand ended the rich brown mud glimmered in the strong sun. The breeze tapped us lightly on bare arms and legs and then flung away to tease the wavelets as they chased it across the shore. Egg salad and peanut butter sandwiches had a rich new flavor, when eaten flat on one's stomach on the warm sand, enveloped by the lush fragrance of salt.

We made castles and tunnels and mud pies. We threw pieces of driftwood for Shanty who retrieved them with extravagant abandon and then came back to shower us with water and sand. We had a contest to see who could get the most skips from a stone hurled flat at the surface of the water. Daddy won.

Around five, the sun began to lose its warmth and the breeze quickened coolly. Jimmy and I were gathering our impedimenta and the youngsters were flirting with the incoming tide. A man and his wife coming across the beach, stopped to chat with them. Their words carried back to us. In an oozy voice the woman said to Karen, "You poor little thing."

Karen pulled her crutches back a few inches and straightened to look at them.

"It must be awful to wear those braces," said the man. Jimmy started toward them but I grabbed his arm.

"Let's let Karen handle this," I whispered.

"You poor child," repeated the woman.

"Why?" asked Karen inquisitively.

Gloria was standing in shocked stillness. I maneuvered into a position behind the couple where I could signal her to be still. Her throat and face were scarlet with anger. She stepped forward, resting her hand on Karen's shoulder. Before she could open her mouth, I gesticulated wildly to attract her attention and placed my finger emphatically on my lips. She gave me a rebellious look, but I shook my head in a firm negative. She glared at me and kept still.

"Why?" Karen repeated not having received an answer.

"Why—why—well—because—" The woman was obviously off balance. The man took a few backward steps in the direction of the gate.

"I'm lucky," said Karen. "You just don't understand." They stared at her.

"You see," Karen explained patiently, "I can see with my eyes, hear music with my ears, and I can speak as well as anybody. Mom says better than a lot of grownups." Crouching a little to keep her balance, she lifted a crutch and waved it. "Good-by."

A few wild flowers came up in our garden and we left them. After all, we couldn't plant anything prettier than daisies and Queen Anne's lace.

One June evening, Jimmy had gone off with his shiny books of scalpels, sponges, clamps and clips. I had Karen and Rory out in the yard. We were equipped with jars, waiting the last few minutes before we could start chasing fireflies. We would then take them into the nursery and enjoy their flashings before we released them, each one carrying off into the night a child's wish. Marvelous thunderheads had accumulated in the west and we were finding all kinds of images in their piled foam. Karen tapped off by herself and Rory and I continued to watch the shifting panorama.

I got up and brushed the grass off my skirt and turned to find Karen standing behind me. "I have something for you," she said with that particular catch in her voice that came when she knew she'd done something special. She shifted her weight and proudly raised her left crutch. Her hand on the bar was not so tight as usual, and there between the third and fourth fingers, hung a daisy.

Marie had been eleven months when she first picked and brought me a flower. Rory—seventeen months. Karen was six weeks short of eight years.

The fireflies came and Karen held the jar while Rory and I chased after them. As I ran around the locust tree, I bumped into him standing very still and looking up

248

through its lace to the sky. We breathed the perfume of the privet blossoms, fresh-cut grass and flowers. Without moving he sighed a great sigh and said, "This is God's property."

The next day we trekked to Brooklyn and when I finally got to bed I was too tired to sleep. Shortly after two I fell into a light doze and was awakened by a strange noise. I had the feeling that it had been going on for some little while. I listened for a few minutes and then got up to investigate. I went into the nursery and there was Karen sitting on the side of her bed, looking pleased as Punch.

"What are you doing?" I whispered.

"I just took myself to the bathroom."

It took a minute for the significance of her words to penetrate my foggy brain. "You did what?" I exclaimed.

"I took myself to the bathroom. I think Daddy needs his sleep. I'm not going to call him any more. I can go all by myself."

The next day I encouraged her to be just as independent in the daytime. Pants greatly complicated the procedure but she did as much as she could alone. I timed this activity when she was wearing just a nightgown; and from the time she got herself out of bed and on to her crutches, down the hall to the bath, all matters properly attended to and back to her room and up on the bed, it took a little more than half an hour.

When it was just too hot to let them play outdoors, she and Rory filled many hours giving therapy to dolls. If I came into the room during the "treatment," I was hushed so I would not "distract" the child.

In Karen's own therapy, Jimmy and I decided that the time had come when Karen should learn to handle distractions during the passive exercises. We were training in movements that she would have to use, not in the isolated quiet of a room, but in the bustle and noise of living. We were always working toward school where Karen would need all these movements in walking, and several

249

hundred youngsters would not stand still and quiet in the corridors while Karen made her way to the classroom. So we began to invite the neighborhood children to drop in at therapy time. I let some of them help a little and their curiosity, interest and participation guaranteed some audience almost every day. It was hard for Karen in the beginning, but by degrees she became able to hold to a particular routine, without a break in rhythm when children walked in and out of the room.

Everything we did with her—she did with her dolls. Her love for babies increased rather than diminished as she grew older. The first week-end in July, Nana came up and took Karen and Rory to Playland. Playland is a large and beautiful amusement park which has every conceivable "ride." Nana was exhausted after three hours of satisfying every whim of both of them.

"Was it wonderful?" Gloria asked Karen when they came in. Mother had fallen on the couch and looked as if she never wanted to move again.

"I had the time of my life," Karen said.

"What did you like best?" Jimmy asked her. "What made you the happiest?"

Karen did not hesitate over her answer. "I saw a baby."

"Dear Lord," my mother gasped.

Chapter 25

THE LOAD OF C.P. WORK grew heavier and heavier.
There were nineteen groups at the second annual meeting of the New York State Cerebral Palsy Association.
What was being done in New York was being done in
many other states as well. The parents were on the march.
A few of us were working very hard toward the activation
of our nation-wide organization. As a springboard, our
State Association was planning the First National Cerebral Palsy Conference for February of 1949. All the work
of our association was on a volunteer basis.

On the home front, we had frequent reminders of the
need for such work. The majority of people still felt
that we should hide away our C.P. children. After
Karen's First Communion, there had been some little talk
that "It's disgusting the way the Killileas exploit their
child." Other tidbits of local comment were, "You can
tell they don't care. You can tell by the way they act."
And, "Letting that child out alone. What kind of a
mother is she?" And "Running off to Syracuse, leaving
her children." And, "The child should be put away. I
wouldn't let mine play with her. How do I know why
she's that way?"

Important outside activities like trips to the zoo had
been beyond us for some time. The Ford was less and less
dependable.

July 25 was our fourteenth wedding anniversary.
Mother was coming for dinner and was due at six-thirty.
When she hadn't arrived at seven we were worried, since
Mother is as prompt as the sun. By eight, we hadn't
heard from her and by eight-thirty, we were frantic. At

twenty minutes to nine, she walked in. I was so relieved to see her all in one piece I was mad and had to bite my tongue to keep from giving her a dressing down. The children had been put to bed in tears over missing a party dinner and were now shrieking and yelling for "Nana."

"Get them up," she said.

"What? It's almost nine o'clock."

"I have your present outside and I want them to see it when you do." They heard her and didn't wait for my summons, but came tumbling out. Marie was thrashing around on her bed in a frenzy of curiosity.

"Jimmy, why don't you carry Marie to that chair in front of the window?" Mother said.

Jimmy complied though completely puzzled.

We clustered at the door and Mother opened it with a flourish. There at the curb stood an Austin sedan.

"Happy anniversary!" she said. I thought that was really underplaying it.

We christened the car Ha'penny. We took turns staying with Marie and taking Karen on excursions. Jones Beach, the Rosedale Stables to ride a pony, the zoo, a picnic in the pine woods at Rye Lake, or just driving. Marie was glad for Karen but frequently made all of us miserable by prolonged bouts of self-pity.

I almost hate to see one problem solved for it seems that immediately we are faced with a new one. We ran true to form. The first of August we ran afoul of the *Law*.

Shanty was Karen's constant companion. He did, however, take two hours off when she was napping. Logically he decided to cool off. The Law was logical too, and decreed that no dogs were allowed on the beach from June 1 to September 15. With a fine disregard for statutes, he headed for the water the minute my back was turned. Obliging neighbors would bring him home and he would be chastised. Or the attendant would summon me to fetch him and again punishment would be

252

metcd out. But I guess he decided that the sport was worth the penalty and he kept it up.

One day Karen and I had just gotten home from Brooklyn when the phone rang. It was the police. Shanty was in jail. The children carried on dreadfully and I had to quiet them down before I went and fetched him. I brought him home and tied him up. In ten days he gnawed through or broke every kind of rope or chain. Karen had to be kept in the yard and she wailed and Shanty wailed with her. Understandably the neighbors complained about the constant cacophony so I tied him in the cellar and added "walking the dog" to my other chores. But walls do not a prison make and he broke out. Kavy came and "sat" and I went looking for him. He was nowhere to be found. Naturally I did not call the police but at nine o'clock they called me. The sergeant shall be nameless for he said, "Come get your * * * dog."

"Yes, sir."

"And you'll have a nice fumigating bill," he said viciously. "Your * * * hound has the cell full of fleas."

If it hadn't been for Karen's need for the * * * dog we'd have found a nice farm for him. And if it hadn't been for her need I never would have taken him to the doctor to see why he limped and I never would have been persuaded to stop at the drugstore on the way home.

When Jimmy came in from a hard day at the office he stopped and stared at the boxes and bottles on the kitchen table—and the bill; $7.85. "What now?" he said listlessly.

"It's for Shanty," Karen piped before I could stop her. "He has a calcium and vitamin deficiency and he needs medicine besides."

Jimmy's jaw dropped. He sucked in air like a dying fish. Before he could speak, Karen turned on the full battery of her charm and smiled confidently into his eyes.

"He's so good to me. He's worth it. Isn't he, Daddy?"

253

Daddy picked her up and sat down with her in his lap. He twisted her braid around under her nose like a mustache, kissed the back of her neck and said, "Yes, sweetheart, he's certainly worth it."

The opening of school in September 1948 dealt harshly with both Marie and Karen. Whether you're nine or eleven, it is a bleak and lonely day when your playmates romp off to school and leave you at home alone. And each child was alone in her grief. Karen was most desolate because Mary Robards had a schedule which made it physically impossible for her to continue coming to the house for home teaching. It was six weeks after school opened before a new teacher was assigned to Karen.

I had been informed that her name was Mrs. Owen and that she was well qualified for the job. It was with surprise that I greeted her, "Betty Weigle, what are you doing here?"

"Marie Lyons!" she exclaimed with equal surprise. We had known each other since childhood and had been out of touch for the past ten years.

From the very beginning Betty and Karen got along like kittens in a basket. Betty was better qualified for the job than most people realized. She had a C.P. sister, which gave her an understanding and sympathy that were precious. Betty not only has a talent for teaching, but a talent for loving and inspiring love. Karen learned rapidly under her tutelage. All except printing. She seemed unable to learn to use a pencil.

"Teach her to write with the typewriter," I urged Betty.

"Nothing doing," said Betty firmly. "I think she can learn to use a pencil and I don't propose to give her an out."

I yielded to her judgment, but as time went on I began to suspect that she was wrong.

She asked me to get her everything I could on teaching the C.P. child. Our State Association had compiled a bibliography. The material was scant, considering the scope of the problem. Betty studied avidly. One day she said with a hopeless regret that brought a lump to my throat, "My sister was born twenty years too soon."

"So many were, for so long," I replied.

"That's one reason I'm grateful for this opportunity to work with Karen."

One of the first things she did was to start a diary for Karen. Karen worked all the harder, with no results that I could see, to write so that she could do her own recording. To say that Betty was amazed at Karen's vocabulary and sentence construction would be a gross understatement. She was dumfounded. Utilizing every asset, she encouraged Karen to compose little verses. Karen's first attempt did not presage another Francis Thompson, but we thought it rather good:

YUM-DUM MY KITTEN

> She is sweet, I love her
> Soft and yellow is her fur.
> She purrs like a percolator
> All day long
> That's the way
> She sings her song.

Marie again worked with Karen and again it helped both of them.

The time had come for Karen to have specific responsibility so I assigned her the care of the floor and rug in Marie's room. "Marie's doing something for you. Here's something you can do for her," I said.

She used the mop by steadying herself with one crutch and leaning against something. The bed—the bureau. She got a fair amount of the dust on the rug but that only made vacuuming more interesting. The vaccum she used the same way. It was a struggle for her to push the machine, change its direction and remain upright. Lots of times she fell. She'd pull herself over to the bed and painfully haul herself erect. Then she'd call me to give her the handle and she'd start again. Sometimes the machine would get away from her and crash into the bureau, chest of drawers, chair or bed. There were deep gouges in all the furniture after a while, but it didn't seem as important as it once would have been.

Kavy's older son, Peter, became our prop. At nine he could fix more things than the average mature male. He became thoroughly familiar with Jimmy's workbench and handled tools with loving care. When bolts or nuts or washers or whatever fell out of Karen's crutches, no longer did we have to put them away and stand her in a chair until Daddy came home. "Don't wuwwy, Kawen," Rory would comfort her. "Peter'll fick it."

Marie inaugurated a sweet custom which holds today and which I expect will hold when I'm old and feeble and totter out the front door. Whenever I went out to do something on C.P. organization work, she'd call the children into her room and say, "Let's say a prayer that Mommy will be successful." Karen would let herself slip down to the floor, Rory would kneel beside the bed and fold his hands and close his eyes, and with grave earnestness they'd recite, "Please, God, help Mommy to help the other kids."

That help was needed was borne out by a file of clippings eloquently bespeaking that today was not soon enough—newspaper stories from Florida to Michigan of parents who, in their frustration, heartbreak and despair had murdered their C.P. child.

And there are endless stories of heroism. I met a woman in Washington who typifies the faith, determination and selfless courage of so many. The family had little education and were very poor. This mother was intelligent and refined. She had fourteen children and her husband died when the last child, a C.P., was less than a year old. The nearest help for her child was an orthopedic clinic in Washington, two and a half miles from her home. She had no money for carfare and for four and a half years she walked this distance, twice a week, carrying her son.

Many times we were so tired and discouraged that we would have liked to quit our C.P. work. To rationalize by saying, "We've been working hard for a long time. We helped get the movement started. We need recreation. Let someone else carry on from here." Then we would come up against a situation with Karen, or pick up the paper and read of a mother abandoning her child, and we would find renewed vigor for the job ahead.

Without Gloria I could not have done the job at all. She handled correspondence, wrote reports, filed, and helped with washing and ironing at night and on weekends. She'll get her crown in Heaven for this, if for nothing else.

I made a lot of mistakes but was saved from many more by Charlie Harwood. He taught me much and, taking my measure early, one of his first lessons was this, "Remember, Marie, more often than not, it pays to indulge in brilliant flashes of silence."

All reports of trips were family affairs and the children began to get a liberal education which will stand them in good stead. Marie particularly enjoyed these reports. Without meeting the people, she came to know them and after a while appraise them. Her social consciousness and sense of geography were far ahead of ours at that age.

The brace problem was far from solved, but by November, after countless adjustments, we had achieved the elimination of the pressure sores. We can only guess at what this meant to Karen.

The next step was Karen's teeth. They were beautiful and strong, but I noticed a few dark spots on two of her molars. Our regular dentist was in Scarsdale and in the past year and a half, due to the Ford's incapacitation, we had been unable to make the trip. We had tried several dentists in near-by towns without being completely satisfied. I now started on a fresh list for Karen. It was difficult for dentists to work on her, since they gave no thought to the necessary emotional conditioning, and I could not do it alone. When she went into a strange office and was plumped right into an uncompromising chair, surrounded by cabinets of gleaming instruments and all manner of terrifying accouterments of the trade, she became panicky. Her ordinary stiffness increased a hundredfold and her jaw would become locked in terror. One man failing, we would try another. Three in succession told me after the first visit, "I'm sorry, Mrs. Killilea, but my schedule is so full that time does not permit me to take on such a difficult and time-consuming patient." I checked with other parents and found that they had the same experience and those with athetoid children who had involuntary movement or facial grimaces were further told, "You cannot bring your child to me. In the waiting room he is a source of embarrassment to my other patients." Finally we found, twenty-nine miles away in New York City, Dr. Stephen Jackson. Many of his confreres scratched their heads over Dr. Jackson, because he liked to work with C.P. children. It was fifty-eight miles for each trip to the dentist until Joe Massucco started practice in Rye.

Late in November Jimmy became ill. "Mostly exhaustion," the doctor opined. "If you want to die before you're forty, keep it up. This extra work is too damn much."

Jimmy railed at the doctor and called him an alarmist but he was scared.

"Your body machine can't take this kind of punishment indefinitely," the doctor insisted. "Nobody's could. You're not being very farsighted so far as Marie and the children are concerned. Think it over."

Jimmy thought it over and went back to a twelve-hour day. Now that he didn't have to rush out after dinner he insisted on assuming part of Karen's therapy. I held out until I felt he was really better and then gratefully gave in.

One morning I wakened to the realization that Christmas was only thirteen shopping days away and I had nothing done. "Buying for Marie is a pretty problem," I thought. "She has enough bed jackets to take her through eight confinements and her library is almost complete."

My worry was wasted. On December 18, Marie was pronounced "cured." Our funds were low, our medical bills mounting higher all the time, but it didn't seem important. We knew she had grown while in bed but we didn't realize how much, until she got up. She was as tall as Gloria.

The arrangement of our house, with the living quarters divided as they were by long steep stairs, was an ever-growing problem, and carrying Karen up and down stairs grew daily more difficult. What we needed was a house with a bedroom and bath on the first floor with a living room, kitchen and office on the first floor also. The future held no promise for such an acquisition.

Gloria had a friend named Russ Lea. He stood six-feet-three inches in his stocking feet and his heart was as big as his frame. He was a very intelligent young man and full of fun. He was a camera man for a television studio and worked some at night which gave him time at home during the day. He lived not far from us and seemed to enjoy nothing so much as being with Karen and Rory. He spent a good deal of time with them.

For some time preceding Christmas we knew the children were up to something. All four of them. For trying periods of time (because there was so much to be done) Jimmy and I would be isolated either upstairs or downstairs.

Christmas morning came, too soon as usual. Russ arrived at five forty-five, bless him, to take movies of the children around the crèche and opening their presents. We went to Mass, came home and had breakfast, and about eleven o'clock Jimmy said, "What was all this hush-hush business?" That our children were ready to burst with their surprise was obvious. It was also obvious that they were watching Rory like three vigilant

259

hawks, lest he spill the beans. They all started talking at once and the gist of it was that we would have to wait until Russ came back in the afternoon because he was in on it too.

He arrived at four o'clock and I could see the sharp outline of a box under his coat. He was so surreptitious about it I was curious. It was not Christmas presents, he had deluged us with those in the morning. That he was in on the surprise we knew, but we couldn't relate the box to whatever was to come. The children directed Jimmy and me to sit on the top step. Russ disappeared with them into the dining room below. Their excitement was contagious. There was much suppressed laughter and talk. We waited a minute or two and Jimmy called down, "Hurry up before I die of curiosity."

"Right away," they yelled back.

Gloria appeared at the foot of the stairs and, lifting Karen, placed her on the bottom step, sideways to the wall and the banister. Karen gripped the rail. We watched in stupefaction. Slowly Karen raised her right foot and placed it on the step above her. Grasping the banister for all she was worth, she made a mighty effort and brought the left foot up and on the step beside the right. Gloria stayed on the step below her and Russ and Marie and Rory stood at the bottom and cheered her on. Twenty minutes later Karen was at the step below us. As she made her final effort she lifted her face to us and with a ravishing smile she said, "Merry Christmas," and threw herself into Jimmy's outstretched arms.

"Merry Christmas," shrieked the others and came charging upstairs.

Jimmy carried Karen into the living room and everybody was talking at once and laughing, except me. As usual, I was crying. Russ went over to the closet and took down a white box. With a courtly bow he presented it to Karen. Jimmy helped her open it and with trembling fingers she lifted out an orchid corsage. "Oh—Russ," and she threw her arms around his neck.

260

"That's for walking upstairs—all by yourself," he said with a suspicious moisture in his eyes.

I took a card from the tissue paper. *To the most wonderful girl in the world,* it read, *with all my love—Your best beau, Russ.*

As we adults sat in sweet fatigue around the fire that night, Jimmy said, "The ways of the Lord are strange. If we could have afforded to buy the kind of a house we were dreaming about, Karen might never have learned to walk upstairs."

In February 1949 we had our First National Cerebral Palsy Conference. We had doctors in C.P. and allied fields coming from all over the country. We had been warned by some experts not to attempt this conference but a few had encouraged us a little and the more optimistic said we should plan on between a thousand and fifteen hundred attendees. In making the arrangements we went to the right place when we approached the Hotel Statler. They welcomed us with open arms. We might have been their wealthiest clients for the service they gave.

This conference is a story in itself. Suffice to say that after three delirious days, nights of little sleep, the final tally showed *twelve thousand* attendees and medical representation from every state and *eighteen* foreign countries.

This conference was, to date, the most important single effort toward the age old problem, and its most important single result was when Lenny Goldenson accepted the leadership of our nation-wide agency—the United Cerebral Palsy Association, Inc.

We had met Lenny and Isabel at our Westchester Treatment Center, where they took their child for treatment. A more beautiful little girl I have never seen. Bright as a new thimble and possessed of consummate charm. From the time when they first learned of the parents' effort in the field, they believed that only through a

261

national organization, devoted exclusively to C.P., could all the solutions be found. Being of great heart, their one wish was to see that *all* children had equal opportunity for training and education, social acceptance, and employment. Lenny was, at this time, vice president of Paramount Pictures, and this industry got behind our movement with manpower, talent and all important media for public education.

Our first nation-wide publicity was a picture of Cardinal Spellman, who had given the Invocation, with three C.P's around him. With pardonable pride I must boast that the lovely little lady of the picture was Karen.

In February and March Jimmy took over all of Karen's therapy. As legislative representative for the State Association I was in Albany anywhere from three to five days a week for these two months. My function was to educate legislators to the scope of this problem: twenty-two thousand C.P.'s in New York State alone; one out of one hundred getting treatment and education; many hundreds improperly placed in mental institutions. I could write a book (what am I saying?) on these months in the state capital.

Our children were getting a practical education in civics. I called home every day and late in March, when the session was drawing to a close and we still did not have our appropriations, Karen asked with deep concern, "Did your bills come out of committee?"

My eternal presence in the corridors and legislative chambers was a constant reminder to the legislators of the letters from constituents on their desks, and visits from others with the same interests at home. I was a spearhead for the ground troops who worked indefatigably on the local front.

No one greener than I ever hit Albany. Due to the kindness and interest of men and women—I wish I could name them all—and the sincere and active concern of all the legislative correspondents, particularly their dean, Leo O'Brien, on March 8, 1949, the state appropriated

$1,103,300 (of a total state budget of $937,000,000) for cerebral palsy.

The day before I left the hallowed halls and the nine pigeons who shared my window sill at the Hotel Wellington (the state having spent $47,500 to chase them from the Education Building), I called home at dinnertime. Rory answered the phone.

"What did you do today?" I asked.

"We had a play," he said.

"Were you in it?"

"Oh, less. I gave a speech on cerebral palsy."

Chapter 26

"PLAY BALL."

It was spring.

Karen hopped around with the robins. Like them she had to eschew snow and ice. She just couldn't walk on it. She had more privileges now, out of deference to her years. The thing that tickled her most was being allowed to go to the "first show" alone with Marie. Jimmy would drive them down and pick them up, but, as Karen said, "Just we girls are going."

She seemed to be falling more than she used to. Jimmy and I debated whether or not we should put a football helmet on her for protection. A young lady, with Karen's keen cosmetic sense, might pick up a complex or two. The decision was taken out of our hands when she fell and had a bad concussion. For three days she was a very sick chick.

We got a helmet although a number of doctors in the field thoroughly disapproved of this practice. They felt that it makes the child afraid. We believed that if the matter were handled properly this need not be so, and with Karen we proved it. Besides, without a helmet, the C.P. would have to be restricted to a chair and deprived of much in the way of experience and socialization.

A side effect of Karen's fall and injury was a spurt of fear, on my own and Jimmy's part, for the other two young ones. We hated to see Marie ride off on her bike. It required tremendous will power to teach Rory to climb a tree. With him, particularly, we had to be on guard constantly not to overprotect. The "Don'ts" we stifled, if strung out on tape, would reach from here to Boston.

Yum-Dum presented Karen with a litter of 99.44%

Persian kittens in the minimum time allotted by nature. When she purruped for her kittens, they came running and I remarked to the children that here was a fine example of prompt obedience. Pets gave Karen a responsibility since we charged her with part of their care. We acquired a turtle and a white mouse (not for long). Shanty tolerated all additions with a fearful curiosity and ill-concealed suspicion. He withdrew in dignified haste when the kittens wanted to play with his feathers, but he did assume the responsibility for their morning toilette. All of which delighted Karen immeasurably.

It was a great day when with Ha'penny we found The Secret Garden. About five miles into Connecticut, it was concealed by a wall which was all but hidden by overgrowth. The old house had burned down long since, and we picnicked on the foundation and wandered through untended glories of peonies, roses, sweet william, sweet peas, and came home with arms full of blooms. Picking some raspberries one evening, Rory looked around him and said, "It's a shiny day, isn't it, Mom?"

"It is," I agreed, thinking how aptly he expressed the light and shadows.

"Daddy, come quick," Karen called. "Look on that flower. Look at that exquisite flutterby." Then turning to me she said, "I bet you wish you could paint it."

Karen's sense of independence had been thwarted by the artistic terrain of our house, which snuggled in a hollow. There was a stretch of lawn in front of it and then a steep bank, then lawn to the street. She couldn't manage the five steps to the street, and it was humiliating for her to have to ask to be taken in to the bathroom. Providentially, it was Sunday when she decided to take matters into her own hands and providentially five of the twelve McShanes were visiting us. Arty had his movie camera with him. Karen walked to the curb at the top of the bank. I saw her begin to crouch and, for no particular reason that I remember, I asked Arty to start the camera. She lowered herself until she was sitting on the curb. This was no mean feat to execute without toppling over. She then took off her crutches and with a mighty heave threw them eight feet down the bank to the lawn. She then lay down on the ground, sideways to the hill, gave herself a push and rolled over and over until she came to rest at the bottom. She poked one crutch until it was beside the other, fitted them on her arms and worked her way to her knees. Jimmy came up and put his arm around me and we watched, not believing what we saw. Arty was following every move with the camera. Karen put the crutch tips about two feet ahead of her, pushed them hard against the ground and straining and sweating began to straighten. She fell. She started again. She fell again. On the third try, when she was half erect, she began to ease the crutches closer to her body. First one and then the other. Little by little she moved them and little by little she straightened, and then—she was erect and walking toward the door. We are glad that we shall have forever a moving picture of this accomplishment and her expression of triumph and satisfaction at its completion.

"If her braces were right, what couldn't she do?" Jimmy asked me.

I had no answer.

Our brats caused quite some scandal that summer by talking to friends and strangers alike about their Mommy and Daddy getting married. July 25 was our wedding anniversary. We had been married at a Nuptial Mass, and this day, fifteen years later, Monsignor McGowan offered a Nuptial Mass for us again and we renewed our marriage vows. Our family was present and a few special friends of all faiths. For Jimmy and me it was a day of rare happiness. As we knelt for the final blessing our hearts were full of thanksgiving for the blessings God had heaped upon us and upon our work, and a serene confidence in the future.

With Marie out of bed and Jimmy no longer working nights, and in spite of trips for adjustments, and consistent disappointments, that summer of 1949 was a happy one.

Early in September, Jimmy and I were awakened one night by a loud thump. We dashed into the nursery. Rory was sitting on the side of his bed, pale as death, his eyes riveted on Karen who was lying beside her bed on the floor. She was lying very still with her eyes open.

We knelt beside her. "Are you all right?" She didn't answer. Her body was limp. Her eyes stayed open and motionless. "Daddy's here, honey. Are you hurt?" No motion, no sound.

"She made an awful noise, Mommy. She jerked," Rory said behind us in a monotone. His hands on the sheet beside him were clutching and unclutching. "I tried to call you. I couldn't."

Jimmy picked Karen up, keeping her flat. I supported her head and we took her into our room and put her on my bed. I picked up the phone and called John. I went back to Rory, soothed him and tucked him in. John was down in less than ten minutes. "Please, please, God, let her be all right," I prayed with frenzied urgency while we waited for him. He examined her thoroughly. "She's had a convulsion," he said, when he was through. Karen had started retching every few minutes and she kept turning her head from side to side and murmuring, "God, please take the pain away." John stayed with her most of the night and in the morning he called Dr. F of Philadelphia in consultation. Dr. F was a neurologist of international repute.

Karen was still retching with tortured regularity when Dr. F arrived. She was fairly alert and her spasticity had returned. Dr. F said there was pressure on part of the brain and he and John agreed that from now on she should be on restricted fluid intake. No more than twenty-two ounces in twenty-four hours. Most of the talk was over our heads but we comprehended fully that Dr. F was a most unusual individual, kind, brilliant and humble. They didn't leave until late in the afternoon.

267

When Dr. F. bade us good-by he said, "She's going to be all right."

Karen assumed the responsibility for her fluids, measuring them and reminding us (as if we needed it) to mark them down. She was also on an almost salt-free diet and was allowed only one teaspoonful of sugar a day. No candy, chocolate, ice cream, frosting or ices. If she was offered any of these things when visiting, she would say, "No thank you," and let it go at that. Birthday parties were the hardest. With all the goodies which are such an important part of a child's party, Karen would accept only a plain cookie or a piece of cake with the icing scraped off.

We had some "dog days" during Indian summer and though she was always thirsty now, during this kind of weather her thirst was excruciating. She was allowed some extra fluid because of what was lost during hot weather through perspiration, but it didn't mitigate the terrific thirst. We tried not to drink in front of her.

One evening when I was putting her to bed, she asked, "Mom Pom, how many ounces do I have left?"

"One," I answered and went to fetch it.

"Good and cold and in the silver cup," she called after me. "It tastes better that way."

When she had drunk it I took the cup and said, "Darling, I know how hard it is—it's just plain awful and you're a wonderful sport about it."

"I don't mind too much"—she lay looking up at me. "You see, Father Felix told me that when Jesus was on the cross His worst suffering was thirst. That helps a lot —to know that."

Rory was not yet five, yet from the day this regime started he never asked for or ate any of the forbidden things in front of her. The first time after her convulsion when he got his usual nickel after a haircut to buy lollypops, he stood hesitating on the street in front of the drugstore.

268

"Go on, son. Mommy has to get home and start dinner."

"I'm not going to buy none sweets," he said. "Can Karen have gum?"

"Yes, she can."

"O.K.," and he dashed into the store and came out with a package of Beechnut.

About six weeks later, Jimmy was helping her get ready for bed. During family prayers, he knelt so that he could watch her.

"What's on your mind?" I asked him later.

"Have you noticed anything in particular about Karen lately?"

"Like what?" I countered.

"It seems to me," he began hesitantly, "that whenever I work with her or help her with something—" He paused.

"Go on," I urged.

He took a deep breath. "Well, she doesn't seem as spastic." He was looking at me for confirmation. "Not a tremendous difference, mind. But a difference."

"Yes, I have noticed it. More markedly in the past two weeks." He was pleased.

"I have been afraid it was just wishful thinking on my part," he said.

"So have I. That's why I didn't mention it."

When we told Dr. F about this, he said it was not unusual. That decreased spasticity sometimes followed when the fluids were restricted. We noticed it most in her hands. By Christmas she was coloring well, staying within the lines of small areas. Encouraged by this, we started Karen on the piano.

She was practicing one afternoon when Frances Giden walked in unexpectedly. She had been out in Kansas, at the Institute of Logopedics for over a year, working as assistant to the research director. She had been getting speech therapy from the boss himself, Dr. Martin Palmer.

She made a fuss over the kids and they made a fuss over her. There was a lot of chatter and I noticed Rory looking at Francie, a frown puckering his forehead. He tilted his head a little to one side as if listening. I could almost see the wheels churning inside his head. He was trying to figure something out. Francie held out her hand to him and said, "I want to see all your Christmas presents." The frown vanished and he smiled. Whatever it was, he had it figured out. He took her hand and said directly, "You don't talk like a C.P. any more."

They showed her their presents. Karen was proudest of her gift from Lou Whiton. Francie's eyes widened in startled appreciation. "Just like the other girls," Karen said holding aloft a pair of black leather Mary Janes with a single strap. With rare understanding, Lou had decided on this gift and had purchased the slippers and had the brace man do what was necessary so they would fit the braces. "Never heard of such a thing," he had told Lou. Then added grudgingly, "It's wonderful. Wish I'd thought of it myself a long time ago."

They couldn't be worn much. There wasn't enough support. But they were worn to church on Sunday and to birthday parties. "Just like the other girls."

270

Chapter 27

FOR A YEAR AND A HALF we had been preparing Karen
for her Confirmation which took place in May of 1950.
We had been somewhat hampered by Rory, who wanted
to be in on almost every instruction. Many of the matters
discussed were beyond the comprehension of a five-year-
old and he promptly forgot them. But his little mind
worked overtime trying to understand the descent of the
Holy Ghost. It may not have kept him awake nights, but
it certainly occupied a good part of his thinking during
the day. About a week before the occasion, he jubilantly
announced at luncheon, "Now I know about the Holy
Ghost. I'll splain it. Just like Santa Claus, he comes
down the chimney."

Confirmation day was as beautiful as Karen's First
Communion day. The recipients were from nine years to
forty. They all wore white gowns, and the girls wore small
red skull caps. Karen was still tiny for her age so we
ordered the smallest size gown, and then had to take up
the sleeves and hem.

The altar was ablaze with candles. The slender
wooden figures carved in Oberammergau that stood behind the altar proper seemed to breathe in the shimmering
light. Bishop Joseph Donohue was officiating and his
throne was set on the top step in front of the tabernacle.
His crimson and snowy surplice was partially hidden by
the full cape of heavy white silk embroidered in gold.
The tall, triangular-shaped miter, symbol of his succession to Peter, rested on his abundant, dark hair. Pendu-
lant folds of gossamer gold hung from each side of the
miter. "Mommy, look," said Rory in a high clear voice.
"The Bishop's hat looks like a butterfly's wings."

Before the service, one of our priests had spoken to the Bishop about Karen's walking difficulty and asked him if he would prefer coming down to the altar rail to her, rather than having her traverse the wide space of the altar floor and six steps. "No, indeed," said this wise man. "No child likes to be different. Tell her to take her time and I shall wait for her."

When Karen's turn came, Jimmy took one of her hands and I the other. She walked between us. Slowly we crossed the sanctuary and more slowly we moved up the steps to the throne. The sponsor stepped forward and the priest attending the Bishop handed him Karen's card. Looking at it the Bishop said, "You are taking the name Marie?" She couldn't kneel, but stood before him, a tiny figure of Faith.

"Yes, Your Lordship," she answered in a steady voice, but I could feel her tremble.

With holy oil, the Bishop anointed Karen's forehead in the form of the cross and spoke, "I confirm thee with the Sign of the Cross and anoint thee with the chrism of salvation." With his hands extended over her head he invoked the Holy Ghost, breathed upon her and then administered a light tap on the cheek—reminder that from this day forth she was a soldier of Christ. Then he leaned forward and with a smile of ineffable tenderness he said, "A special blessing for you, my child."

We retraced our steps. Karen clutching our hands. She walked surer, straighter than she ever had before. The voice of supplication filled the church and our hearts echoed, *"Veni, Creator Spiritus*— Come, Holy Ghost, Creator, come . . ."

A month later Marie brought home a report card which called for a reward. Her average was good and we were most specially pleased with straight A's in Co-operation and Courtesy. She was highly satisfied with herself and to top all this she had won a swimming medal.

She requested her own reward—her first grown-up

party. It was a supper party from seven-thirty to ten-thirty. There were fifteen guests from twelve to sixteen.

Jimmy and I felt that this affair would provide a proving ground of Karen's socialization. We knew the normal attitude of children individually, but we also knew that frequently individual behavior is at sharp variance with group behavior. And how would Marie react? And Karen?

I gave Karen and Rory an early supper in the nursery and shortly thereafter bundled the little man, protesting, into bed. While I was so engaged Marie came in and said, "I wish you'd let Karen stay up until nine. Just as a special treat."

"I think that's a swell idea," I said.

After their supper and eleven gallons of punch, the youngsters trooped upstairs for dancing. They were a little slow getting started, the girls not wanting to dance together and the boys not sure that dancing with girls was manly. I offered to teach them the polka and nothing was slow thereafter.

Karen was sitting on the couch, attended by two young swains and the three of them were conversing animatedly. The rest of the crowd were stamping and spinning in the authentic Polish steps. Marie danced over to the couch and excused herself to her partner. She bent and picked up Karen, quite a load, and whirled her away. Two of the boys asked to have a turn "dancing with Karen" and it was ten o'clock before Jimmy polkaed her off to bed.

Karen's companions, in her own age group, had outgrown "sit-down" games and moved on to "Hide and Seek," "King of the Hill," jumping rope, baseball, tag. One morning, Karen spent twenty minutes working her way to a group, only to have it disintegrate shortly after she arrived. The youngsters had decided to roller skate. "Mom Pom, will you buy me a pair of roller skates?"

Whispering the routine prayer for guidance, before answering a significant question, I sat down beside her forlorn little figure. Speaking very matter-of-factly, I said, "No, Snickle-britches, because you're not going to be able to roller skate." I took her crutches and sat her beside me. I pulled two pieces of sour grass, handed one to her and nibbled on the other. "You know, darling, I have always wanted to draw and paint. Lots of times I've ached with the desire to portray an interesting face or a beautiful scene. But I can't. My hands are not right for the job. That's the way it is with you and roller skating. Your legs are not right for the job." She was staring at me.

"Every person in this world, at some time or another, wants to do something he can't. You're no different. But the happy people are those who forget about what they can't do and work at the things they can do." I put my arm around her shoulders.

"You have a much sweeter voice than any of the other children, perfect pitch and tempo. Maybe it's time we started you on singing lessons. What do you say?"

"Oh, Mom, could I?"

"I don't see why not."

"Boy, oh, boy. Will the other kids be jealous."

"I'll talk it over with Daddy. In the meantime," I said, rising and handing her the crutches, "I have a pile of brochures that have to be folded and put in envelopes. Want to help?"

"Do you think I could?"

"Of course."

"Maybe Ruth Ann and Kathy could come too," she suggested.

I called the youngsters and they were thrilled to play real "office." I instructed them and they spent a happy hour and a half finishing the job unassisted, even to sealing the envelopes and stamping them. We invited them to stay for dinner, and on the whole I felt we'd pulled through fairly well.

We developed many activities for Karen. Jimmy had her help him paint the rowboat. We took her with us to get bait and she became very quick at pinning the elusive fiddlers under her crutch tip. After she had helped snare her bait, we took her fishing for blackfish.

We bent over backward about not asking Glo and Marie to take Karen with them, because we never wanted them to feel that they were saddled with her. Most of the time, however, they asked to have her go. Rory was a good companion to her also and provided much entertainment with his antics and words. She was such a good audience that he was always trying to outdo himself. Many of our windows were only a few feet off the ground and she found it highly amusing when he decided that he would forswear the ordinary mode of egress and ingress and went in and out through these windows. Because of her reaction, it took us just that much longer to recondition him to using doors. "If *only* I could write so I could keep a diary on him," she said more than once. "And he's going to be a poet. Today he said our house grew beside our garden and the other day when we were walking with Marie he told us that the birches were Dalmatian trees. If I could write—"

Karen attended all the neighborhood birthday parties and although there were many games in which she could not participate, she became, with Marie's careful tutoring, most expert at pinning the tail on the donkey, and brought home a prize for this excellence from almost every party.

One night, late in August, Gloria stood waiting to hand Karen her helmet after supper. She was beside Karen's chair swinging it by the elastic that went under the chin. Suddenly she stopped and looked at the helmet as if she had never seen it before. She sat down and studied it intently.

"What's on your so-called mind?" asked Marie, with the heavy humor of the adolescent.

"I was just thinking . . ." Gloria's voice trailed off.

"That's obvious," Marie said. "What about?"

"About what a wonderful pocketbook this would

make for teen-agers." She looked up, her face bright with the exciting idea. "I could just line it with denim or some other material and draw the surplus into a pouch with a drawstring." As she spoke, a lot of further ideas came crowding each other. She rattled on, "We could have them made in the different school colors."

"There couldn't be too many different combinations," I said. "I really think you have something."

A few weeks later she went on vacation and she made herself a timetable. By the end of the vacation she had seen a patent lawyer and the design was filed. She also visited the concerns that make such products and developed an impressive knowledge of costs and materials. Once launched there was no stopping her or slowing her down and before many moons had passed she had five more original designs and was working through one of the largest firms in youth styles.

In September, when Rory was five and a half and Karen was ten, Karen had to face up to one of her biggest heartaches yet.

Rory started to school.

It was not only the loneliness but the emphasis, as never before, on her isolation from this broadest phase of every other child's life. Kindergarten only lasted half a day, but from September on Karen's mornings were bleak.

Betty helped the situation some by having Karen go to her house to school instead of coming to ours, and by arranging Karen's time in the morning. Karen's progress in her work was good and she was consumed with a desire to write. "I'll never learn. I just can't write," she would cry bitterly, as day after day she failed in the attempt.

In spite of Betty's efforts to keep us optimistic, Jimmy and I grew more and more disheartened. "When you boil it down," Jimmy said, "the pen is mightier than the crutch."

All that first winter of Rory's schooling, Karen would say, "When I was in kindergarten—" and then go on to recite some fabulous adventure or routine of school activity which was entirely the product of her imagination.

In the fall I had been invited to speak to the Rye Kiwanis Club and had given my "Once Upon a Time" talk, which is Karen's story synopsized.

At five o'clock Christmas afternoon, we were gathered around the tree and there was a knock on the door. In walked a delegation from the Kiwanis Club, headed by Mr. Knapp and Jack Chambers. They were carrying something huge, covered over with a raincoat. As soon as the introductions were over, Jack with a superb gesture whisked away the coat. "Merry Christmas," they chorused and with charming formality presented Karen with an exquisite stand and cage which housed a beautiful gold canary. She had wanted a bird for years. But the cost had put it beyond our reach. All she could say was, "Oh, no. Oh, oh, oh, oh."

They stayed a while and before they left the bird began to sing. A few tentative chirps first as though trying out the acoustics, and then a full-throated song of infinite sweetness and wide range. With the first chirp, Karen forgot everyone in the room and sat spellbound. I got a kick out of watching her and also her benefactors. They were looking at Karen and every face expressed an immense gratification.

Chapter 28

FOR THE PAST FEW YEARS, Jimmy and I had elected to
spend New Year's Eve at home, alone. We took a lot of
kidding about it and were labeled anti-social.

I dressed with as much care for New Year's Eve 1951
as if I'd been appearing at the smartest clubs in New
York. Jimmy was charged with supplying the best fire of
the year and a bottle of sparkling Burgundy. (Two bottles last year and this, because we got the children up at
midnight for the uncorking and a toast.) Not Gloria, of
course. She was twenty-one and at that age New Year's
Eve meant lots of people and lights and noise. (It's not
too much of a strain for me to remember that far back.)

When the three younger ones were settled, we pulled
the couch over in front of the fire and relaxed blissfully.
I had taken care of my responsibilities for the evening; I
had a pile of records, both dance and classical, and in
the icebox, wrapped in wax paper, were two platters of
very dainty, very succulent, very expensive sandwiches.
It was a cold night and the wind tore through the
branches of the pines and hurled its evil voice through
the windowpanes. I got up and drew the drapes and returned to my snug haven. The fire burned brightly and,
it seemed, defiantly.

Jimmy made us a highball and I turned on the radio.
The muted sounds of music and pre-midnight hysteria
edged into the room.

Habitually we did some recapitulating in the last hours
of each year.

"We've certainly come a long way with Karen," Jimmy
mused, sipping his drink.

"We have that," I assented, holding my glass so the pale fluid would pick up the firelight.

"I remember, all too well," he said reflectively, "seven years ago tonight . . ." His voice trailed off.

I remembered, too. I remembered when he had said, "You know, sweetheart, we don't have one problem—we have five, if we're going to think of Karen as a whole child," and he had ticked off on his fingers the five phases of growth.

Now we sat silent. The fire chortled and hissed. Jimmy lit a cigarette for me and one for himself. The smoke curled around his hand as it rested on his knee.

"Darling, just look at Karen, the whole child she is now. Look at her unbelievable development, physically, spiritually, emotionally, socially—why in these last three she's head and shoulders above most youngsters."

"If she could only learn to write," he said, and his voice yearned over the thought.

"I know. I feel the same way. And then I feel ungrateful." I drew my legs up under me and sat sideways facing him.

"Today we know," he went on, "that there's something equally important, something outside the child, without which so many of her accomplishments will be wasted. I mean her acceptance by the world at large."

"I think about it all the time," I said. "Sure she's accepted in Rye, but later—will the world accept C.P.'s for what they are and what they can do?"

"That," said Jimmy, "is the sixty-four-dollar question."

"Well, we should have the answer soon," I reminded him. "Our campaign will tell us first, whether people know; second, if they care; and third, if they accept."

"Here's hoping," he raised his glass.

"Here's hoping and praying," I responded, raising mine.

"Let's dance."

The next four months gave us our answer to this all-important question.

Had I known ahead of time what work was in store, I would have pulled a Rip Van Winkle act and I think Lenny and the whole Executive Committee of the U.C.P.A. would have bedded down too. Also Gloria and Marie who assumed so much of household responsibility.

There were flying trips to Canada, Chicago, Kansas, Washington. We had affiliates in twenty-one states, Canada and South Africa. Every day our ranks were swelled by individuals who wanted to guarantee the right answer to our question. Bob Hope, Bing Crosby, Jane Pickens, Arthur Godfrey, Maurice Tobin, Jack Benny, Kate Smith, Jinx McCrary, Grantland Rice, A. Ansara, Earl Hudson—these were just our chairmen, the leaders. They were backed by the motion-picture industry, members of the "fourth estate," radio, television. Our National Sports Committee alone numbered over one thousand. This was sensational and we were vastly encouraged; but the American public, the man on the street—did he know? Did he care? Did he accept?

We put a small notice in *The New York Times* in January. We asked for Christmas cards to use in treatment centers and schools.

And we got our answer to the sixty-four-dollar question.

At the last count, the American public knew enough, cared enough, accepted enough, that they sent the Karens of their country *sixty-eight million cards.*

In March of 1951 it looked as though Rory's nightly prayer, "Please God, give Mommy strong bones to lift Karen and lots of money for C.P." was going to be answered. The bones were holding up nicely and the campaign plans seemed a guarantee of financial success. This financial success was all important. We had a goal of five million dollars. This money would provide funds for research under the guidance of Dr. Sidney Farber toward the improved treatment and ultimate prevention of cerebral palsy, and funds to enlarge existing facilities for diagnosis, treatment and education, and for the important recruiting and training of all necessary personnel, on a large scale. Financial success would mean hope for the 96 out of every 100 C.P.'s who now were not getting treatment or education. And further, it would hold promise for the C.P. child, born every 53 minutes, somewhere in the country.

In the same month, we stole an afternoon off for the circus and were just as carefree as we had been B.C.P. We acquired the usual collection of hats, sticks, hideous hollow metal horses, pictures of the side shows, the giant's ring, whistles and another pet, a chameleon which we promptly christened Morpheus. All the acts were supercolossal, but as always the hit of the show was Emmett Kelly, his classic nonsense enthralling the children of all ages.

Karen laughed until she cried, when he begged the tiny fish from the seal trainer by mutely holding out his frying pan with his inimitable suppliant pathos. Then came the aerialists—"daring daredevils hurtling through space in death-defying leaps with no nets." While the audience sat in horrified fascination, Karen watched Emmett Kelly as he scuffed his weary way into the center ring, hauled a trunk into the middle, pulled a deck of cards from his pendulous pockets and started a game of solitaire. At this, we all gave way to hysterical mirth. Of all the wonderful, exciting entertainment, it was Emmett Kelly that Karen talked about for weeks after.

The day after the circus, I gave a talk to our National Sports Committee, again "Once Upon a Time" and *Billboard* reviewed it generously. Bill Boley, our volunteer advertising expert, felt that it would provide excellent material for the major radio show of our campaign and asked Alan Sloan, a script writer, to get in touch with me. Alan is one of the best in his line and had volunteered his services.

When Alan called me, I told him if he was going to write about Karen and her family, he should spend some time with us. He properly construed this as an invitation and asked if Tuesday, April 10, would be agreeable. It was.

Alan came about ten in the morning. Karen was out "baby sitting" at Dempseys' across the street and he and I took a few minutes to get acquainted. I liked him immediately. He was intelligent and sensitive and I could see that he would fit in and not make the children "guest" conscious, which would spoil everything.

Edna Dempsey dropped Karen in front of the house about ten-thirty. Alan and I stood waiting for her in the doorway as she crutched toward us. She was wearing the helmet and in spite of it she was pretty. She had on a dress of blue, green and cinnamon stripes. A white piqué Peter Pan collar framed her lively face. When she lowered her eyes I could see the faint blue tracing on the lids at the root of the heavy lashes. Her sensitive chin was sporting a few new freckles. Her eyes seemed to laugh even when her face was serious.

"Karen, may I present Mr. Sloan. Alan, this is Karen."

"How do you do," said Karen, her smile trickling from her eyes to her lips, and sat down to visit until Betty came for school work. She arrived at eleven and I told her that Alan and I would like to sit in on the lesson. "Delighted," she said. "I was going to ask you today anyway."

"Go in and wash and go to the johnny," I said in an aside to Karen. She put on her crutches and tapped off.

"Can she do—eh—all of those things herself?" Alan asked in surprise.

"As of last week—all," I answered proudly. "It takes some time, but you and Betty can chat and I'll set up the table and chairs in the nursery."

"Does she need a special table and chair?" he asked.

"No more."

282

Fifteen minutes later, Karen was at her table, ready to start. "Karen, I'm amazed at the way you get on and off chairs," Alan said to her.

"Oh, it took me a long time to learn and it was hard work, but I don't need help any more," said Karen, taking off her helmet.

Betty sat beside Karen, I perched on the foot of the bed, and Alan elected to sit on the floor in front of the table, whence he could look up at her. It was an unusually warm day and the casements were flung wide. The sunshine drenched the room, plucked the glints from Karen's hair and tossed them back in a golden sheen. The smells and sounds of spring skipped across the window sill. The warm thump of a ball on a mitt, the sibilant shout of a hose, the patter of a pair of robins, building a nest in the bush beneath the window.

Karen was sitting straight and tall, her knees bent and her feet flat on the floor. Her hands were clasped in her lap and she was darting quick glances from Betty to Alan to me.

"Could you be sunburned?" I asked her, noticing her high color.

"Nope. Just excited," she answered with that catch in her voice that means "surprise."

"How come?" I asked.

"You'll see," she said, her eyes crinkling with anticipatory mirth. "Won't she, Betty?"

"Yes in-n-n-deed." Betty had a funny little smile on her face. She was stacking books on the bureau. She picked up a piece of 8½ x 11 bond paper and came back to the table.

Karen said, "You're going to be amazed and delighted. I'll bet you will—"

"Hush. No hints," said Betty.

"Hurry!" Karen urged in a stage whisper.

Betty picked up a pencil and using the edge of a crayon book, drew two horizontal lines across the paper, a half inch apart. She moved down an inch and drew two more lines. Then two more, until they went down to the bottom of the sheet.

"Trolley tracks?" I inquired, moving around beside the table. "Aren't you a little old for that sort of thing?"

Betty smiled and said nothing. She put the paper on a slant in front of Karen, took two tiny pieces of Scotch tape and fastened the paper down at the top corners. By this time my curiosity was immense. Betty looked at her watch.

"Ready?" she said to Karen.

"Uh-huh," was the breathless answer.

She handed her pencil to Karen, a regular Eberhard Faber, #2. Karen took it in her left hand and put her right forearm and hand flat on the table. I saw the fingers tense. Karen gave me a quick look, she was no longer smiling, and put the pencil point to the paper. She put the point on the bottom line of the first pair and slowly moved it upward to the line above. It stopped and then still more slowly began moving in an arc—out, around, down. It was back at the starting point. And there, for all the world to see, was the letter "D."

I was witnessing a miracle.

Karen didn't look up. She bent closer, her flush deepened. She placed the point and, faltering, moved it up again. This line was not so squiggly as the first. She followed the top line over a bit, lifted the point, moved it down, made a horizontal line, lifted it again. She started to place it on the starting point. The pencil shot off to the side, laboriously she worked it back and after a struggle found the point and drew another horizontal line, parallel to the two above. I saw the letter "E."

I believe that Karen was now unaware of our presence. She had clamped her teeth so tightly on her lower lip, there was a wide, white line. The intensity of her effort produced overflow motion in her legs and they stiffened out some in front of her, causing her to slip down in her chair a little. Her feet were no longer flat, but resting on the heels with the toes slightly elevated.

284

No one spoke. No one moved. We were holding our breath.

Karen started another letter. She ran the first line at a slant, which ended up slightly curved instead of straight, and we saw her painstakingly form the letter "A." Then —and this took much longer than the others—the letter "R." I wiped my wet palms on the side of my skirt.

"Holy Mother," I said under my breath, "She's not *copying!* She's doing it *all* alone!" I stared at the word "DEAR."

"F," prompted Betty, and Karen started another word. The letters stumbled across the page, Betty prompting occasionally, and Karen started on the pair of lines below. A half hour, a century later, letters faint and unsure, but undeniably legible, stared up at us.

DEAR FUNNIEST CLOWN IN THE WORLD

Again she set the pencil point, but it was too much. I bent over her. The tears coursed down my cheeks and splashed on the page. I put my arms about her and sobbed against her braids.

"I told you she'd cry, Betty." Karen's voice was muffled against my shoulder. I eased my embrace. She turned her face. "Oh, Mom Pom, I can *write!* I can write all by *myself!*" I turned and threw my arms around Betty. She held me a moment, started to say something and stopped. I swallowed a couple of times, tried to speak to Karen, choked and tried again.

"You blessed, wonderful, adorable child!" I pushed the table aside and knelt in front of her. I put my head in her lap. She locked her hands around my neck and squeezed. "Mom Pom," she said in hushed breathlessness, "I can't hardly believe it. I can't hardly believe it," she repeated.

"I can't believe it, either. I just can't. Oh, Jimmy!" and as I thought of his happiness, the tears ran heavier than before.

"Hey, Mom, look at him." She pushed my head up. I remembered Alan. "Mom, he's crying too." I swiveled around. He was, unashamedly. Wiping his eyes and blowing his nose, he said with a quavery laugh, "Who isn't?" and pointed to Betty.

"This is one of the happiest moments of my life," she sniffled, looking at her watch. "It took thirty-six minutes! We've been working at it seven months."

"Mom!" Karen was pulling my arm. "Mom Pom," she called for my attention.

"What is it, you wonderful child, you!"

"I can walk. I can talk. I can read. I can *write*. Mom Pom, I can do *anything!*"